T0135218

Intelligent Wavelet Based Techniques for Advanced Multimedia Applications

Rajiv Singh • Swati Nigam • Amit Kumar Singh
Mohamed Elhoseny

Intelligent Wavelet Based Techniques for Advanced Multimedia Applications

 Springer

Rajiv Singh
Department of Computer Science
Banasthali Vidyapith
Banasthali, Rajasthan, India

Amit Kumar Singh
Department of Computer Science
& Engineering
National Institute of Technology
Patna, Bihar, India

Swati Nigam
Department of Computer Science
Banasthali Vidyapith
Banasthali, Rajasthan, India

Mohamed Elhoseny
Faculty of Computers and Information
Mansoura University
Dakahliya, Egypt

ISBN 978-3-030-31875-8   ISBN 978-3-030-31873-4   (eBook)
https://doi.org/10.1007/978-3-030-31873-4

This Springer imprint is published by the registered company Springer Nature Switzerland AG.
The registered company address is: Gewerbestrasse 11, 6330 Cham, Switzerland

Foreword

The book titled *Intelligent Wavelet Based Techniques for Advanced Multimedia Applications* is a significant effort on the innovative use of wavelet for demanding applications of multimedia. The book intends to enhance the understanding of opportunities and challenges in wavelet-based multimedia for real-world applications at the global level.

It is a challenge for any researchers and scholars to identify the most popular topics on wavelet-based multimedia in any instant of time due to rapid progress on research and development.

This book summarizes the popular intelligent multimedia applications in wavelet domain in terms of image fusion, image and video watermarking, object tracking, camouflaged person identification, activity recognition, and emotion recognition using facial expressions.

The book focuses on identifying new directions to students, researchers, programmers, and industry professionals. Given this, summarizing the vast literature in multimedia in wavelet domain and identifying the most cutting-edge phenomena is a huge task. I hope the readers will find the book of great value in its visionary words.

I congratulate the authors for this book and look forward to seeing it in print soon.
Email: aboitcairo@fci-cu.edu.eg

Founder and Chair of the Scientific
Research Group in Egypt, Professor at
Cairo University, Faculty of Computers
& Artificial Intelligence, Information
Technology Department, Giza, Egypt

Aboul Ella Hassanien

Preface

Wavelet transforms are useful in many signal, image, and video processing applications, especially for multimedia security and surveillance. Some interesting applications of wavelets in security and surveillance are watermarking, fusion, steganography, object detection, tracking, motion recognition, intention recognition etc. Wavelets are well capable of analyzing signals, images, and video sequences at different resolution levels, popularly known as multiresolution analysis. Multiresolution analysis is advantageous in multimedia security and surveillance applications. It provides flexibility in the selection of different resolution levels, which leads to better accuracy. Wavelets provide directional information, which is very useful in determining certain aspects related to object characterization in various directions. Furthermore, recently sparse representation has become an advancement to analyze wavelet coefficients. It is observed that a few wavelet transforms possess invariance property, which makes them suitable for many vision applications. Recently, wavelet transforms, together with sparse representations, are found very useful in various potential applications. Wavelets have been explored for several image and signal processing applications; however, multiresolution analysis and sparse representation have not been explored for advanced multimedia applications in the area of image processing and computer vision.

Outline of the Book and Chapter Synopsis

In view of above, this book presents state-of-the-art intelligent techniques and approaches, design, development, and innovative use of wavelet for demanding applications of multimedia. We have provided potential thoughts and methodologies that help senior undergraduate and graduate students, researchers, programmers, and industry professionals in creating new knowledge for the future to develop efficient wavelet-based novel approach for multimedia applications. Further, key role and great importance of wavelet transform as a mathematical tool is elaborated in the book. The book has been organized into ten chapters to provide complete theoretical and experimental details of the advanced mutlimedia applications of wavelet transforms in image processing and computer vision domains. A brief and orderly introduction to the chapters is provided below.

Chapter 1 presents a brief introduction on the development of multimedia in the wavelet domain. Further, key role of wavelet transform in intelligent multimedia applications, along with key challenges in real life, is discussed. The applications include image fusion, image and video watermarking, object tracking, person identification, emotion recognition using facial expressions, and activity recognition.

Chapter 2 discusses the basic foundations of classical and new generation wavelet transforms, along with their merits and demerits. It includes the discrete wavelet transform (DWT), dual tree complex wavelet transform (DTCWT), curvelet transform (CVT), contourlet transform (CT), and nonsubsampled contourlet transform (NSCT).

Chapter 3 provides the potential importance of complex wavelet transforms for image fusion. This chapter provides an overview of medical image fusion in complex wavelet domain and evaluates the performance of fusion methods using qualitative and quantitative techniques. The experimental study on three sets of medical images proved that the method is superior to existing fusion methods in transform and spatial domains.

Chapter 4 describes the embedding of mutiwatermark in transform domain. The method uses a combination of nonsubsampled contourlet transform (NSCT), discrete cosine transform (DCT), and multiresolution singular value decomposition (MSVD) to imperceptibly hide watermarks into medical cover image. A series of experimental outcomes proved that the method is robust against various kinds of geometrical attacks and superior to similar state-of-the-art techniques.

The basic concepts of video watermarking, their importance and key characteristics, are elaborated in Chapter 5. Further, a brief review and the comparative analysis of various state-of-the-art video watermarking techniques are presented with a general embedding and extraction procedure in wavelet domain.

Chapter 6 presents an algorithm for the tracking of moving human objects in videos. This algorithm exploited a newly emerged adaptive wavelet technique that is based on curvelet transform coefficients. Results show that the proposed algorithm offers better performance in terms of the Euclidean distance and the Bhattacharyya distance.

Chapter 7 introduces a camouflaged person identification technique that integrates discrete wavelet coefficients with a support vector machine classifier. This method is capable of handling background and foreground ambiguity for camouflaged persons and shows improved performance for CAMO_UOW video dataset.

Chapter 8 analyzes real world human activity recognition problems. The method uses discrete wavelet transform and a multiclass SVM classifier to develop an activity recognition framework. Experimental evalaution over Weizmann and KTH datasets shows the better performance of the proposed method in terms of recognition accuracy.

Chapter 9 presents a biometric emotion prediction technique in wavelet domain. The approach reduced the image dimensions and preserved the perceptual quality of the original images. Downsampled features are classified using a multiclass SVM classifier that has a one-versus-all architecture. This system is trained with benchmark JAFFE and CK+ facial expression datasets. The result study on JAFFE and CK + facial expression datasets proved that the wavelet-based approach achieved good recognition rate and was found superior to similar approaches.

Finally, Chapter 10 discusses the recent challenges in the visual information processing that are directly related to societal benefits. Its major components are healthcare, education, transportation, and security. A methodological enhancement of the techniques and their evaluation parameters are being discussed to provide future research directions to the wavelet-based multimedia applications.

We especially thank the Series Editor, Advanced Sciences and Technologies for Security Applications, *Prof. Anthony J Masys,* for his continuous support and great guidance.

We are grateful to *Prof. Aboul Ella Hassanien*, Faculty of Computers & Artificial Intelligence, Information Technology Department, Cairo University, Egypt, for his inspirational forewords for the book.

We would also like to thank the publishers at Springer, in particular *Annelies Kersbergen*, associate editor, Security Science, Springer, for their helpful guidance and encouragement during the creation of this book.

We are sincerely thankful to all the authors, editors, and publishers whose works have been cited directly/indirectly in this manuscript.

Special Acknowledgments

The first and second authors gratefully acknowledge the authorities of Banasthali Vidyapith, Rajasthan, India, for their kind support in coming up with this book.

The third author gratefully acknowledges the authorities of the *National Institute of Technology Patna*, India, for their kind support in coming up with this book.

The fourth author gratefully acknowledges the authorities of *Mansoura University, Egypt*, for their kind support in coming up with this book

Banasthali, India	Rajiv Singh
Banasthali, India	Swati Nigam
Patna, India	Amit Kumar Singh
Dakahliya, Egypt	Mohamed Elhoseny

Contents

About the Authors

Rajiv Singh is an assistant professor at the Department of Computer Science, Banasthali Vidyapith, Rajasthan, India. He has received Doctor of Philosophy in Computer Science from the Department of Electronics and Communication, University of Allahabad, India. His research areas of interests are information fusion, computational cognitive science, medical image processing, computer vision, context aware computing, and information security. He has published more than 25 papers in refereed conferences and journals. He has served as reviewer for reputed journals like *Information Fusion, IEEE Transactions on Biomedical Engineering, IEEE Transactions on Circuits and Systems for Video Technology, IEEE Transactions on Image Processing, IEEE Transactions on Industrial Electronics, IEEE Transactions on Computational Imaging, The Visual Computer*, and many conferences. He is a professional member of IEEE and ACM and a life member of Computer Society of India (CSI).

Swati Nigam is an assistant professor at the Department of Computer Science, Banasthali Vidyapith, Rajasthan, India. She has been a postdoctoral fellow under the National Post Doctoral Fellowship scheme of the Science and Engineering Research Board, Department of Science and Technology, Government of India. Earlier she has been awarded Senior Research Fellowship by the Council of Scientific and Industrial Research, Government of India. She has received PhD in Computer Science from the Department of Electronics and Communication, University of Allahabad, India. She has authored more than 20 articles in peer-reviewed journals, book chapters, and conference proceedings. She is a designated reviewer of several SCI journals like *IEEE Access, Computer Vision and Image Understanding, Journal of Electronic Imaging*, etc. She has been a publication chair, publicity chair, TPC member, and reviewer of various conferences. She is a professional member of IEEE and ACM. Her research interests include object detection, object tracking, and human activity recognition.

Amit Kumar Singh is an assistant professor with the Computer Science and Engineering Department, National Institute of Technology at Patna (An Institute of National Importance), Patna, India. He has authored over 90 peer-reviewed journal, conference publications, and book chapters. He has authored two books entitled *Medical Image Watermarking: Techniques and Applications*, Springer, in 2017, and *Animal Biometrics: Techniques and Applications*, Springer, in 2018. He has also edited three books titled *Smart Networks Inspired Paradigm and Approaches in IoT Applications*, Springer, in 2019; *Handbook of Multimedia Information Security: Techniques and Applications*, Springer, in 2019; and *Security in Smart Cities: Models, Applications, and Challenges*, Springer, in 2019. He currently serves as the associate editor of *IEEE Access* and is a former member of the editorial board of *Multimedia Tools and Applications* (Springer). He has edited various international journal special issues as a guest editor, such as *IEEE Consumer Electronics Magazine*; *IEEE Access*; *Multimedia Tools and Applications*, Springer; *International Journal of Information Management*, Elsevier; *Journal of Ambient Intelligence and Humanized Computing*, Springer; etc. His research interests include data hiding, biometrics, and cryptography

Mohamed Elhoseny is an assistant professor at the Faculty of Computers and Information, Mansoura University, Egypt, where he is also the director of the Distributed Sensing and Intelligent Systems Lab. Dr. Elhoseny has authored or coauthored over 100 ISI journal articles, conference proceedings, book chapters, and several books published by Springer and Taylor & Francis. His research interests include network security, cryptography, machine learning techniques, and intelligent systems. Dr. Elhoseny serves as the editor-in-chief of the *International Journal of Smart Sensor Technologies and Applications* and as an associate editor of several journals such as *IEEE Access*.

List of Figures

List of Tables

Chapter 1
Wavelets and Intelligent Multimedia Applications: An Introduction

Abstract With the great development of multimedia technology and applications, it becomes important to provide a thorough understanding of the existing literature. This aim can be achieved by analysis of state of the art methodologies of multimedia applications. Wavelet transforms have been found very useful in a large variety of multimedia applications. It ranges from simple imaging to complex computer vision applications. One of the major advantages of the wavelet transform is that it meets the need of majority of applications and can be combined with machine and deep learning for performance enhancement. These applications include image fusion, image and video watermarking, object tracking, activity recognition, emotion recognition etc. This chapter aims to provide a brief introduction to the development of multimedia applications in the wavelet domain. Some major multimedia applications of the wavelet transforms have been discussed with their relevance and real life applications.

Keywords Wavelets · Multimedia applications · Machine learning · Intelligent systems · Image processing · Computer vision

1.1 Introduction

The emergence of multimedia technology for processing visual information [1, 2] has influenced to explore the possibility of the development of the intelligent applications. The applications may range from image processing to computer vision [3–6]. Some of these applications are biometric scanners [7], expression recognition [8], object recognition [9], object tracking [10], behavior understanding [11] etc. These applications may include low or high computational requirements. But, based on the importance of these applications, the computation cost can be afforded. For example, a video surveillance system [12] includes the complete monitoring of the subjects to identify abnormal behavior. The key steps in video surveillance include object identification followed by tracking and activity recognition. Thus, a complete solution requires many steps to be completed and it should provide a fully automatic system to detect and predict abnormal behavior of the subjects. Such a multimedia system is highly desirable for surveillance and monitoring to avoid major security threats against humanity like 26/11 and 9/11.

Another example of multimedia application in image processing is image fusion [13] which merges complementary information from multiple registered source images into single composite image for better perceptual and visual representation. For example, visible and thermal imaging sensors, having different and complementary information are successfully used for fusion to elicit all the pertinent information. Multimodality image fusion has been proved advantageous as it provides more accurate and non-redundant information in less time with reduced cost and storage. The continuous development of medical imaging sensors and their complementary nature have influenced the researchers and scientists to explore image fusion for clinical applications. Therefore, the concept of image fusion has been explored in a variety of potential applications such as concealed weapon detection, remote sensing, military surveillance, image retrieval, object tracking, object recognition, information security and biometrics [13–15]. Thus, for multimedia applications, we require better solutions as their applications are directly related to the societal benefits [16, 17].

To provide solutions to the multimedia applications, many methods have been suggested in spatial and transform domain. Spatial domain methods are simple that directly manipulates the intensity of the image sequence to provide solutions for multimedia applications. However, These are not efficient and lack in providing robustness. With the advancement of the algorithm design, many other methods have been suggested for the solution of multimedia problems. But, among these solutions, wavelet transforms have become a very useful mathematical tool to be obtain solutions for multimedia applications such as video surveillance, image fusion, image and video watermarking, behavior understanding, etc. [18–24].

The applications of wavelet transform is not limited to these aforementioned applications only, it also integrates machine and deep learning concepts for many applications. For example, a wavelet support vector machine (WSVM) has been suggested by Zhang et al. [25], which integrated wavelet kernel with support vector machines for classification. Similarly, magnetic resonance image (MRI) classification has been performed using wavelets as a feature using SVM and neural network [26]. Brain tumor classification method is proposed using wavelet based feature extraction and combining it with random forest classifier [27]. Motivated by the successful integration of wavelet transforms and machine learning, deep learning has also been integrated with wavelet transforms for several applications [28–32]. Some recent multimedia applications of wavelet transform indicate that it can be widely used for healthcare [33–36], computer vision [37, 38] by integrating machine and deep learning techniques. Moreover, modern application areas like internet of things (IoT), data analytics are some other possible research area where wavelet transforms can be explored [39, 40]. Based on the applications of wavelets for multimedia, in this chapter, we highlight the motivations and provide a background by discussing the problems, covered in this book.

1.2   Motivations and Objectives

Wavelet transforms are useful in many signal, image and video processing applications, especially for healthcare [41], multimedia security [42] and surveillance [43]. Wavelets are well capable of analyzing signal, image and video at different resolution levels, popularly known as multiresolution analysis [44–46]. This multiresolution analysis is advantageous in many multimedia applications and can be seen in literatures [10, 22, 23, 37–40, 47]. It provides flexibility in selection of different resolution levels that leads to better accuracy. Wavelets provide directional information which is very useful in determining certain aspects related to object characterization in various directions [48]. Furthermore, recently sparse representation has become an advancement to analyze wavelet coefficients. It has been observed that wavelet transforms possess invariance property [49, 50] which makes them suitable for many vision applications.

Thus, wavelet transforms together with sparse representations have great impact in the development of intelligent multimedia applications. Wavelets have been explored for several image and signal processing applications, however, multiresolution analysis has not been explored for multimedia applications fully. Here, we would like to explore the diverse applications of multimedia security and surveillance, and wish to include several classical and advanced wavelet transforms for this purpose. The contents of this book will focus on intelligent techniques including the concept of machine and deep learning for multimedia systems particularly image and vision applications. It will provide a complete understanding of semantic information of images with the help of simple and straightforward examples, case studies on benchmark datasets.

The objective of this book is to provide understanding of different multimedia applications and promote research focusing the intelligent wavelet based techniques for advanced multimedia applications. It will cover recent and state of the art research topics in the wavelet domain to demonstrate the usefulness of classical and new generation wavelet transforms. Image fusion, image and video watermarking, object tracking, person identification, activity recognition and emotion recognition are some major application areas that have been discussed in this book.

1.3   Wavelet Transforms and Intelligent Multimedia Applications

As discussed in the Sect. 1.2, wavelet transforms have certainly gained popularity to handle simple and complex multimedia problems. Researchers and scientists have been influenced and proposed many scientific theories followed by experimental demonstrations to validate the successful applications of wavelet transforms in

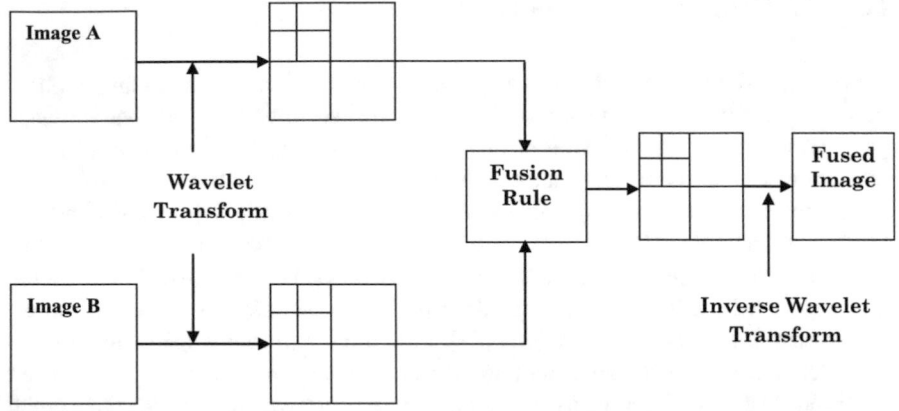

Fig. 1.1 Basic framework for image fusion in wavelet domain

intelligent multimedia applications. In this section, we highlight some major problems that have been solved using wavelet transforms.

1.3.1 Image Fusion

Wavelet transforms have been widely used for image fusion [51]. It includes infrared and visible image fusion, medical image fusion and other complementary imaging systems. A general framework of wavelet domain fusion has been shown in Fig. 1.1 for two input source images. From Fig. 1.1, it is clear that initially source images are decomposed using forward wavelet transforms to obtain wavelet coefficients and fusion rules are applied on these coefficients to obtain fused wavelet coefficients. Fused image is obtained using inverse wavelet transform.

The primary focus of fusion imaging is to develop fusion rules, and provide a complete framework for fusion of multisensory images in wavelet domain. The evaluation of fusion results is another key issue which can be addressed in using reference and non-reference fusion metrics. Thus, research in image fusion has a great possibility to be explored in wavelet domain as wavelet coefficients acts as a feature that has been combined using different fusion rules. In addition to this, fusion process must be robust and tolerant of noise or other artifacts which makes it more challenging for the development of fusion rules.

1.3.2 Image Watermarking

Image watermarking is a kind of data hiding technology that provides copyright protection, content authentication and broadcast monitoring [52]. In wavelet domain

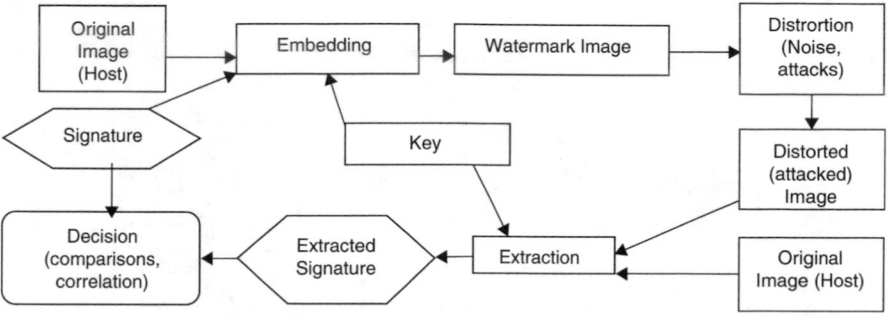

Fig. 1.2 Wavelet domain watermarking framework

techniques, we use wavelet transforms for cover data and embed secret message into wavelet coefficients that makes it more robust. A common framework for watermarking in wavelet domain has been given in Fig. 1.2. Wavelet domain techniques require more computations but are robust against common image processing operations such as existing image compression standards (JPEG, MPEG, JPEG2000, etc.), low-pass filtering, rotation cropping, and addition of noise. One of the major reasons for selecting wavelet transforms is multiresolution representation of image and compatibility with the international data compression standards like JPEG2000. One of the key challenges in image watermarking is to select appropriate wavelet transforms and proper subband to embed secret message so that the watermarked image is imperceptible and robust against various geometrical and signal processing attacks.

1.3.3 Video Watermarking

Image watermarking ensures the security of image data and this concept can be extended to provide copyright protection and unauthorized use of the video data. Video piracy is one of the key factors which can be avoided using video watermarking. The voluminous availability of video data over Internet and availability of high speed internet poses several challenges of copyright violation and illegal distribution of data. Like image watermarking, wavelet transforms can be used to provide solutions for the copyright protection and contribute significantly to avoid video piracy. A framework for video watermarking has been shown in Fig. 1.3. The steps of the video watermarking are similar to the image watermarking, except that it requires video frame selection for embedding and extraction of secret message. The key challenges in video watermarking in wavelet domain are selection of video frames, video compression schemes, sampling and quantization.

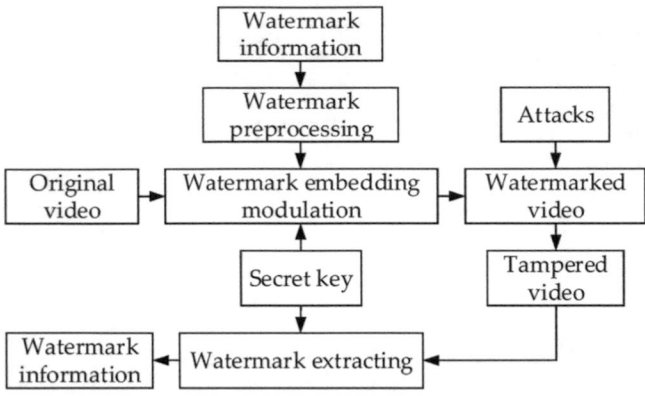

Fig. 1.3 A common framework for video watermarking

1.3.4   Object Tracking

Object tracking is one of the key steps in video surveillance system, widely used in public places to capture the abnormal activity of the human subjects. It can be defined as the process of locating object's position with respect to time. Object tracking can be done for single as well as for multiple objects. In addition to the video surveillance, object tracking can be used for clinical applications, biomechanical applications, human robot interaction, entertainment, education, and training etc. Wavelet transforms have been found to provide better solutions for object tracking as it is a key step for video surveillance system and tracks the subjects to prevent any kind of illegal activity [53, 54]. Furthermore, variants of wavelet transform such as complex wavelet transform provides shift invariance which is highly desirable for locating moving objects. However, we must consider some of the challenges such as changing shape of objects, occlusion, noise and blur, intensity variation etc. for the development of the efficient object tracking algorithms (Fig. 1.4).

1.3.5   Person Identification

Object tracking requires human detection either single or multiple for applications like video surveillance. With the increase of feature extraction algorithms, person identification has been involved as a key research area in computer vision and is a fundamental step of video surveillance system. Person identification in video sequence is a challenging problem as number of human objects, contrast, pose and background may vary in video frames. Thus, an invariant person identification algorithm is always required to provide an effective human motion analysis. These challenges can be handled with wavelet transforms as it provides better representation using directional selectivity and can handle shift as well by making use of

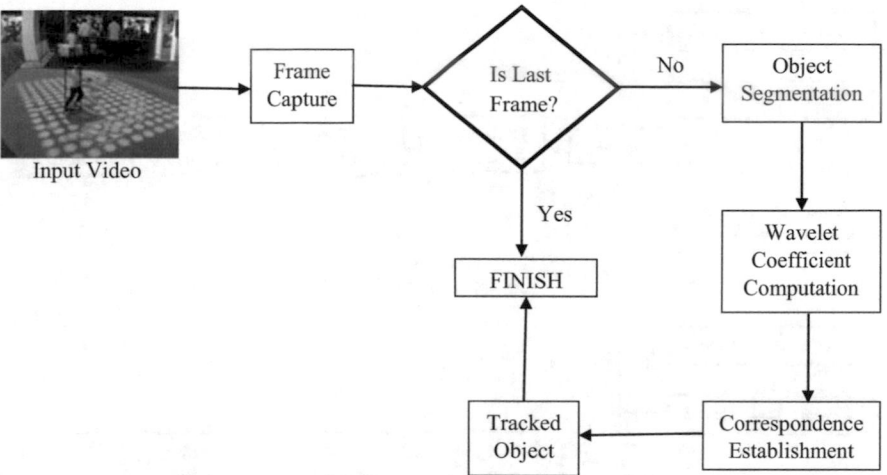

Fig. 1.4   A common framework for object tracking in wavelet domain

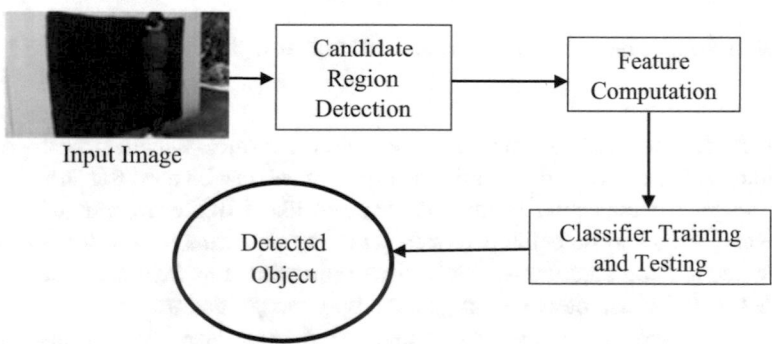

Fig. 1.5   Object detection framework

redundant wavelet transforms which provides shift invariance. Wavelet coefficients can act a feature vector and can be combined with local binary patterns (LBP) to develop robust and invariant person identification algorithms [55]. A framework for person identification has been shown in Fig. 1.5.

1.3.6   Activity Recognition

Activity recognition is a promising and challenging research area of multimedia security, especially for video surveillance. It can be defined as the actions performed to complete some task [56]. Recognition of human activities has been challenging as we have to find correspondence between different video sequence using labeled data.

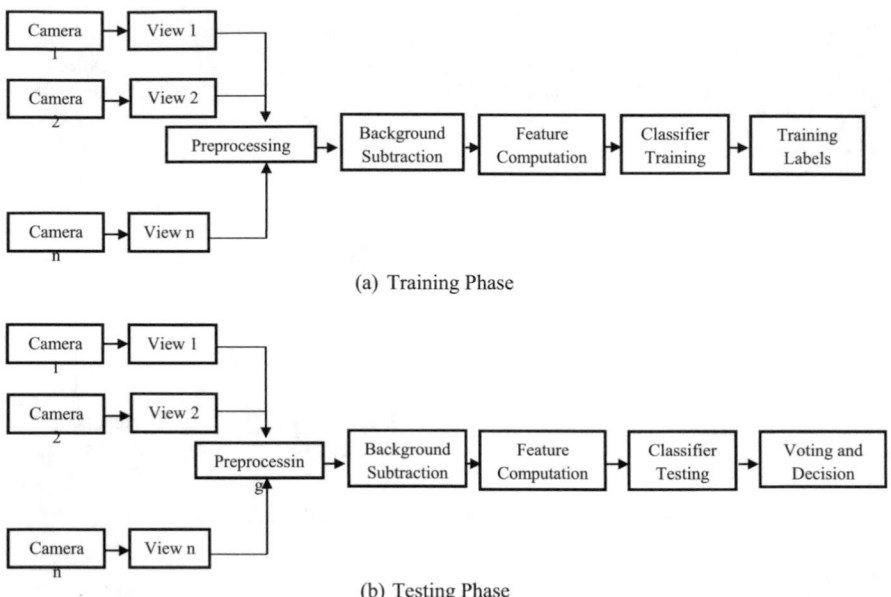

Fig. 1.6 A generic structure of the activity recognition process

It includes feature learning and training of pattern classifier. Wavelet transforms can contribute significantly in the activity recognition and can be used to learn classifier using wavelet coefficients. Feature descriptors like LBP, histogram of oriented gradients (HoG) can be combined with wavelet transforms to develop intelligent activity recognition algorithms. These algorithms should be invariant against environment variation and other challenges. Activity recognition involves action recognition, human-human, human-robot and multiple human interactions. Crowd behavior prediction [57] is an extension of simple activity recognition problem and can be explored using wavelet transform. Thus, activity recognition has a lot of scope as it is less explored in wavelet domain. A framework for activity recognition has been shown in Fig. 1.6.

1.3.7   Emotion Recognition Using Facial Expressions

Emotion recognition is the one of the crucial step of the human behavior analysis that predicts the psychological aspects of the human beings [58, 59]. Facial expressions have been widely used to recognize human emotions. The muscles of human face changes and these changes correspond to communicate feelings to human-human or human-machine interactions. Facial expression recognition problem can be understood using Fig. 1.7 [22] and is widely applicable in biometrics, security,

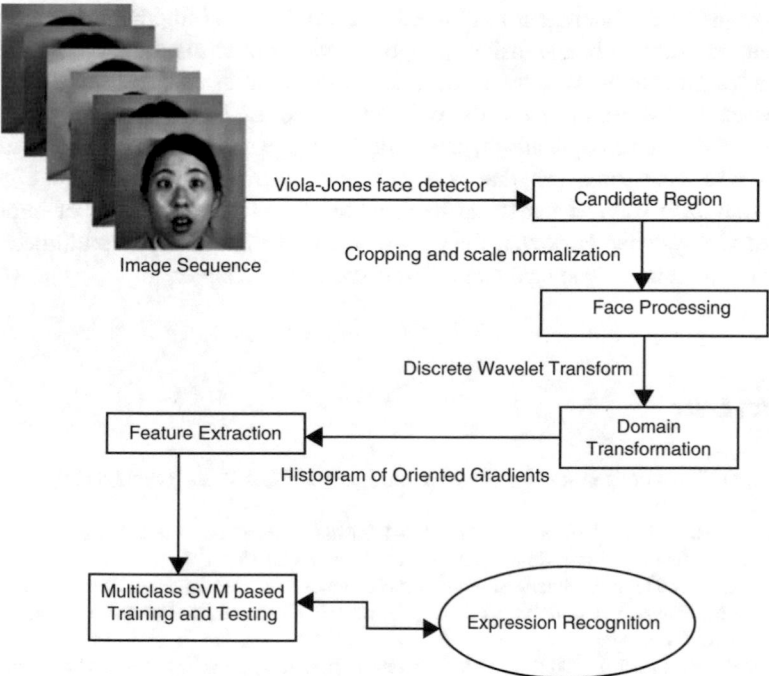

Fig. 1.7   A framework for emotion recognition using facial expressions

surveillance, etc. From Fig. 1.7, it is clear that wavelet transform can be integrated with other feature descriptors and used to identify emotions using facial expression. The six standard emotions based on facial expressions are *angry*, *disgust*, *fear*, *happy*, *sad* and *surprise*. These expressions have been widely used to identify human emotion in computer vision. One additional expression, without these six expressions is called neutral expression. Thus, in total seven benchmark facial expressions are used for emotion recognition. Emotion recognition is a challenging problem in computer vision as these standard expressions are not enough to recognize human behavior. We need some other methodology to identify the psychological behavior of the human beings. One such possibility is to integrate speech and other multimodal information to identify human behavior. Several other factors are age, gender, ethnic background and level of expressiveness.

1.4   Summary

The chapter summarizes the relevance and provides a basic idea of multimedia problems in wavelet domain so that the readers could connect themselves to this book and understand the basic framework. In this chapter, we have provided a background to the intelligent multimedia applications and highlighted some major applications such as image fusion, image and video watermarking, object tracking, person identification, activity recognition and emotion recognition using facial expressions. The usefulness of the wavelet transforms has influenced to use them in many multimedia applications, especially in image and vision based applications. It has also been observed that machine and deep learning techniques can be integrated with wavelet transform to provide efficient development of intelligent multimedia systems. However, the development of the intelligent multimedia systems should consider the challenges discussed in this chapter.

References

1. Marr D (1976) Early processing of visual information. Philos Trans R Soc Lond B Biol Sci 275 (942):483–519
2. Posner MI, Nissen MJ, Klein RM (1976) Visual dominance: An information-processing account of its origins and significance. Psychol Rev 83(2):157–171
3. Jain AK (1989) Fundamentals of digital image processing. Prentice Hall, Englewood Cliffs
4. Sonka M, Hlavac V, Boyle R (2014) Image processing, analysis, and machine vision. Cengage Learning, Stamford
5. Forsyth DA, Ponce J (2002) Computer vision: a modern approach. Prentice Hall Professional Technical Reference, Upper Saddle River
6. Schalkoff RJ (1989) Digital image processing and computer vision, vol 286. Wiley, New York
7. Jain AK, Ross A, Prabhakar S (2004) An introduction to biometric recognition. IEEE Trans Circuits Syst Video Technol 14(1):4–20
8. Lyons M, Akamatsu S, Kamachi M, Gyoba J (1998, April) Coding facial expressions with gabor wavelets. In: Proceedings third IEEE international conference on automatic face and gesture recognition. IEEE, Seoul, pp 200–205
9. Prokop RJ, Reeves AP (1992) A survey of moment-based techniques for unoccluded object representation and recognition. CVGIP: Graph Model Image Process 54(5):438–460
10. Yilmaz A, Javed O, Shah M (2006) Object tracking: A survey. ACM Comput Surv (CSUR) 38 (4):13–es
11. Pantic M, Pentland A, Nijholt A, Huang TS (2007) Human computing and machine understanding of human behavior: A survey. In: Artifical intelligence for human computing. Springer, Berlin, Heidelberg, pp 47–71
12. Hu W, Tan T, Wang L, Maybank S (2004) A survey on visual surveillance of object motion and behaviors. IEEE Trans Syst Man Cybern Part C Appl Rev 34(3):334–352
13. Li S, Kang X, Fang L, Hu J, Yin H (2017) Pixel-level image fusion: A survey of the state of the art. Inf Fusion 33:100–112
14. James AP, Dasarathy BV (2014) Medical image fusion: A survey of the state of the art. Inf Fusion 19:4–19
15. Jiang D, Zhuang D, Huang Y, Fu J (2011) Survey of multispectral image fusion techniques in remote sensing applications. In: Image fusion and its applications, pp 1–23.
16. Jain AK, Dorai C (1997) Practicing vision: Integration, evaluation and applications. Pattern Recogn 30(2):183–196
17. Vernon D (1991) Machine vision-automated visual inspection and robot vision. NASA STI/Recon Technical Report A, 92.
18. Kingsbury N, Magarey J (1998) Wavelet transforms in image processing. In: Signal analysis and prediction. Birkhäuser, Boston, pp 27–46

19. Rioul O, Vetterli M (1991) Wavelets and signal processing. IEEE Signal Process Mag 8 (ARTICLE):14–38
20. Mallat S (1999) A wavelet tour of signal processing. Elsevier, San Diego
21. Mallat SG (1989) A theory for multiresolution signal decomposition: The wavelet representation. IEEE Trans Pattern Anal Mach Intell 11(7):674–693
22. Nigam S, Singh R, Misra AK (2018) Efficient facial expression recognition using histogram of oriented gradients in wavelet domain. Multimed Tools Appl 77(21):28725–28747
23. Singh R, Khare A (2014) Fusion of multimodal medical images using Daubechies complex wavelet transform–a multiresolution approach. Inf Fusion 19:49–60
24. Singh S, Rathore VS, Singh R (2017) Hybrid NSCT domain multiple watermarking for medical images. Multimed Tools Appl 76(3):3557–3575
25. Zhang L, Zhou W, Jiao L (2004) Wavelet support vector machine. IEEE Trans Syst Man Cybern B Cybern 34(1):34–39
26. Chaplot S, Patnaik LM, Jagannathan NR (2006) Classification of magnetic resonance brain images using wavelets as input to support vector machine and neural network. Biomed Signal Process Control 1(1):86–92
27. Usman K, Rajpoot K (2017) Brain tumor classification from multi-modality MRI using wavelets and machine learning. Pattern Anal Applic 20(3):871–881
28. Liu P, Zhang H, Zhang K, Lin L, Zuo W (2018) Multi-level wavelet-CNN for image restoration. In: Proceedings of the IEEE conference on computer vision and pattern recognition workshops. IEEE, Salt Lake City, pp 773–782
29. Kang E, Min J, Ye JC (2017) A deep convolutional neural network using directional wavelets for low-dose X-ray CT reconstruction. Med Phys 44(10):e360–e375
30. Kanarachos S, Christopoulos SRG, Chroneos A, Fitzpatrick ME (2017) Detecting anomalies in time series data via a deep learning algorithm combining wavelets, neural networks and Hilbert transform. Expert Syst Appl 85:292–304
31. Hassairi S, Ejbali R, Zaied M (2015, November) Supervised image classification using deep convolutional wavelets network. In: 2015 IEEE 27th international conference on tools with artificial intelligence (ICTAI). IEEE, Vietri sul Mare, pp 265–271
32. Ye JC, Han Y, Cha E (2018) Deep convolutional framelets: A general deep learning framework for inverse problems. SIAM J Imaging Sci 11(2):991–1048
33. Diker A, Avci D, Avci E, Gedikpinar M (2019) A new technique for ECG signal classification genetic algorithm wavelet kernel extreme learning machine. Optik 180:46–55
34. Subasi A, Kevric J, Canbaz MA (2019) Epileptic seizure detection using hybrid machine learning methods. Neural Comput & Applic 31(1):317–325
35. Ghasemzadeh A, Azad SS, Esmaeili E (2019) Breast cancer detection based on Gabor-wavelet transform and machine learning methods. Int J Mach Learn Cybern 10(7):1603–1612
36. Khagi B, Kwon GR, Lama R (2019) Comparative analysis of Alzheimer's disease classification by CDR level using CNN, feature selection, and machine-learning techniques. Int J Imaging Syst Technol 29(3):297–310
37. Kiaee N, Hashemizadeh E, Zarrinpanjeh N (2019) Using GLCM features in Haar wavelet transformed space for moving object classification. IET Intell Transp Syst 13:1148–1153
38. Moghaddam HA, Zare A (2019) Spatiotemporal wavelet correlogram for human action recognition. Int J Multimed Inf Retr 8:1–14
39. Bolouri K, Azmoodeh A, Dehghantanha A, Firouzmand M (2019) Internet of things camera identification algorithm based on sensor pattern noise using color filter array and wavelet transform. In: Handbook of big data and IoT security. Springer, Cham, pp 211–223
40. Chen YT, Lai WN, Sun EW (2019) Jump detection and noise separation by a singular wavelet method for predictive analytics of high-frequency data. Comput Econ 54:1–36
41. Aldroubi A, Unser M (1996) Wavelets in medicine and biology. CRC Press, Bosa Roca
42. Dhawas NA, Patil D, Sambhaji A (2019) Invisible video watermarking for data integrity and security based on discrete wavelet transform–a review. Invisible video watermarking for data integrity and security based on discrete wavelet transform–a review (May 18, 2019)

43. Tsakanikas V, Dagiuklas T (2018) Video surveillance systems-current status and future trends. Comput Electr Eng 70:736–753
44. Burrus CS, Gopinath RA, Guo H, Odegard JE, Selesnick IW (1998) Introduction to wavelets and wavelet transforms: A primer, vol 1. Prentice hall, New Jersey
45. Strang G, Nguyen T (1996) Wavelets and filter banks. SIAM, Wellesley
46. Mallat SG (1988) Multiresolution representations and wavelets
47. Pajares G, De La Cruz JM (2004) A wavelet-based image fusion tutorial. Pattern Recogn 37 (9):1855–1872
48. Daubechies I (1990) The wavelet transform, time-frequency localization and signal analysis. IEEE Trans Inf Theory 36(5):961–1005
49. Simoncelli EP, Freeman WT, Adelson EH, Heeger DJ (1991) Shiftable multiscale transforms. IEEE Trans Inf Theory 38(2):587–607
50. Selesnick I, Baraniuk R, Kingsbury N (2005) The dual-tree complex wavelet transform. IEEE Signal Process Mag 22:123–151
51. Pajares G, De La Cruz JM (2004) A wavelet-based image fusion tutorial. Pattern Recogn 37 (9):1855–1872
52. Gangadhar Y, Akula VG, Reddy PC (2018) An evolutionary programming approach for securing medical images using watermarking scheme in invariant discrete wavelet transformation. Biomed Signal Process Control 43:31–40
53. Rui T, Zhang Q, Zhou Y, Xing J (2013) Object tracking using particle filter in the wavelet subspace. Neurocomputing 119:125–130
54. Guo Q, Cao X, Zou Q (2018) Enhanced wavelet convolutional neural networks for visual tracking. J Electron Imaging 27(5):053046
55. Chan AD, Hamdy MM, Badre A, Badee V (2008) Wavelet distance measure for person identification using electrocardiograms. IEEE Trans Instrum Meas 57(2):248–253
56. Siddiqi M, Ali R, Rana M, Hong EK, Kim E, Lee S (2014) Video-based human activity recognition using multilevel wavelet decomposition and stepwise linear discriminant analysis. Sensors 14(4):6370–6392
57. Wang J, Xu Z (2016) Spatio-temporal texture modelling for real-time crowd anomaly detection. Comput Vis Image Underst 144:177–187
58. Goldman AI, Sripada CS (2005) Simulationist models of face-based emotion recognition. Cognition 94(3):193–213
59. Busso C, Deng Z, Yildirim S, Bulut M, Lee CM, Kazemzadeh A et al (2004) Analysis of emotion recognition using facial expressions, speech and multimodal information. In: Proceedings of the 6th international conference on multimodal interfaces. ACM, State College, pp 205–211

Chapter 2
Wavelet Transforms: From Classical to New Generation Wavelets

Abstract Wavelet transforms have become an important mathematical tool that has been widely explored for visual information processing. The wide range of wavelet transforms and their multiresolution analysis facilitate to solve complex problems ranging from simple to complex image and vision based problems. The present chapter aims to provide an overview of existing wavelet transforms ranging from classical to new generation wavelets. This chapter discusses the basics of the discrete wavelet transform (DWT) followed by new generation wavelet transforms and highlights their useful characteristics. Other than DWT, the present chapter provides a brief review on dual tree complex wavelet transform (DTCWT), curvelet transform (CVT), contourlet transform (CT), contourlet transform (CNT), nonsubsampled contourlet transform (NSCT) to provide fundamentals and understanding of the wavelet transforms.

Keywords Wavelet transforms · Discrete wavelet transform · Complex wavelet transform · New generation wavelets · Applications of wavelet transforms

2.1 Introduction

Wavelets and multiscale transforms have been significantly used for a variety of multimedia applications ranging from simple imaging to complex vision based methods [1–3]. Though, it was the Fourier transform, which introduced the idea of using transforms in signal and image processing applications using time-frequency analysis [4]. However, Fourier transform lacked in handling non-stationary signals and providing localized information in time-frequency analysis. Later, short term Fourier transform (STFT) has been developed, also called windowed Fourier transform to overcome the shortcomings of classical Fourier transform. STFT provides time-frequency localization with fixed window size with a very little flexibility. These drawbacks led to a new mathematical theory, called wavelet analysis, has been found to be more useful than Fourier transform and capable of handling stationary as well as non-stationary signals [5]. Wavelet transform provides another representation of signals in form of wavelet coefficients, can be processed for any

© Springer Nature Switzerland AG 2020

R. Singh et al., *Intelligent Wavelet Based Techniques for Advanced Multimedia Applications*, https://doi.org/10.1007/978-3-030-31873-4_2

application in science and engineering. The present chapter aims to provide a literature review over existing classical and new generation wavelet transforms to explore the possibilities in various engineering applications and to give strong foundations to the subsequent chapters of the book.

2.2 Wavelet Transforms

Wavelet transforms have been developed from the word 'wavelet' which is similar to a small wave. We can define 'wave' as an oscillating function in time or space [6], e.g. sinusoid signals. Wave analysis is provided by Fourier transform, which converts the signals into sinusoids. A function $\psi(t)$ is called wavelet (mother wavelet) if it is of finite energy and satisfies following conditions [7]:

- The function $\psi(t)$ should have wave like nature and integrates to zero:

$$\int_{-\infty}^{\infty} \psi(t)dt = 0.$$

- The function $\psi(t)$ should have finite energy and duration:

$$\int_{-\infty}^{\infty} |\psi(t)|^2 dt < \infty.$$

- The function $\psi(t)$ should satisfy admissibility condition that can be used in analysis and synthesis of signals.

$$C = \int_{-\infty}^{\infty} \frac{|\widehat{\psi}(\omega)|^2}{|\omega|} d\omega, \quad 0 < C < \infty$$

where, $\widehat{\psi}(\omega)$ is Fourier transform of $\psi(t)$.

The difference between a wave and wavelet can be understood by Fig. 2.1. It can be easily observed that the sinusoid wave has infinite duration and energy whereas wavelet has finite energy and concentrated around one point.

For a function $x(t)$, continuous wavelet transform (CWT) [8, 9] is given by:

$$W(a,b) = \frac{1}{\sqrt{|a|}} \int x(t) \psi^* \left(\frac{t-b}{a} \right) dt$$

where, $\psi^*(t)$ denote the complex conjugate of mother wavelet $\psi(t)$, a is real nonzero scale parameter and b is real parameter that shifts the mother wavelet, so that $CWT_f(a,b)$ shows the local information about $f(t)$, at time $t = b$.

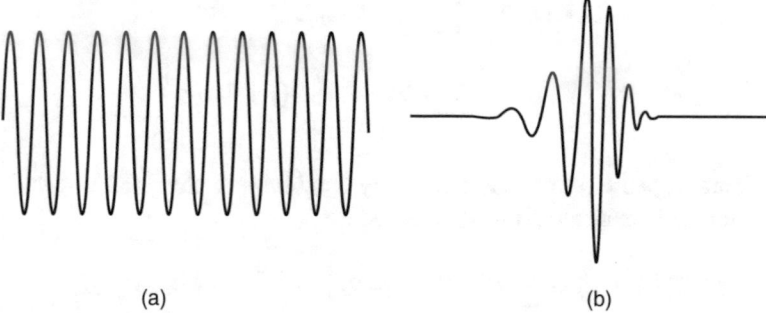

(a)   (b)

Fig. 2.1 (a) A wave and (b) a wavelet

CWT introduces redundancy in computation of wavelet transforms and does not provide multiresolution analysis (MRA) of signals [10]. DWT can be considered as a sampled version of CWT. But, it has been introduced independently and handles the drawbacks of CWT efficiently.

2.2.1   Discrete Wavelet Transform

For majority of signal processing and practical implementation of wavelet transforms, only DWT has been explored [11, 12]. DWT provides dyadic decomposition of input signals using shifted and dilated versions of mother wavelet $\psi(t)$ and of a scaling function $\phi(t)$ [6, 13] which are given by

$$\phi(x) = \sqrt{2}\sum_{k} l(k)\phi(2x - k)$$

$$\psi(x) = \sqrt{2}\sum_{k} h(k)\phi(2x - k)$$

where $l(k)$ and $h(k)$ are approximation and wavelet coefficients respectively. The scaling and wavelet functions are further used to decompose a given image $F(x)$ using equation

$$F(x) = \sum_{k} C(j,k)\phi_{j,k}(x) + \sum_{j}\sum D(j,k)\psi_{j,k}(x)$$

where $C(j,k)$ and $D(j,k)$ are scaling and wavelet coefficients at scale J and can be computed by following relation:

$$C(j,k) = \sum_k l(k-2m)\, C(j+1,k)$$

$$D(j,k) = \sum_k h(k-2m)\, C(j+1,k) \tag{2.5}$$

The original signal can be reconstructed by combining scaling and wavelet coefficients, and mathematically, it is represented by

$$C(j+1,k) = \sum_k C(j,k)l(m-2k) + \sum_k D(j,k)h(m-2k)$$

This forward and backward analysis of signals facilitates to have multiscale signal representations at varying scales. Directional information into three spatial orientations; namely, horizontal, diagonal and vertical has been provided by DWT, which are combinations of scaling and wavelet functions as given below:

$$\phi_{LL}(x,y) = \phi(x)\phi(y), \quad \psi_{LH}(x,y) = \phi(x)\psi(y)$$
$$\psi_{HL}(x,y) = \psi(x)\phi(y), \quad \psi_{HH}(x,y) = \psi(x)\psi(y)$$

DWT decomposition process in two dimension has been given in Fig. 2.2 which shows the multiscale representation of a given image at different levels.

DWT coefficients are real valued and represent the visual information, which is local in space and frequency. Thus, for any signal and image processing applications,

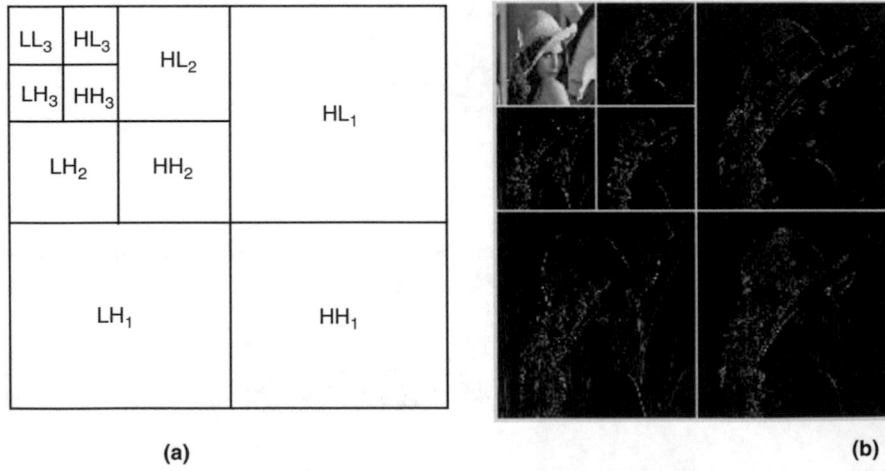

(a)   (b)

Fig. 2.2 Decomposition process in Discrete Wavelet Transform (DWT). (**a**) DWT decomposition up to level 3, (**b**) Two level decomposition of Lena image

one can use DWT for extraction of local information with multiresolution analysis. Further, DWT enables the detection of edges in the form of large magnitude wavelet coefficients by representing three directional edges: vertical, horizontal and diagonal. Using this property, we can develop edge sensitive signal and image processing algorithms.

The wavelet coefficients obtained after DWT decomposition are approximately decorrelated. Therefore, during practical implementation, if a few wavelet coefficients changes, then this would not lead to the other wavelet coefficients. Moreover, the most essential information of signal is represented by high magnitude wavelet coefficients, which represents salient information such as edges, corners etc. For these advantages, DWT has been well explored in many image and vision based applications [14–18].

However, DWT has lacked in providing shift invariance, high directionality and phase information. It has been found that these properties enables better reconstruction of signals and images and can be explored for applications like object tracking, action recognition etc.

Shift sensitivity can be defined as the imbalanced change in transform coefficients due to input signal shift. DWT [19] has been found shift sensitive due to the use of downsamplers in its implementation. This shift sensitivity arises in DWT as it is critically sampled, and it violates Nyquist criterion [20]. To achieve shift invariance, a transform must satisfy Nyquist criterion.

The two dimensional DWT provides only three spatial orientation through wavelet coefficients. These orientations are horizontal, vertical and diagonal. For applications like medical imaging, watermarking etc. high directional information can be utilized for efficient representation of images [21] and a replacement of DWT is highly desired.

As DWT provides real valued wavelet coefficients, it is not able to provide phase information. Phase information has been exploited in many signal/image processing applications [22, 23]. It provides greater robustness in signal-processing applications. Since real valued wavelet transforms do not provide phase information, therefore, one cannot achieve accurate and robust results for complex vision based applications.

Lifting wavelet transform (LWT) [24] and integer wavelet transform (IWT) [25] are a few other wavelet transforms which provide faster implementation. These are used to enhance the computational speed of wavelet domain methods. In addition to this, redundant discrete wavelet transform (RDWT) [26] is an undecimated wavelet transform and provides shift invariance at the high computational cost than DWT and others. These can be treated as real valued wavelet transforms as they provide real valued wavelet coefficients after decomposition. Hence, except RDWT, no other real valued wavelet transform is capable of providing shift invariance. In order to reduce the cost and redundancy, RDWT should be replaced with computationally efficient wavelet transforms.

2.2.2   Complex Wavelet Transforms

As discussed in Sect. 2.1, DWT and other wavelet transforms provide limited functionality. Hence, a new family of wavelet transforms, called complex wavelet transforms has been introduced by Kingsbury [27] and Lina & Mayrand [28]. These transform provides complex wavelet coefficients, i.e. in the form of $a + ib$ and capable of handling the shortcomings of DWT and other wavelet transforms. In this section, we discuss a brief implementation of these wavelet transforms and present characteristics of complex wavelet transforms, proposed by Kingsbury and Lina.

2.2.2.1   Dual Tree Complex Wavelet Transform (DTCWT)

(DTCWT) [21, 27, 29] has been proposed by Kingsbury to overcome the limitations of DWT. It is approximately shift invariant transform and computationally efficient than RDWT. In comparison to DWT, it provides better directional selectivity and is a redundant transform with limited redundancy. This redundancy is independent of scale and for one dimensional signal, it is 2:1. More specifically, for m-dimensional signal, this redundancy is $2^m : 1$. DTCWT enables perfect reconstruction using short linear phase filters at the cost of limited increased computation, i.e. 2^m times for m-dimensional signals.

One of the major concerns of DTCWT implementation is shift invariance. It has been observed that this shift invariance can be introduced in DTCWT using DWT tree. For this purpose, sampling rate should be doubled at every level of the DWT decomposition tree with evenly spaced samples. Removing downsampling by 2 after level 1 is the one possible way to double the sampling rate. DWT tree based decomposition and reconstruction has been shown in Fig. 2.3.

To provide perfect reconstruction, DTCWT uses odd and even length filters in two different trees alternatively at different levels. Latter, it was found that this filtering scheme is not fully symmetrical; hence, a Q-shift dual tree structure has been used for DTCWT. Both, even-odd filtering scheme and Q-shift has been exploited for design and analysis of DTCWT.

In order to find inverse of DTCWT, biorthogonal filter is used for DWT trees. These filters are made to achieve perfect reconstruction using 2-band reconstruction, can be seen in Fig. 2.3. The outputs obtained from the two trees have been averaged for reconstruction of signals. The system obtained with above specification is a wavelet frame with redundancy two. If analysis and synthesis filter banks have similar frequency responses, then it fulfills the condition of tight frame. Therefore, the DTCWT provides energy preservation during signal and image transformation.

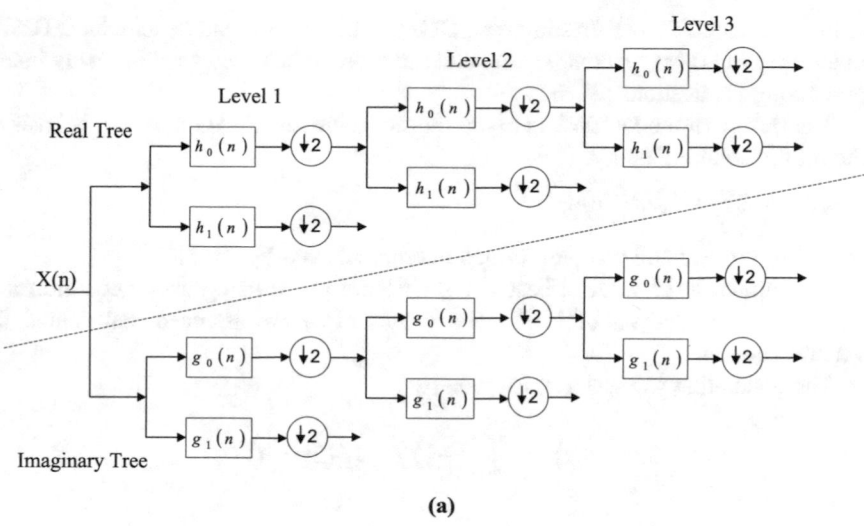

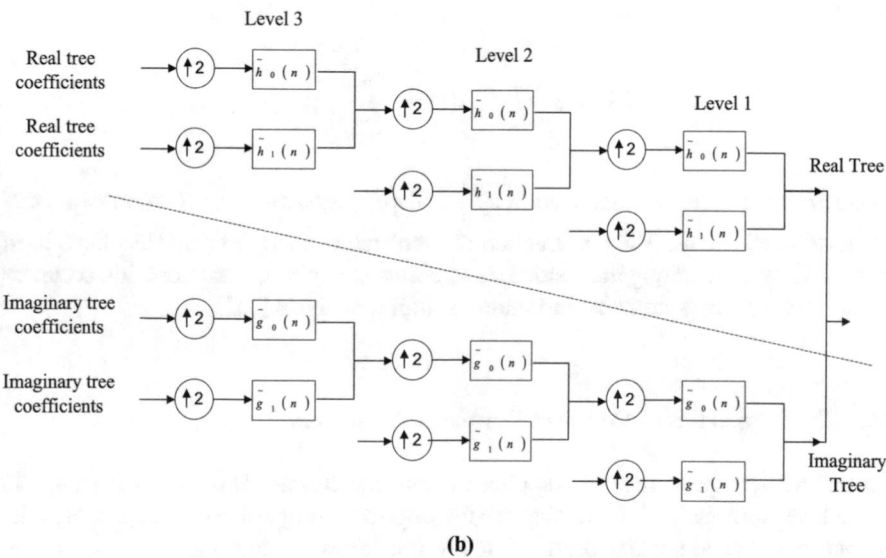

Fig. 2.3 The wavelet tree decomposition and reconstruction in DTCWT [27]

2.2.2.2   Discrete Complex Wavelet Transform (DCxWT)

Like DTCWT, DCxWT is the complex version of basic DWT and originally proposed by Lina [28, 30, 31]. DTCWT uses real filter banks in the implementation, whereas complex filter banks has been used for the implementation of DCxWT. Thus, it can be said that DCxWT is a complete complex wavelet transform and is less redundant than DTCWT. In summary, DCxWT has been found better than DTCWT in terms of redundancy, computation and therefore, it has been used for many image processing applications [22, 32].

The design of the DCxWT is based on the following equation, which is basis of the multiresolution theory:

$$\phi(x) = 2\sum_{k} a_k \phi(2x - k)$$

where a_k are real and complex valued coefficients and $\sum a_k = 1$.

One dimensional wavelet bases $\{\psi_{j,\ k}(t)\}$ are given using above equation and multiresolution analysis of $L^2(R)$. The values of a_k are assumed real valued for general solution.

The generating wavelet $\psi(t)$ is given by

$$\psi(t) = 2\sum_{n} (-1)^n \overline{a_{1-n}} \phi(2t - n)$$

Here $\psi(t)$ and $\phi(t)$ share the same compact support $[-N, N + 1]$.

Any function $f(t)$ can be decomposed into complex scaling function and mother wavelet as:

$$f(t) = \sum_{k} c_k^{j_0} \phi_{j_0,k}(t) + \sum_{j=j_0}^{j_{max}-1} d_k^j \psi_{j,k}(t)$$

where j_0 is a given resolution level, $\left\{c_k^{j_0}\right\}$ and $\left\{d_k^j\right\}$ are known as approximation and detailed coefficients. The construction of Daubechies complex wavelets have been provided by considering the conditions of compact support, orthogonality, accuracy of approximation, symmetry and multiresolution analysis [31].

2.2.2.3   Properties of Complex Wavelet Transforms

In this section, properties of complex wavelet transforms (DTCWT and DCxWT) have been summarized. Following are the important properties of complex wavelet transforms that are found useful in many image processing and computer vision applications [33].

(i) **Symmetry**: It has been found that except 'Haar' wavelet, none of the real orthogonal wavelets are symmetric. However, the DTCWT [34] and DCxWT [30] can be made symmetric which is required for easier handling of boundary value problems for finite length signals [35].

(ii) **Low Redundancy**: The DTCWT offers a limited redundancy of 2 : 1 for 1-dimensional signal and 2^n : 1 for n-dimensional signal whereas the DCxWT has no such redundancy. This lower redundancy of the DTCWT provides an efficient computation than RDWT, wavelet packet transform (WPT) and other advanced wavelet transforms like CVT, CNT and NSCT. Furthermore, since, the DCxWT has no redundancy, therefore, it is superior to the DTCWT and above wavelet transforms.

(iii) **Shift Invariance**: Both complex wavelet transforms (DTCWT and DCxWT) are shift invariant in nature. Kingsbury [29] clearly demonstrated the shift invariance of these transforms in their work. This property of complex wavelet transforms yield better reconstruction of signals and images.

(iv) **Phase Information**: Since complex wavelet transforms decompose original signals into real and imaginary components, therefore, they provide phase information. It has been found that phase of complex wavelet transforms (DTCWT and DCxWT) plays an important role in image modeling [36–38].

(v) **Directionality**: The DTCWT provides better directional information [29] into six spatial orientations which are $\pm 15^0$, $\pm 45^0$, $\pm 75^0$. Thus, use of the DTCWT enables to incorporate high directionality. Unlike DTCWT, the DCxWT has only three spatial orientations as it is the complex version of basic DWT. However, the DCxWT has better directional selectivity than pyramid transforms.

Till now, we have discussed the transforms which are suitable for many applications, but these are not efficient to provide better and effective analysis for different geometrical shapes. For these reasons, the concepts of wavelet transforms have been extended to introduce new generation wavelet transforms to provide multiscale geometrical analysis [39] and facilitate higher directional selectivity than DTCWT.

2.2.3   Curvelet Transform

Candes et al. [40–42] have introduced curvelet transform (CVT) to overcome the shortcomings of the wavelet representation and handle singularities along curves and provide multiscale geometric analysis. CVT has been found suitable for capturing directional information in many orientations. Hence, it is well suited for capturing geometrical features and gives sparse representation including edges, better than wavelets. This property can be utilized in linear inverse problems to model statistical parameters to extract objects from noisy data. Furthermore, CVT can be used for the modeling of wave propagation geometry and image reconstruction. Thus, like wavelet transform, CVT can be explored for various multimedia applications, particularly in image and vision based applications. In order to understand CVT implementation, we should consider analysis and synthesis components separately.

2.2.3.1   Analysis

CVT analysis is very similar to the wavelet decomposition and includes subband decomposition, smooth partitioning, renormalization and ridgelet analysis.

- **Subband decomposition**

  Subband decomposition is the very first step of CVT decomposition. Any given input object is decomposed into several subbands using filter banks. For a given input object x, the decomposition can be performed using filter banks $P_0(\Delta_s, s \geq 0)$, given by,

$$x \rightarrow (P_0 x, \Delta_1 x, \Delta_2 x, \ldots)$$

- **Smooth Partitioning**

  After subband decomposition, window based smooth partitioning should be performed so that subbands can be centralized. This process can be done for given object x using following equation

$$h_Q = w_Q . \Delta_s x$$

where w_Q is a window function operated over subbands.

The dyadic squares can be defined as

$$Q = \left[\frac{k_1}{2^s}, \frac{k_1 + 1}{2^s} \right] \times \left[\frac{k_2}{2^s}, \frac{k_2 + 1}{2^s} \right] \in Q_s$$

where Q_s represented all dyadic squares, k_1 and k_2 denotes first and last high pass filters that implies that grid is in between them.

- **Renormalization**

  Renormalization is performed to convert every square grid to unit scale. This helps in reducing number of computations. For renormalization, an operator T_Q is defined for each Q as

$$(T_Q x)(x_1, x_2) = 2^s f(2^s x_1 - k_1, 2^s x_2 - k_2)$$

where x_1, x_2 are ridge lines along first and last high pass filter. This operation is used for renormalization of each subband or sub-image. The renormalization of each subband is done as

$$g_Q = T_Q^{-1} h_Q$$

Here we get g_Q as renormalized subband image.

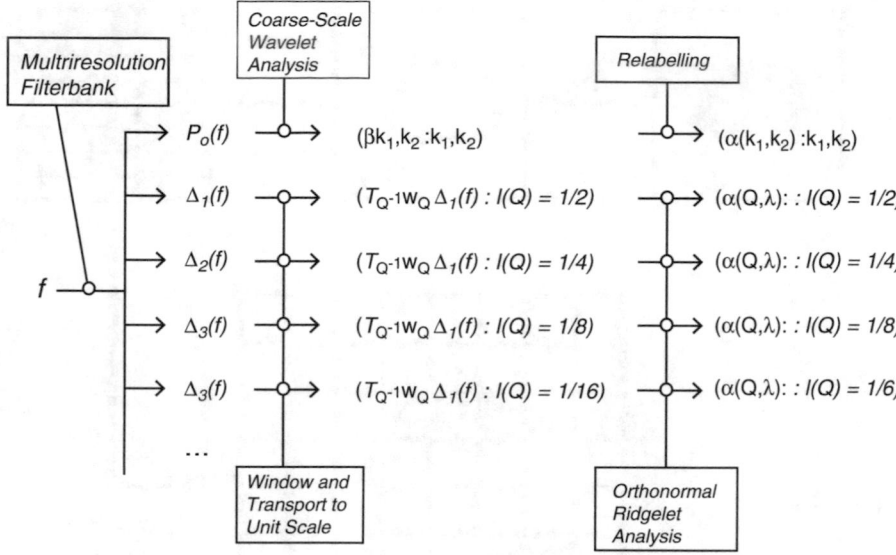

Fig. 2.4 Steps involved in curvelet transform

- **Ridgelet analysis**

    Finally, ridgelet analysis has been performed to obtain CVT coefficients. The organization of curvelet transform has been shown in Fig. 2.4 and the spatial decomposition process of CVT can be understood from Fig. 2.5.

2.2.3.2   Synthesis

CVT synthesis is same as the inverse wavelet transform and includes ridgelet synthesis, renormalization, smooth integration and subband recomposition. Hence, it can be seen that these are the reverse process of analysis which is used to obtain input object x.

CVT was initially developed for continuous domain and then it has been implemented in discrete domain. Thus, grid sampling for CVT is difficult in discrete domain and geometrical representations are done in rectangular grids. This limits the performance of CVT and hence, another new generation wavelet transform, known as contourlet transform (CNT) has been introduced to overcome this problem.

2.2.4   *Contourlet Transform*

The development of multiscale geometrical transforms has been influenced by CVT that enables better representation than wavelet transforms. Contourlet transform

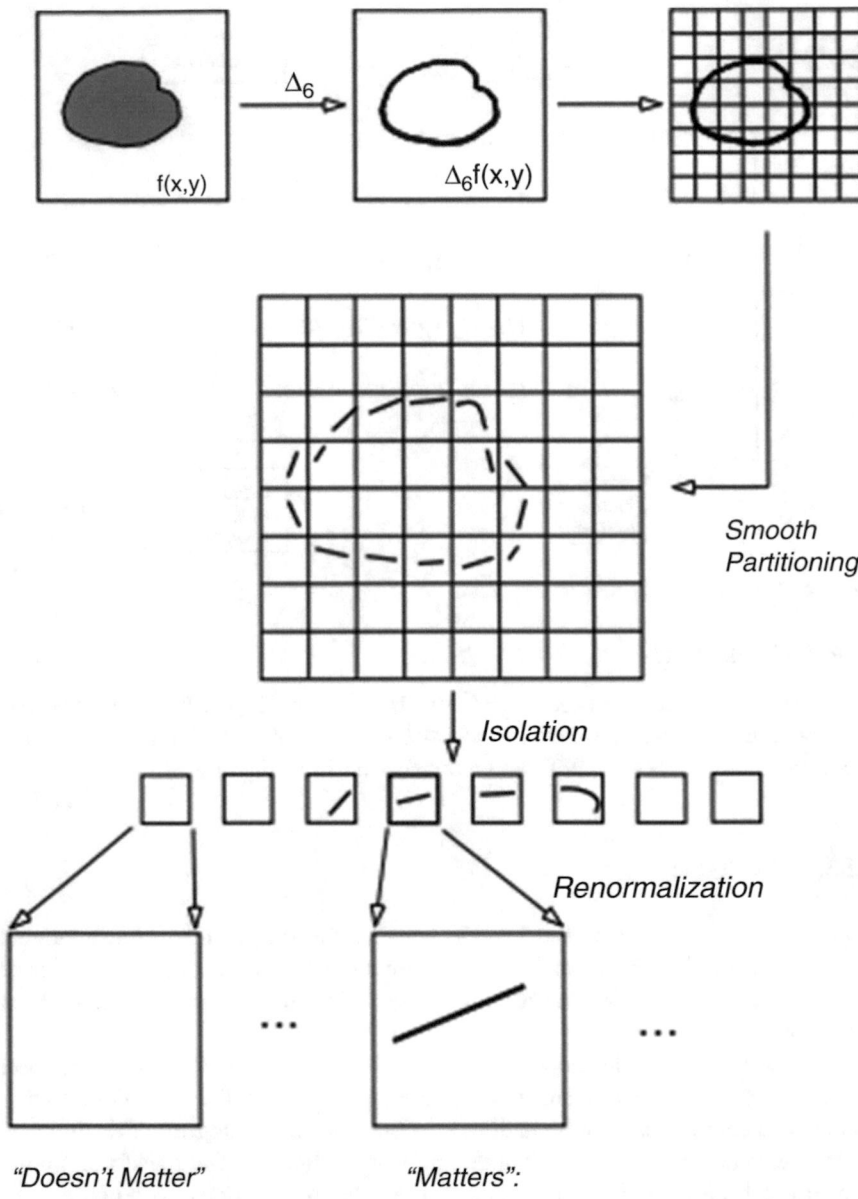

Fig. 2.5 Decomposition process of curvelet transform

(CNT) has been proposed by Do and Vetterli [43, 44] to address the shortcomings of existing transforms. CNT provides better representation of curves and geometry than wavelet transforms and can be seen in Fig. 2.6.

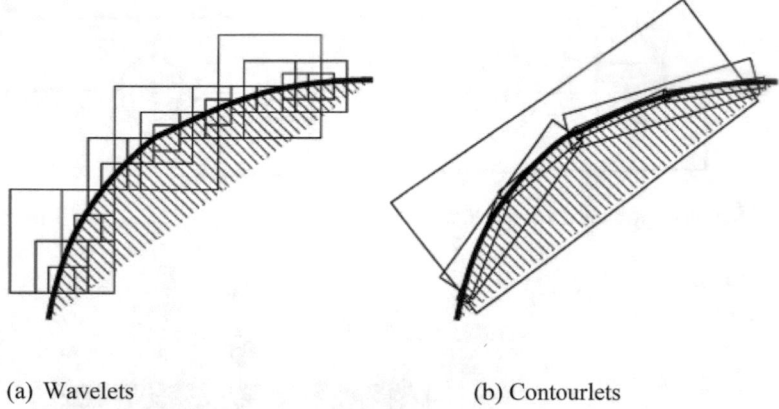

(a) Wavelets   (b) Contourlets

Fig. 2.6   The comparison of wavelet and contourlet scheme

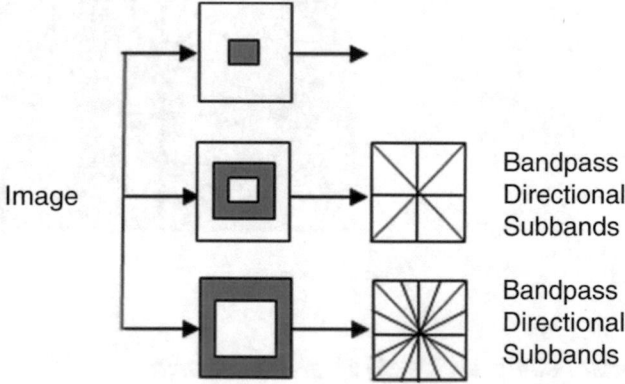

Fig. 2.7   Filter bank structure of contourlet transform

Sparse representation is another important property possess by CNT, which makes it useful for linear inverse problems. CNT also provides better directional selectivity in different ordinations. Thus, it is well suited for the processing of natural images and can be used in applications like image fusion and watermarking which aim to obtain high quality image. The implementation of CNT includes two pass filter banks shown in Fig. 2.7 to obtain sparse representations. In the first pass, Laplacian pyramid is used to capture point discontinuities and provides bandpass image. Laplacian decomposition process is shown in Fig. 2.8.

After Laplacian decomposition, directional filter banks have been used to obtain linear structures from point singularities. For this purpose, $l$level tree decomposition is performed to obtain 2^lsubbands for frequency partitioning, as shown in Fig. 2.9. Thus, CNT implementation includes Laplacian pyramid and directional filter banks to provide multiscale geometrical information of the source images.

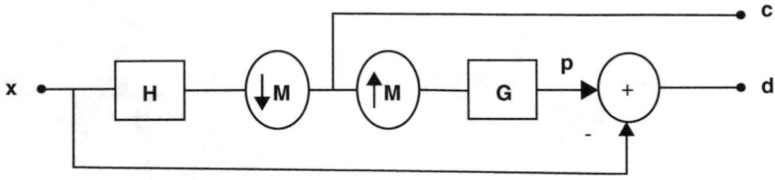

Fig. 2.8 Laplacian pyramid decomposition

Fig. 2.9 The iterated
frequency partitioning

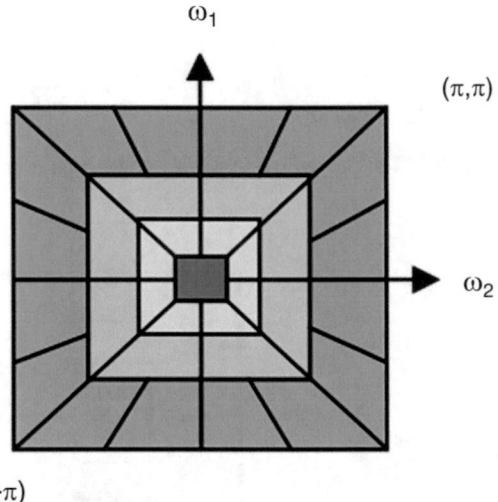

2.2.5   *Nonsubsampled Contourlet Transform*

CNT is well suited and provides better representation of geometrical information
than wavelet transforms and CVT. But, CNT is shift sensitive transform as it uses
downsampling in two level implementation using Laplacian pyramid and
difrectional filter banks. We have already discussed that shift invariance is highly
desirable for robust image and vision based algorithms. Due to these limitations, a
redundant version of contourlet transform, known as nonsubsampled contourlet
transform (NSCT) has been introduced [45, 46]. NSCT is shift invariant multiscale
transform and well capable of providing rich directional information.

NSCT implementation does not use downsampling and due to redundancy it is
less constrained than CNT. Like CNT, NSCT construction includes two steps and
both are shift invariant as downsamplers have been removed during its implementation. Nonsubsampled pyramid filter banks (NSPFB) and nonsubsampled directional filter banks (NSDFB) are used for the construction of NSCT, shown in

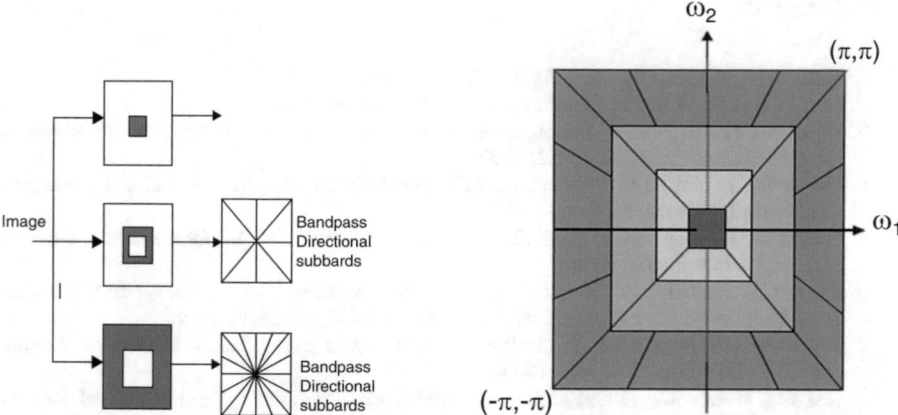

Fig. 2.10 The nonsubsampled contourlet transforms. (**a**) Nonsubsampled filter bank structure. (**b**) The iterated frequency partitioning

Fig. 2.10. NSPFB provides multiscale decomposition and the NSDFB enables to capture directional information of the source images.

We have discussed a few wavelet transforms and new generation transforms and found that the use of these transform can enhance the performance of multimedia applications [46–50]. Also, we have flexibility to choose these transforms as per our requirement. The selection of wavelet transforms must be application oriented as these require more number of computational steps and may not be applicable for every class of problems.

2.3 Summary

In this chapter, we aimed to provide a brief description of the various wavelet transforms used till now for signal, image and computer vision applications. The chapter started with basics of wavelet transform followed by introduction of DWT, The shortcomings of DWT has been discussed and the background for evolution of multiscale geometric transforms has been provided. The development of multiscale geometric transforms will enhance the performance of the algorithms at the cost of computational time and space. Hence, choice of wavelet transform for a particular application must consider the nature of data and complexity of the application for the real time and practical implementations. The number of transforms discussed, in this chapter, are limited. However, many applications can be developed using these and further enhancement can be used by considering more than one wavelet transform, i.e. by making hybrid combination of two different wavelet families.

References

1. Mallat S (1996) Wavelets for a vision. Proc IEEE 84(4):604–614
2. Mallat SG (1988) Multiresolution representations and wavelets.
3. Mallat SG (1990) Multiresolution approach to wavelets in computer vision. In: Wavelets. Springer, Berlin/Heidelberg, pp 313–327
4. Daubechies I (1990) The wavelet transform, time-frequency localization and signal analysis. IEEE Trans Inf Theory 36(5):961–1005
5. Sifuzzaman M, Islam MR, Ali MZ (2009) Application of wavelet transform and its advantages compared to Fourier transform.
6. Burrus CS, Gopinath RA, Guo H, Odegard JE, Selesnick IW (1998) Introduction to wavelets and wavelet transforms: a primer, vol 1. Prentice hall, Upper Saddle River
7. Raghuveer MR, Bopardikar AS (1998) Wavelet transforms: introduction to theory and applications. Pearson Education Asia, Delhi
8. Heil CE, Walnut DF (1989) Continuous and discrete wavelet transforms. SIAM Rev 31 (4):628–666
9. Antoine JP, Carrette P, Murenzi R, Piette B (1993) Image analysis with two-dimensional continuous wavelet transform. Signal Process 31(3):241–272
10. Pons-Llinares J, Antonino-Daviu JA, Riera-Guasp M, Lee SB, Kang TJ, Yang C (2014) Advanced induction motor rotor fault diagnosis via continuous and discrete time–frequency tools. IEEE Trans Ind Electron 62(3):1791–1802
11. Shensa MJ (1992) The discrete wavelet transform: wedding the a trous and Mallat algorithms. IEEE Trans Signal Process 40(10):2464–2482
12. Meurant G (2012) Wavelets: a tutorial in theory and applications, vol 2. Academic, Boston
13. Strang G, Nguyen T (1996) Wavelets and filter banks. SIAM, Wellesley
14. Li H, Manjunath BS, Mitra SK (1995) Multisensor image fusion using the wavelet transform. Graph Models Image Process 57(3):235–245
15. He C, Zheng YF, Ahalt SC (2002) Object tracking using the Gabor wavelet transform and the golden section algorithm. IEEE Trans Multimedia 4(4):528–538
16. Wang Y, Doherty JF, Van Dyck RE (2000) Moving object tracking in video. In: Proceedings 29th applied imagery pattern recognition workshop. IEEE, Los Alamitos, pp 95–101
17. Lai CC, Tsai CC (2010) Digital image watermarking using discrete wavelet transform and singular value decomposition. IEEE Trans Instrum Meas 59(11):3060–3063
18. Shih FY, Chuang CF, Wang PS (2008) Performance comparisons of facial expression recognition in JAFFE database. Int J Pattern Recognit Artif Intell 22(03):445–459
19. Strang G (1989) Wavelets and dilation equations: a brief introduction. SIAM Rev 31 (4):614–627
20. Simoncelli EP, Freeman WT, Adelson EH, Heeger DJ (1991) Shiftable multiscale transforms. IEEE Trans Inf Theory 38(2):587–607
21. Selesnick I, Baraniuk R, Kingsbury N (2005) The dual-tree complex wavelet transform. IEEE Signal Process Mag 22:123–151
22. Singh R, Khare A (2014) Fusion of multimodal medical images using Daubechies complex wavelet transform–a multiresolution approach. Inf Fusion 19:49–60
23. Singh R, Srivastava R, Prakash O, Khare A (2012) Multimodal medical image fusion in dual tree complex wavelet transform domain using maximum and average fusion rules. J Med Imaging Health Inf 2(2):168–173
24. Sweldens W (1996) The lifting scheme: a custom-design construction of biorthogonal wavelets. Appl Comput Harmon Anal 3(2):186–200
25. Calderbank AR, Daubechies I, Sweldens W, Yeo BL (1998) Wavelet transforms that map integers to integers. Appl Comput Harmon Anal 5(3):332–369
26. Fowler JE (2005) The redundant discrete wavelet transform and additive noise. IEEE Signal Process Lett 12(9):629–632

27. Kingsbury N (2001) Complex wavelets for shift invariant analysis and filtering of signals. Appl Comput Harmon Anal 10(3):234–253
28. Lina JM, Mayrand M (1995) Complex daubechies wavelets. Appl Comput Harmon Anal 2 (3):219–229
29. Kingsbury NG (1998) The dual-tree complex wavelet transform: a new technique for shift invariance and directional filters. In: IEEE digital signal processing workshop, vol 86. Citeseer, Bryce Canyon, pp 120–131
30. Lina JM (1998) Complex daubechies wavelets: filters design and applications. In: Inverse problems, tomography, and image processing. Springer, Boston, MA, pp 95–112
31. Clonda D, Lina JM, Goulard B (2004) Complex Daubechies wavelets: properties and statistical image modelling. Signal Process 84(1):1–23
32. Lina JM (1997) Image processing with complex Daubechies wavelets. J Math Imaging Vision 7 (3):211–223
33. Shukla PD (2003) Complex wavelet transforms and their applications. Glasgow (United Kingdom)), M. Phil. Thesis, Dept. of Electronic and Electrical Engineering, University of Strathclyde.
34. Kingsbury N (2000) A dual-tree complex wavelet transform with improved orthogonality and symmetry properties. In: Proceedings 2000 international conference on image processing (Cat. No. 00CH37101), vol 2. IEEE, Vancouver, pp 375–378
35. Lawton W (1993) Applications of complex valued wavelet transforms to subband decomposition. IEEE Trans Signal Process 41(12):3566–3568
36. Miller M, Kingsbury N (2008) Image modeling using interscale phase properties of complex wavelet coefficients. IEEE Trans Image Process 17(9):1491–1499
37. Lina JM, Drouilly P (1996) The importance of the phase of the symmetric Daubechies wavelets representation of signals. In: Proc. IWISP, vol 96, p 61
38. Lina JM, Gagnon L (1995) Image enhancement with symmetric Daubechies wavelets. In: Wavelet applications in signal and image processing III, vol 2569. International Society for Optics and Photonics, Bellingham, pp 196–207
39. Candès EJ, Donoho DL (2001) Curvelets and curvilinear integrals. J Approx Theory 113 (1):59–90
40. Candès EJ (2003) What is a curvelet? Not Am Math Soc 50(11):1402–1403
41. Candes EJ, Donoho DL (2000) Curvelets: a surprisingly effective nonadaptive representation for objects with edges. Stanford Univ Ca Dept of Statistics, Stanford
42. Candes E, Demanet L, Donoho D, Ying L (2006) Fast discrete curvelet transforms. Multiscale Model Simul 5(3):861–899
43. Do MN, Vetterli M (2005) The contourlet transform: an efficient directional multiresolution image representation. IEEE Trans Image Process 14(12):2091–2106
44. Do MN, Vetterli M (2003) Contourlets. Stud Comput Math 10:83–105
45. Da Cunha AL, Zhou J, Do MN (2006) The nonsubsampled contourlet transform: theory, design, and applications. IEEE Trans Image Process 15(10):3089–3101
46. Zhou J, Cunha AL, Do MN (2005) Nonsubsampled contourlet transform: construction and application in enhancement. In: IEEE international conference on image processing 2005, vol 1. IEEE, Genova, pp I–469
47. Fang L, Zhang H, Zhou J, Wang X (2019) Image classification with an RGB-channel nonsubsampled contourlet transform and a convolutional neural network. Neurocomputing.
48. Yang HY, Liang LL, Zhang C, Wang XB, Niu PP, Wang XY (2019) Weibull statistical modeling for textured image retrieval using nonsubsampled contourlet transform. Soft Comput 23(13):4749–4764
49. Najafi E, Loukhaoukha K (2019) Hybrid secure and robust image watermarking scheme based on SVD and sharp frequency localized contourlet transform. J Inf Secur Appl 44:144–156
50. Subasi A, Ahmed A, Aličković E, Hassan AR (2019) Effect of photic stimulation for migraine detection using random forest and discrete wavelet transform. Biomed Signal Process Control 49:231–239

Chapter 3
An Overview of Medical Image Fusion in Complex Wavelet Domain

Abstract Fusion of multisensor images has shown a potential application in various application domains such as security, medical imaging etc. The recent developments in medical imaging sensors have been a great motivation for fusion due to their complementary nature. This chapter aims to address medical image fusion in complex wavelet domain and provides a detailed study of fusion methods. The wavelet transforms based fusion methods are ahead of other methods in terms of signal representation, complementary information and redundancy. These properties make wavelet transforms suitable for multisensory image fusion. The fusion experiments have been demonstrated over several sets of medical images for different fusion rules in complex wavelet domain. Visual and quantitative evaluation of the proposed fusion results with state-of-the-art fusion methods showed the effectiveness and goodness of the complex wavelet transform based fusion methods.

Keywords Image fusion · Wavelet transforms · Fusion rules · Fusion metrics · Quantitative evaluation

3.1 Introduction

Medical image fusion is an emerging and challenging area of research to obtain relevant and complementary information from fusion of multisensory images [1–3]. Image fusion enables the merging of two or more source images to obtain complementary information to be utilized by various application domains such as remote sensing, security, concealed weapon detection etc. For example, clinical applications of medical image fusion have shown its usefulness in diagnostics and healthcare [4, 5]. Similarly, infrared and visible image fusion has been performed to address biometric security [5, 6]. However, fusion methods are highly sensitive as medical images are of low contrast and may carry noise during the process of acquisition. In the same way, infrared imaging is sensitive towards temperature change and visible imagery only provides high resolution information, but cannot work in different weather conditions. Therefore, a proper fusion methodology is often desired for multisensory image fusion [7].

© Springer Nature Switzerland AG 2020

R. Singh et al., *Intelligent Wavelet Based Techniques for Advanced Multimedia Applications*, https://doi.org/10.1007/978-3-030-31873-4_3

Recent advancements in wavelet based image processing have shown its importance in image fusion and a detailed tutorial over these methods can be found in [8, 9]. These literatures clearly show the importance and acceptability of the wavelets for multisensory image fusion. The aim of present chapter is to provide a necessary background and literature in the context of this book to understand fusion imaging. For this purpose, fundamental concepts such as challenges, requirements, classification, and approaches of image fusion, have been elaborated by providing relevant literature review of the subject.

3.2   Background and Literature

It has been already discussed that fusion methods are challenging due to complementary nature of imaging modalities. In summary, following are the key requirements for fusion methods [10, 11]:

- Fused image must contain all complementary information.
- Fusion process should be robust against any kind of noise or miss-registration.

Image fusion can be performed at pixel level, feature level and decision level [12–14]. This classification can be understood using Fig. 3.1.

Fusion methods can be implemented either in spatial domain or in transform domain [15]. Fused image can be obtained in spatial domain by using direct manipulation into intensity values of source images. Mathematically, spatial domain fusion [16] for n source images could be defined as:

$$I_F(x, y) = \Gamma\{I_1(x, y), I_2(x, y), \ldots, I_n(x, y)\}$$

where $I_1(x, y), I_2(x, y), \ldots, I_n(x, y)$ are n source images, $\Gamma(\bullet)$ is fusion rule, and $I_F(x, y)$ is fused image.

Some of the spatial domain image fusion methods are Averaging, weighted averaging, brovey transform [17], IHS [18], PCA [19], linear [20] and sharp fusion [21]. These methods may introduce visual artifacts which has been reported in [5] for sharp fusion method [21] (Fig. 3.2).

Local energy based fusion rule has been considered in the sharp fusion method which led to this kind of visual artifacts. To avoid such kind of visual artifacts, transform domain fusion has been preferred over spatial domain fusion.

In transform domain, we apply fusion rules on transform coefficients and inverse transform is used to obtain fused image. Similar to spatial domain, if $\Gamma(\bullet)$ is fusion rule, $I_1(x, y), I_2(x, y), \ldots, I_n(x, y)$ be n source images, then mathematical definition of transform domain fusion [16] can be given as:

$$I_F(x, y) = T^{-1}[\Gamma(T\{I_1(x, y)\}, T\{I_2(x, y)\}, \ldots, T\{I_n(x, y)\})]$$

where T denotes forward transformation, and T^{-1} is inverse transformation.

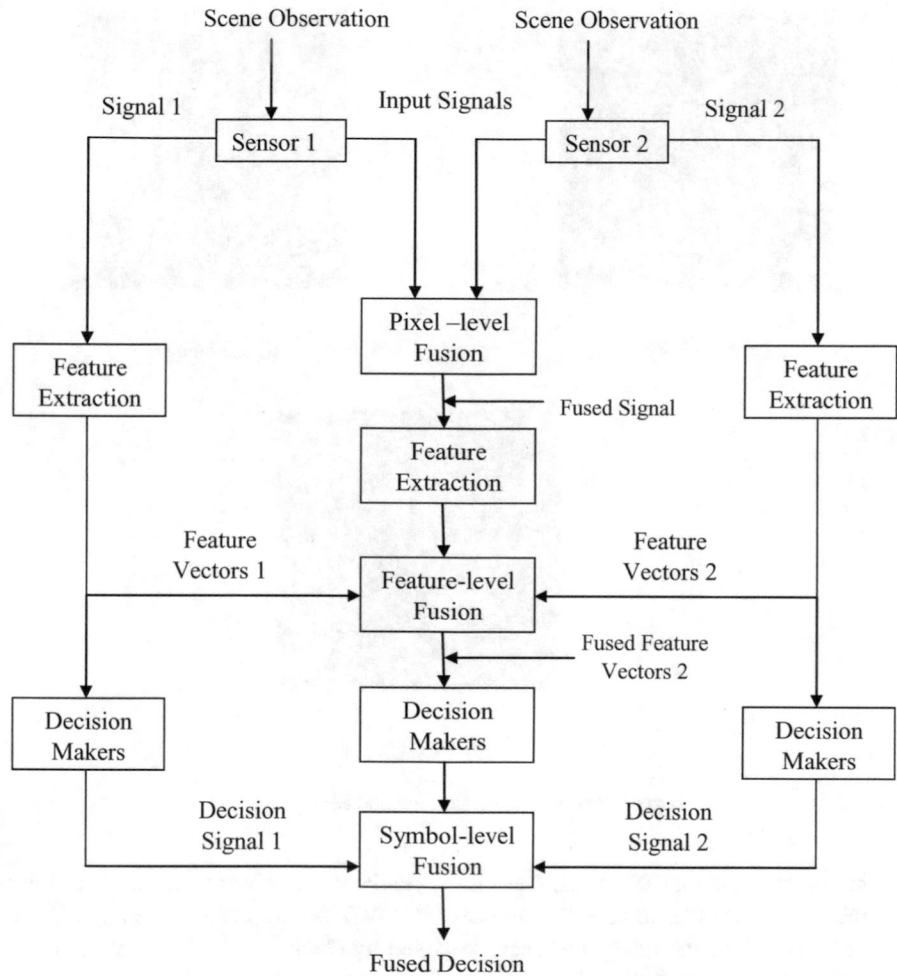

Fig. 3.1 Image fusion classification

The commonly used transforms for fusion are- pyramid and wavelet transforms [22]. Laplacian pyramid [23], gradient pyramid [24], contrast pyramid [25], ratio of low pass pyramid [26], morphological pyramid [27], and FSD pyramid [28] are a few methods which have been commonly used for fusion. These methods are limited in performance due to absence of directional information. Blocking effect is another disadvantage of pyramid based fusion methods [22, 29].

Hence, wavelet domain [30] fusion methods have been used and preferred over pyramid based fusion methods. The family of wavelet transforms could be divided into real and complex wavelets. Since, this work focused on complex wavelets; therefore, in order to provide a foundation, and to make a clear understanding of the research work, analysis of image fusion in real wavelet domain is highly required.

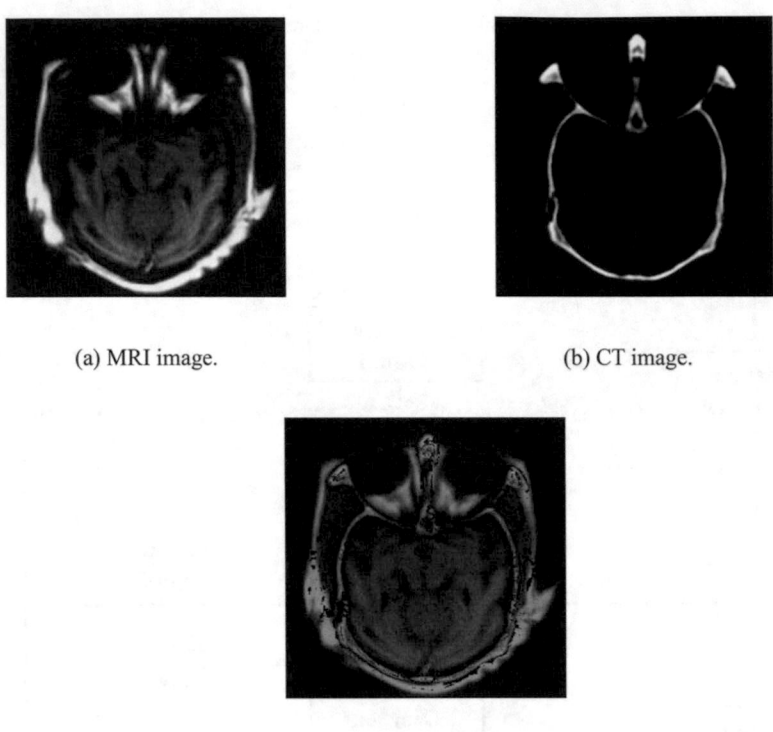

(a) MRI image.   (b) CT image.

(c) Fused image.

Fig. 3.2 Visual artifacts generated by sharp fusion method [21]

It has been found that DWT decomposition yields an effective representation of the signals. Thus, it order to take the advantage of DWT decomposition, a simple DWT based medical image fusion has been proposed by Cheng et al. [31]. They applied weighted fusion rule on wavelet coefficients for merging of medical images. Another pixel and region based multiresolution fusion for MRI and CT images are discussed in [32]. It gives a way to segment and fuse images using multiresolution transforms. Similar to this, a region energy based approach has been proposed [33] which uses weighted scheme for high frequency bands. These works have been continued in [34, 35] and a maximum rule has been chosen for multimodal image fusion. Apart from the conventional rules, a statistical measure based fusion has been reported for selection of wavelet coefficients [36]. In this method, high pass bands are fused using local variance, and edge based fusion has been applied to low pass wavelet coefficients. Similarly, local entropy and variance based approaches [37–39] have been followed to fuse multimodality medical images.

Lifting wavelet transform (LWT) [40, 41] based fusion methods have been used to reduce computational complexity associated with DWT. This motivated to use LWT for MRI and CT image fusion [42, 43]. Multiwavelet transform (MWT) [44–47] is another wavelet transform which has been used for medical image fusion and able to improve compression ratio. However, none of the above wavelet transforms are capable of decomposing high frequency bands and not able to capture local information provided by high frequency bands. Therefore, wavelet packet transform (WPT) [48] has been used to provide a tree like decomposition of low and high frequency bands and gives a choice for best basis selection to perform medical image fusion [49] using self-adaptive operator.

The above wavelet domain methods are shift sensitive and lacks in providing rich directional information. Therefore, redundant discrete wavelet transform (RDWT) [50–53] based image fusion method has been used to facilitate shift invariant image fusion. It provides perfect reconstruction using redundant representation of images and signals; therefore, it is also referred as stationary wavelet transform (SWT) [51]. The SWT based fusion schemes [52, 53] have shown its importance in medical image fusion.

The family of real wavelet domain provides efficient representation of images using multiresolution approach, but, they have several limitations and are shift sensitive as well (except SWT). The shortcomings of the real valued wavelet transforms such as shift sensitivity, lack of phase information and poor directionality have been overcome by the use of complex wavelet transforms. This chapter uses the Dual tree complex wavelet transform (DTCWT), and the Discrete complex wavelet transform (DCxWT) to overcome the limitations of real valued wavelet transforms.

3.3   Methodology and Experiments

Here, We discuss the properties of complex wavelet transform with the help of simulated results and show the importance of these properties in image fusion [54–57].

- **Shift Invariance**

  To avoid the merging and visual artifacts during fusion process, shift invariance is highly desired. Further, it was shown that miss-registration could occur, if shift invariance has not been taken into account while implementing fusion rules. DTCWT provides shift invariance in 2-D by using Gabor like filters and more suitable than SWT due to its low computation cost. Thus, by using DTCWT, quality fused images could be obtained. Experimentally, it was found that reconstruction using DTCWT has better image representation than DWT and has been shown in Fig. 3.3. Similarly, DCxWT is also capable of providing shift invariance and can be analyzed in the same way.

- **High Directionality**

  The DTCWT provides higher directional information in 2-D by dividing sub-bands into six spatial orientations which are $\pm 15^0$, $\pm 45^0$, $\pm 75^0$. Comparison of directional information for DWT and DTCWT is illustrated in Fig. 3.4. From Fig. 3.4, it is clear that DTCWT provides higher directional information through its

Componets of reconstructed 'disc' images

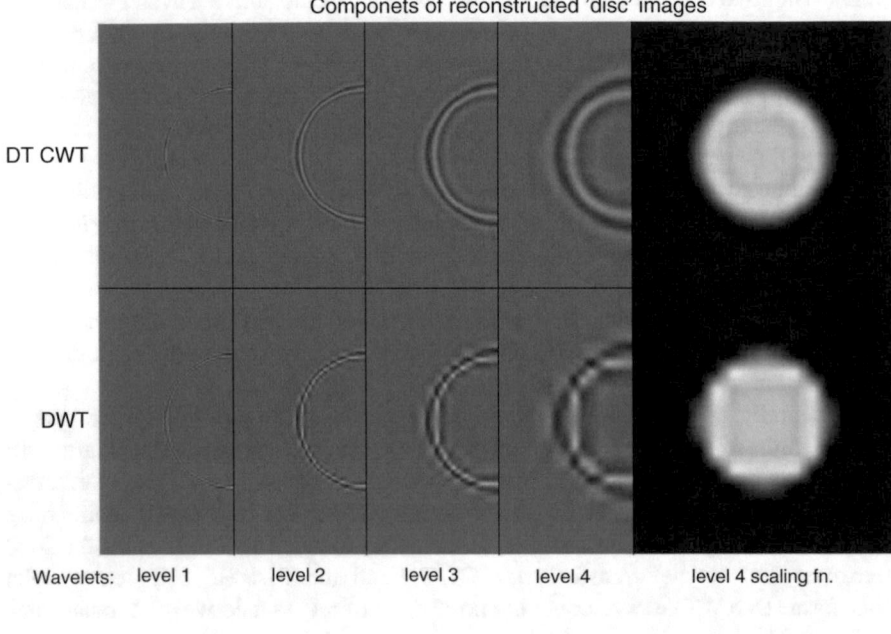

DT CWT

DWT

Wavelets: level 1   level 2   level 3   level 4   level 4 scaling fn.

(a)

Accumulated reconstructions from each level of DT CWT

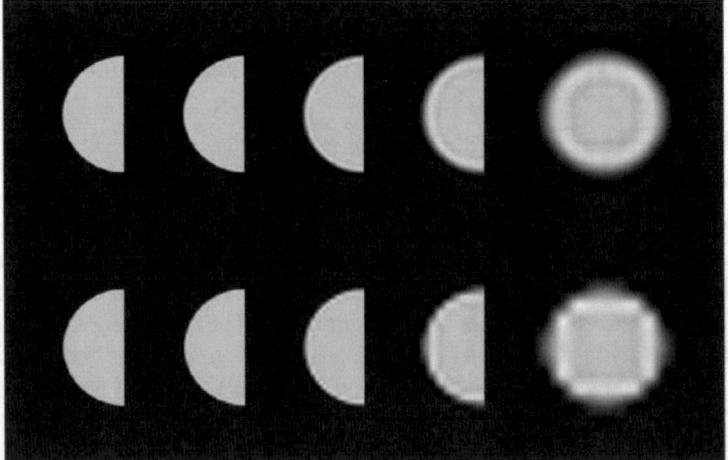

Accumulated reconstructions from each level DWT

(b)

Fig. 3.3 (**a**) Reconstruction of circular disc image for DTCWT and DWT wavelet and scaling coefficients up-to 4 levels, (**b**) Reconstruction of circular disc image for DTCWT and DWT scaling coefficients up-to 4 levels

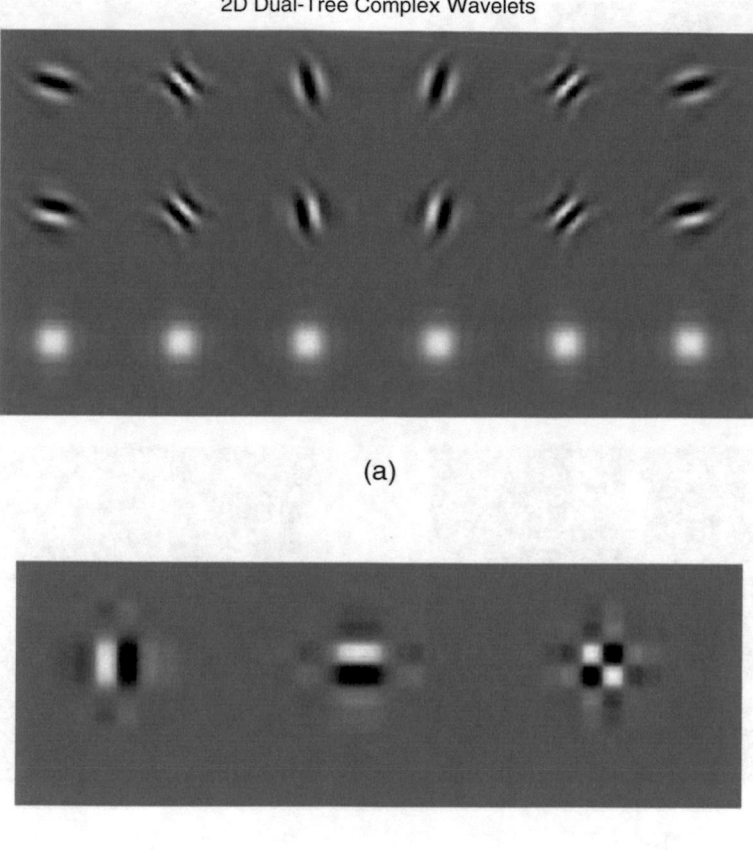

Fig. 3.4 (**a**) Six orientations displayed on the first (second) row are interpreted as the real (imaginary) part and magnitude of the six complex wavelets are shown on the third row for DTWCT, (**b**) three different orientations (horizontal, vertical and diagonal) for DWT

real and imaginary coefficients in 12 orientations (6 for real wavelet coefficients and 6 for imaginary wavelet coefficients). Therefore, by using DTCWT, we are able to capture high directional information from the fusion process. However, the DCxWT is limited in providing direction information and has only three spatial orientations (horizontal, vertical and diagonal), similar to DWT (shown in Fig. 3.4b).

- **Phase Information**

It has further been analyzed that phase information plays an important role in image fusion. Figure 3.5 shows the reconstruction of images using imaginary coefficients only. Thus, it can be seen that fusion rule based on complex wavelet transforms can improve the quality of fused images.

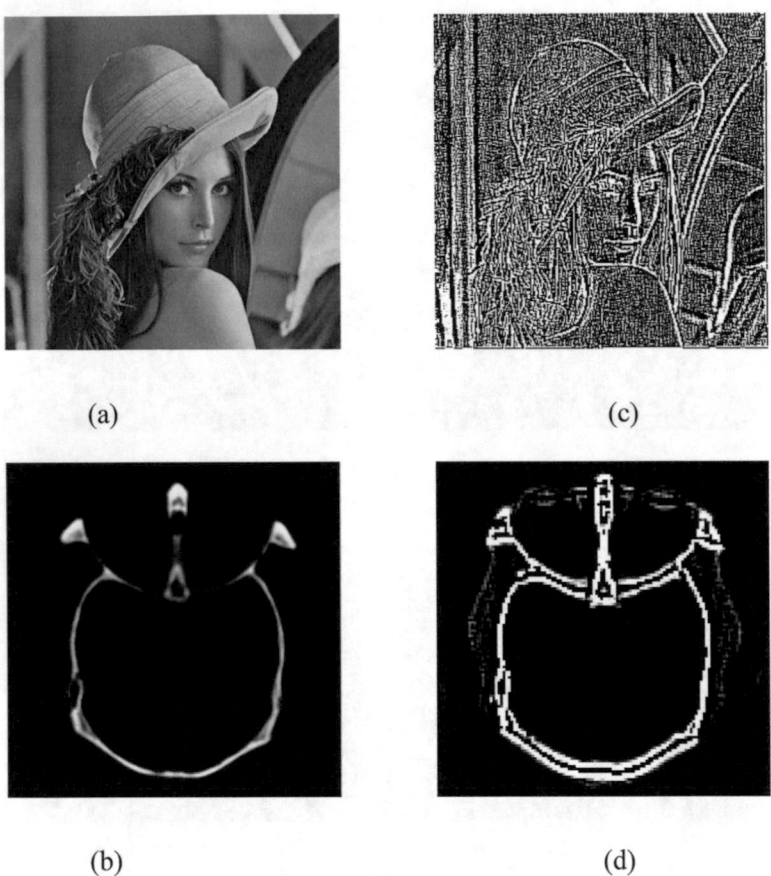

Fig. 3.5 (a) Lena image, (b) medical image, (c) and (d) imaginary parts of the scaling coefficients of the Lena and medical image respectively

The fusion method described in this chapter uses maximum saliency fusion rule for DTCWT and DCxWT. The general framework for wavelet transform based image fusion could be easily understood from Fig. 3.6. The steps of image fusion method are as follows.

(i) Initially source images are decomposed into low pass and high pass wavelet coefficients using complex wavelet transform.
(ii) Apply maximum and average fusion rules to obtained fused complex wavelet coefficients.
(iii) Reconstruct fused image using inverse complex wavelet transform.

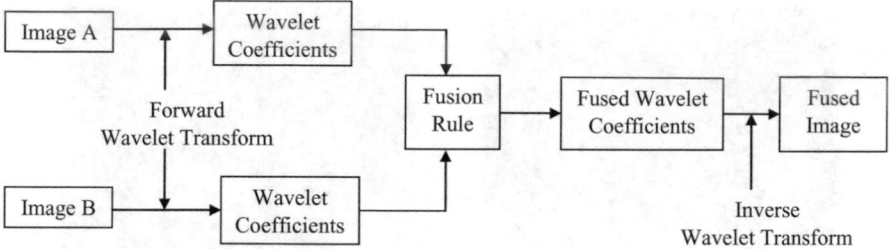

Fig. 3.6 General image fusion framework

3.4   Fusion Results and Discussions

This section shows fusion results for medical images in complex wavelet domain (DTCWT and DCxWT) using Avg-Max and Max-Max fusion rules. The fusion rules have been experimented with three sets of medical image pairs of size 256×256 shown in Figs. 3.7a, b, 3.8a, b, 3.9a, b respectively. The proposed method has been experimented at level 2 for DTCWT and DCxWT. The fusion results have been shown in Figs. 3.7, 3.8 and 3.9 for Avg-Max and Max-Max fusion rules for proposed approach. We have performed qualitative and quantitative comparisons to evaluate fusion results obtained by the proposed method. For qualitative evaluation of fusion results, we have selected popular transform and spatial domain fusion methods separately. The transform domain fusion methods, which are taken for comparison of proposed approach, are gradient pyramid (GP), contrast pyramid (CP), ratio pyramid (RP), discrete wavelet transform (DWT) fusion methods. Similarly, two spatial domain methods principal component analysis (PCA) and sharp fusion methods have been compared with our fusion approach. The quantitative evaluation of the proposed fusion rules have been done with non-reference fusion measures; edge strength (Q), fusion factor (FF), fusion symmetry (FS) and entropy (E). The qualitative and quantitative analysis of the fusion results have been elaborated in following sections.

3.4.1   Qualitative Evaluation

The first set of medical images is brain CT and MRI, shown in Fig. 3.7a, b. The CT image shows the bony structure while MRI provides information about soft tissues. The results for proposed Avg-Max and Max-Max fusion rules for DTCWT and DCxWT have been shown in Fig. 3.7c–f respectively. The results for DTCWT and DCxWT fusion methods have been compared with GP, CP, RP, DWT, PCA, and sharp fusion methods, which are shown in Fig. 3.7g–l. It can be easily concluded that the proposed method outperforms these fusion methods and has good visual representation of fused image. The fused images with GP, CP, RP PCA and sharp fusion

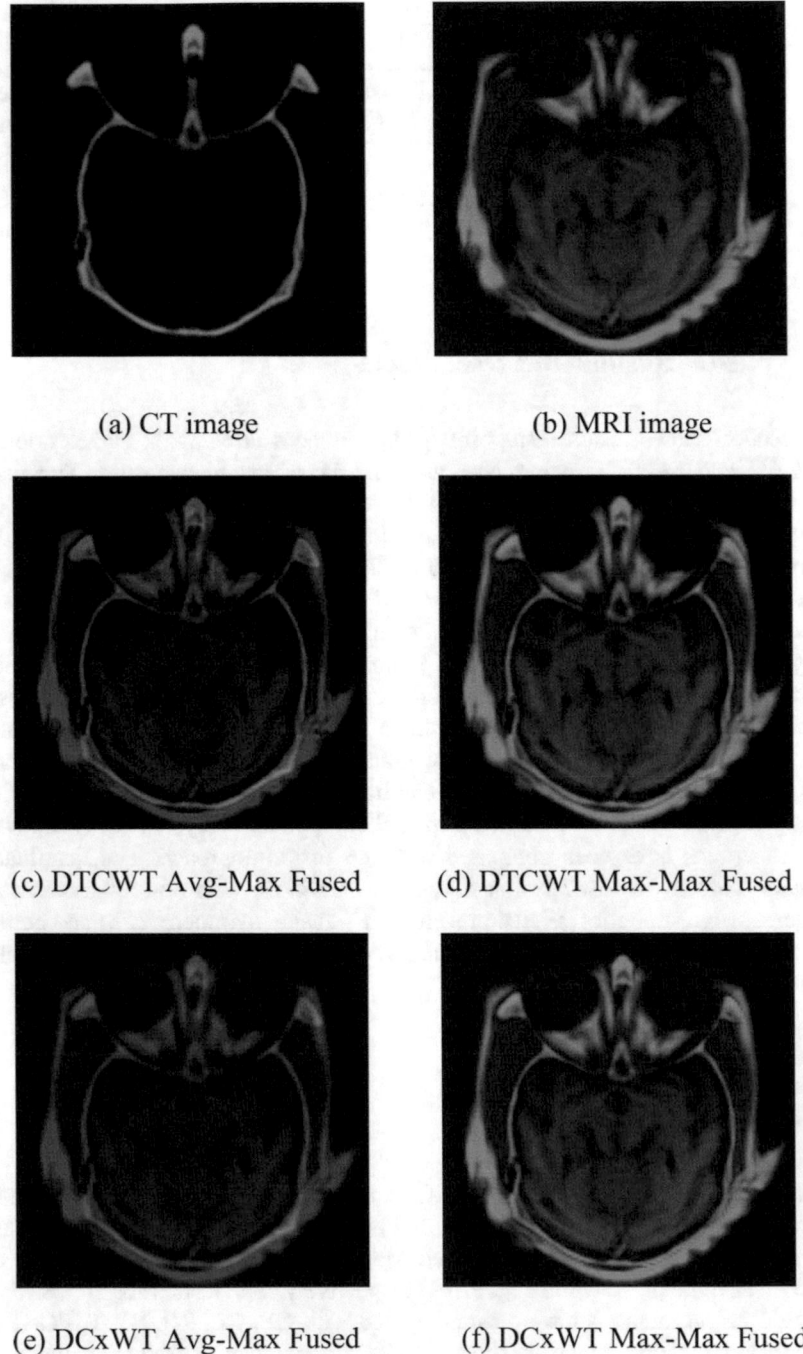

(a) CT image   (b) MRI image

(c) DTCWT Avg-Max Fused   (d) DTCWT Max-Max Fused

(e) DCxWT Avg-Max Fused   (f) DCxWT Max-Max Fused

Fig. 3.7 Fusion results for first set of medical images

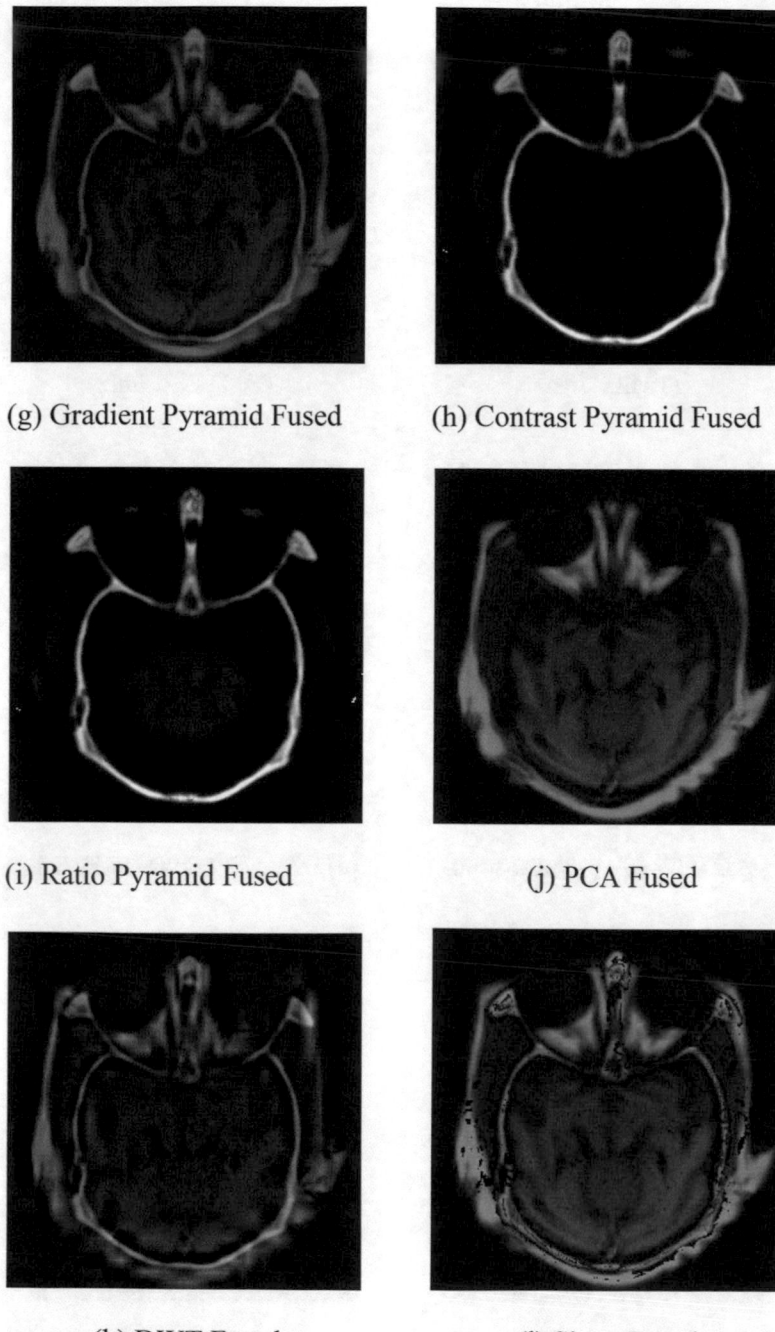

(g) Gradient Pyramid Fused   (h) Contrast Pyramid Fused

(i) Ratio Pyramid Fused   (j) PCA Fused

(k) DWT Fused   (l) Sharp Fused

Fig. 3.7 (continued)

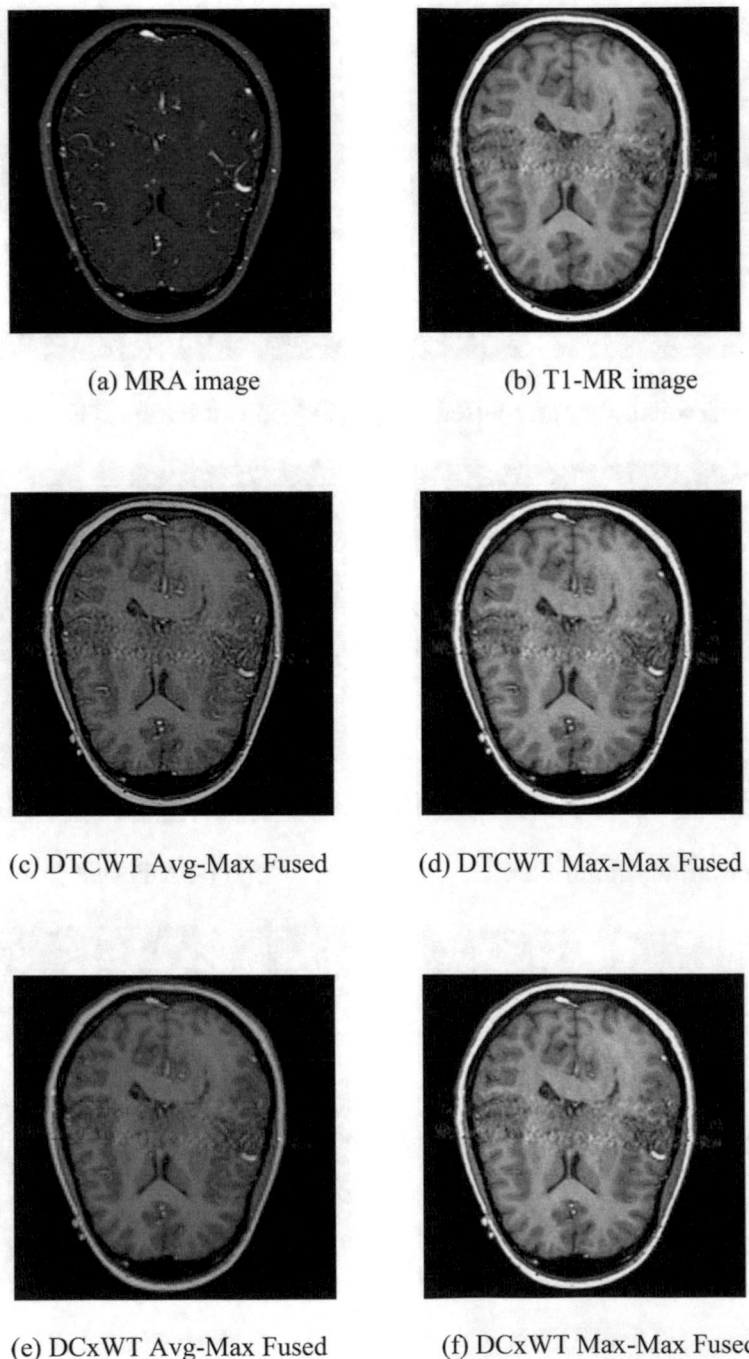

(a) MRA image   (b) T1-MR image

(c) DTCWT Avg-Max Fused   (d) DTCWT Max-Max Fused

(e) DCxWT Avg-Max Fused   (f) DCxWT Max-Max Fused

Fig. 3.8 Fusion results for second set of medical images

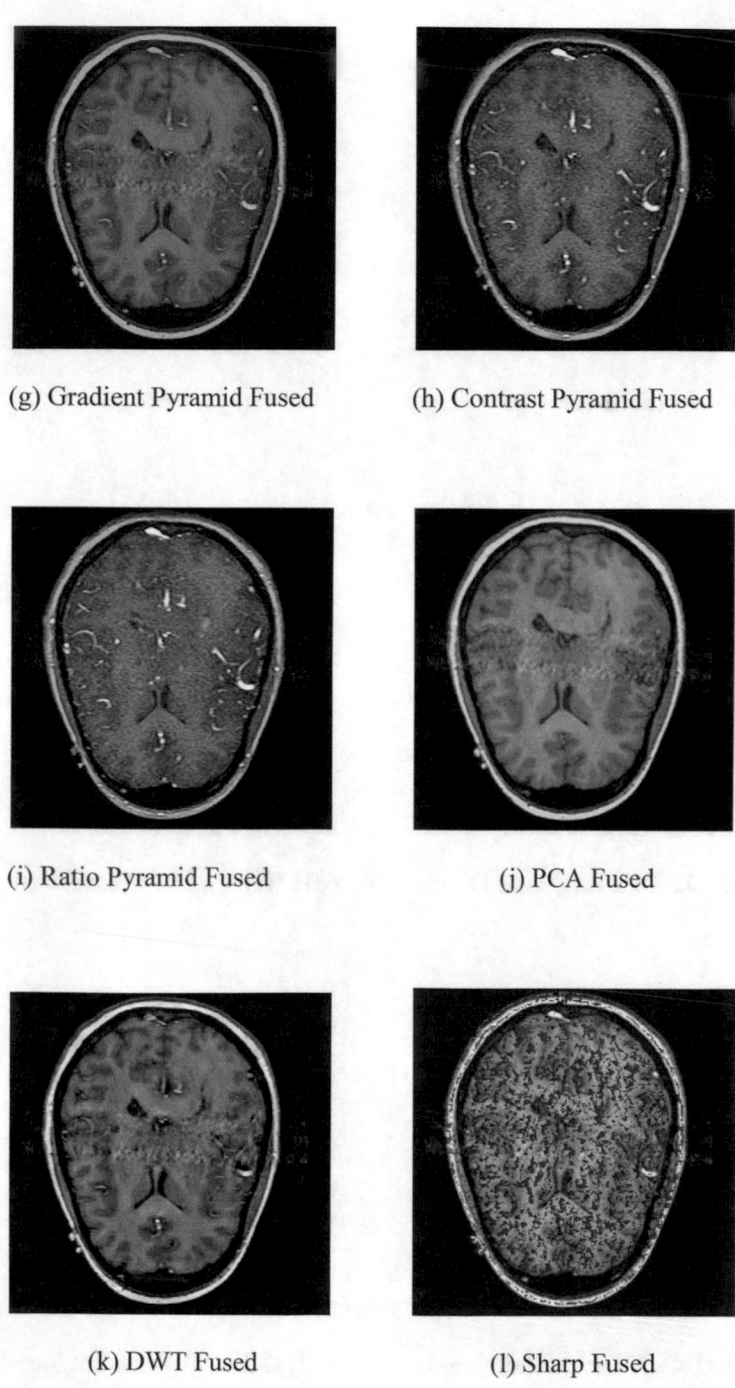

(g) Gradient Pyramid Fused   (h) Contrast Pyramid Fused

(i) Ratio Pyramid Fused   (j) PCA Fused

(k) DWT Fused   (l) Sharp Fused

Fig. 3.8 (continued)

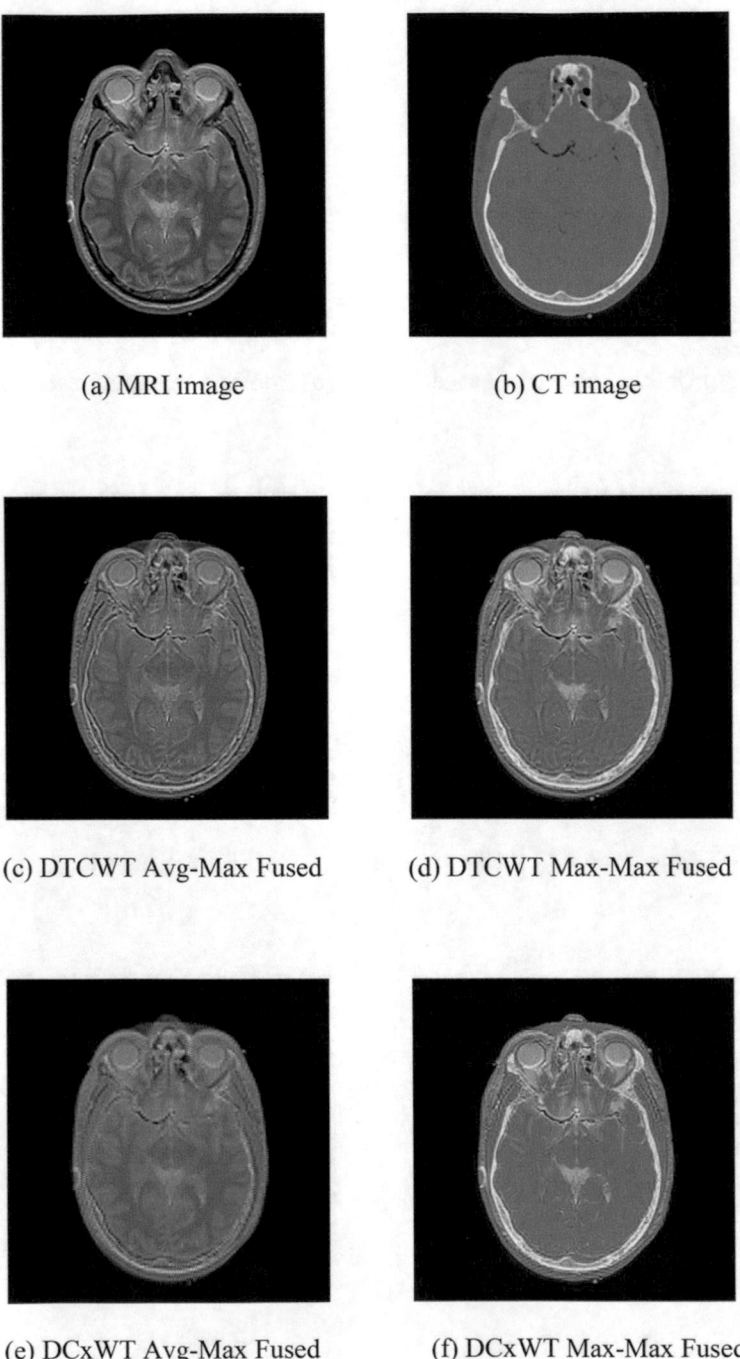

(a) MRI image   (b) CT image

(c) DTCWT Avg-Max Fused   (d) DTCWT Max-Max Fused

(e) DCxWT Avg-Max Fused   (f) DCxWT Max-Max Fused

Fig. 3.9 Fusion results for third set of medical images

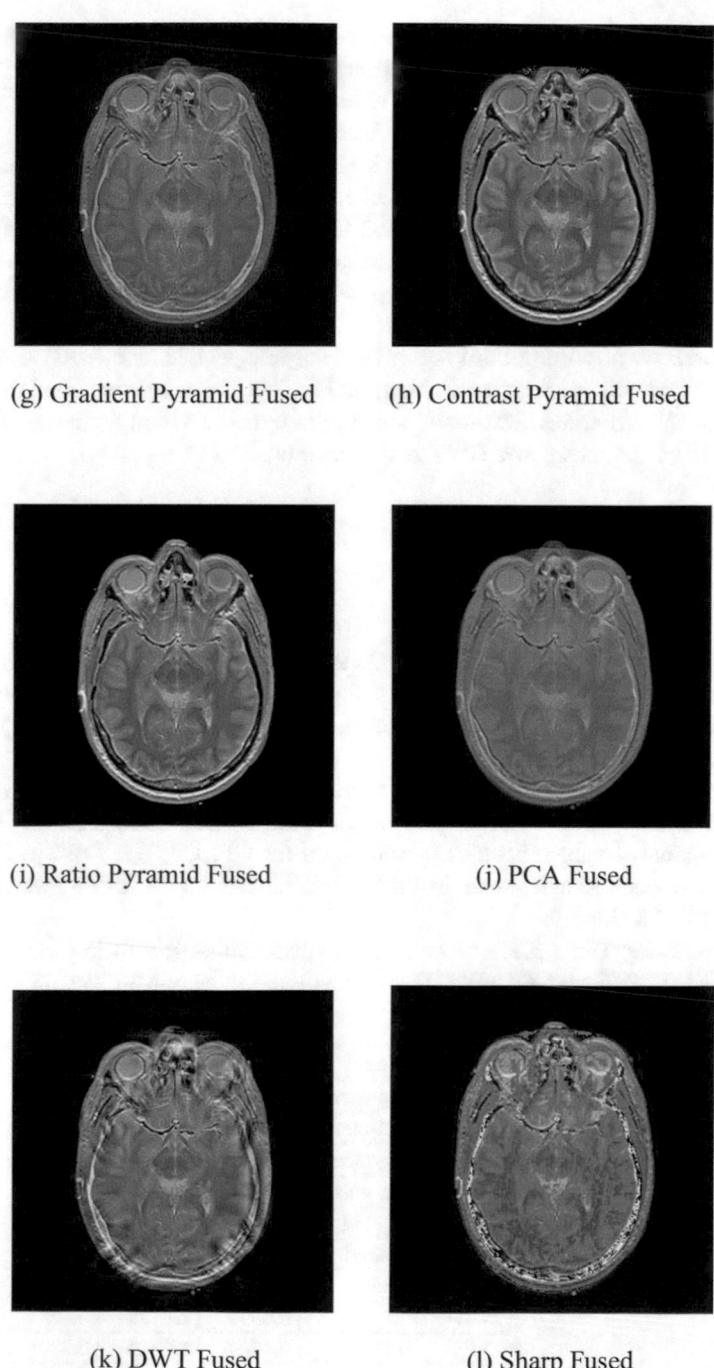

(g) Gradient Pyramid Fused   (h) Contrast Pyramid Fused

(i) Ratio Pyramid Fused   (j) PCA Fused

(k) DWT Fused   (l) Sharp Fused

Fig. 3.9 (continued)

methods are not able to capture the information from CT and MRI pairs. Moreover, sharp fusion method [21] generates visual artifacts, reported in [5]. Further, the DTCWT and DCxWT fusion results with Max-Max fusion rules has the better quality than DWT and other compared fusion methods.

The second set of medical images is MRA (magnetic resonance angiogram) and T1-MR image which is shown in Fig. 3.8a, b. The comparison of proposed fusion results with GP, CP, RP, PCA, sharp, and DWT fusion methods is demonstrated in Fig. 3.8c–l. This comparison clearly indicates that the fused images with Avg-Max and Max-Max fusion rules have better quality and contrast in comparison to other fusion methods.

Similarly, on observing third set of medical images (CT and MRI) and fusion results for these images which are shown in Fig. 3.9, It can be concluded that again the proposed method has been found superior in terms of visual representation over GP, CP, RP, PCA, sharp and DWT fusion methods.

3.4.2   Quantitative Evaluation

The qualitative evaluation of fusion results is not sufficient to analyze fusion results. Therefore, we evaluated fusion results for medical images quantitatively using non-reference fusion metrics, namely; edge strength (Q), fusion factor (FF), fusion symmetry (FS), and entropy (E).

These measures Q, FF, FS and E are computed for the proposed fusion results, i.e. for Avg-Max and Max-Max fusion rules using DTCWT and DCxWT. Further, these quantitative values have been computed for GP, CP, RP, DWT, PCA, and sharp fusion methods and shown in Tables 3.1, 3.2 and 3.3 for fusion results shown in Figs. 3.7, 3.8 and 3.9.

On observing Table 3.1, one can easily observe that the fusion measures for proposed DTCWT and DCxWT fusion method for Max-Max fusion rules has

Table 3.1 Fusion Measures for first set of medical images

Fusion Method	Q	FF	FS	E
DTCWT Avg-max	0.5137	1.0497	0.3278	5.3070
DTCWT max-max	0.7663	1.9166	0.3748	5.9323
DCxWT Avg-max	0.3651	1.2244	0.3566	5.2107
DCxWT max-max	0.7793	2.2756	0.3747	5.8674
Gradient pyramid	0.5784	1.0243	0.3027	5.4698
Contrast pyramid	0.2542	0.9452	0.2721	1.9243
Ratio pyramid	0.2658	0.9901	0.0843	3.5655
PCA	0.6395	2.6305	0.4284	5.6220
DWT	0.4269	1.0342	0.2345	5.5227
Sharp	0.5602	1.4048	0.3785	5.9748

Table 3.2 Fusion Measures for second set of medical images

Fusion Method	Q	FF	FS	E
DTCWT Avg-max	0.5454	3.8389	0.1126	5.6921
DTCWT max-max	0.6159	4.5984	0.1751	6.0259
DCxWT Avg-max	0.3957	3.7650	0.1066	5.4480
DCxWT max-max	0.6398	4.8974	0.1935	5.9307
Gradient pyramid	0.2825	2.9948	0.0959	6.2998
Contrast pyramid	0.2511	2.9112	0.0523	5.8564
Ratio pyramid	0.2492	2.8954	0.0424	5.8947
PCA	0.3219	3.2834	0.1038	6.0242
DWT	0.2970	2.8311	0.0791	5.9870
Sharp	0.3704	3.7095	0.1127	5.9812

Table 3.3 Fusion Measures for third set of medical images

Fusion Method	Q	FF	FS	E
DTCWT Avg-max	0.5558	3.6085	0.0353	5.1271
DTCWT max-max	0.5676	4.2109	0.0304	5.3482
DCxWT Avg-max	0.2621	3.1136	0.0100	4.7946
DCxWT max-max	0.5391	4.4757	0.0213	5.2397
Gradient pyramid	0.5228	3.1159	0.0185	5.7497
Contrast pyramid	0.6475	3.2326	0.0605	4.5518
Ratio pyramid	0.6313	3.6672	0.1385	4.8964
PCA	0.3722	3.8902	0.0401	4.6139
DWT	0.4366	3.0704	0.0280	5.2558
Sharp	0.3953	3.3191	0.0041	5.0626

highest values for Q, FF and E measures than any of GP, CP, RP, DWT, PCA, and sharp fusion methods. However, the proposed fusion method lacks in providing the lowest values for FS measure. But for this case, we considered the majority of fusion measures for quantitative evaluation. The overall evaluation of fusion measures indicates the goodness of Max-Max fusion rule in complex wavelet domain. Moreover, the Avg-Max fusion rule for DTCWT and DCxWT are superior to most of the compared fusion methods and can be verified easily from Table 3.1.

Similarly, observations of Table 3.2 implies that the proposed DTCWT and DCxWT fusion method for Avg-Max and Max-Max fusion rules have higher values of fusion measures than any of the GP, CP, RP, DWT, PCA, and sharp fusion methods. These implications has also been observed for third set of medical images, and the measures shown in Table 3.3 indicates the effectiveness of Avg-Max and Max-Max fusion rules in DTCWT and DCxWT domain.

Thus, qualitative and quantitative evaluation of DTCWT and DCxWT fusion methods with Avg-Max and Max-Max fusion rules showed the effectiveness over transform domain fusion methods (GP, CP, RP, DWT) as well as spatial domain fusion methods (PCA and sharp).

3.5 Summary

In this chapter, we have provided an overview of medical image fusion in complex wavelet domain and discussed fusion results for medical images. The performance of the image fusion methods has been improved using complex wavelet transforms with shift invariance, high directionality and phase information properties. Results have been shown for three sets of medical images, and compared with transform domain fusion methods (GP, CP, RP, DWT), PCA and sharp fusion methods. Qualitative and Quantitative evaluation with non-reference fusion metrics showed that complex wavelet transform based methods outperforms other spatial and transform domain fusion methods. This fusion study can be extended for medical signal and video fusion for healthcare applications by implementing intelligent fusion rules in wavelet domain.

References

1. Blum RS, Liu Z (2005) Multi-sensor image fusion and its applications. CRC Press, Boca Raton
2. Li H, Manjunath BS, Mitra SK (1995) Multisensor image fusion using the wavelet transform. Graph Model Image Process 57(3):235–245
3. Pohl C, Van Genderen JL (1998) Review article multisensor image fusion in remote sensing: concepts, methods and applications. Int J Remote Sens 19(5):823–854
4. James AP, Dasarathy BV (2014) Medical image fusion: a survey of the state of the art. Inf Fusion 19:4–19
5. Singh R, Khare A (2014) Fusion of multimodal medical images using Daubechies complex wavelet transform–a multiresolution approach. Inf Fusion 19:49–60
6. Singh S, Gyaourova A, Bebis G, Pavlidis I (2004) Infrared and visible image fusion for face recognition. In: Biometric technology for human identification, vol 5404. International Society for Optics and Photonics, Bellingham, pp 585–596
7. Ma J, Ma Y, Li C (2019) Infrared and visible image fusion methods and applications: A survey. Inf Fusion 45:153–178
8. Pajares G, De La Cruz JM (2004) A wavelet-based image fusion tutorial. Pattern Recogn 37 (9):1855–1872
9. Amolins K, Zhang Y, Dare P (2007) Wavelet based image fusion techniques—An introduction, review and comparison. ISPRS J Photogramm Remote Sens 62(4):249–263
10. Rockinger O (1996) Pixel-level fusion of image sequences using wavelet frames. In: Proceedings of 16th leeds annual statistical research workshop, pp 149–154.
11. Rockinger O, Fechner T (1998) Pixel-level image fusion: The case of image sequences. In: Signal processing, sensor fusion, and target recognition VII, vol 3374. International Society for Optics and Photonics, Bellingham, pp 378–388
12. Petrovic V (2001) Multisensor pixel-level image fusion (Doctoral dissertation, University of Manchester).
13. Lewis JJ, O'callaghan RJ, Nikolov, SG, Bull DR, Canagarajah CN (2004) Region-based image fusion using complex wavelets. In: Seventh international conference on information fusion (FUSION). vol 1, pp 555–562
14. Zhao Y, Yin Y, Fu D (2008) Decision-level fusion of infrared and visible images for face recognition. In: 2008 Chinese control and decision conference. IEEE, pp 2411–2414
15. Stathaki T (2011) Image fusion: algorithms and applications. Elsevier, Amsterdam

16. Mitianoudis N, Stathaki T (2007) Pixel-based and region-based image fusion schemes using ICA bases. Inf Fusion 8(2):131–142
17. Chibani Y (2006) Additive integration of SAR features into multispectral SPOT images by means of the à trous wavelet decomposition. ISPRS J Photogramm Remote Sens 60(5):306–314
18. Daneshvar S, Ghassemian H (2010) MRI and PET image fusion by combining IHS and retina-inspired models. Inf Fusion 11(2):114–123
19. Naidu VPS, Raol JR (2008) Pixel-level image fusion using wavelets and principal component analysis. Def Sci J 58(3):338–352
20. Clevers JGPW, Zurita-Milla R (2008) Multisensor and multiresolution image fusion using the linear mixing model. In: Stathaki T (ed) Image fusion: algorithms and applications. Academic Press/Elsevier, London, pp 67–84
21. Tian J, Chen L, Ma L, Yu W (2011) Multi-focus image fusion using a bilateral gradient-based sharpness criterion. Opt Commun 284(1):80–87
22. Hamza AB, He Y, Krim H, Willsky A (2005) A multiscale approach to pixel-level image fusion. Integrated Comput-Aided Eng 12(2):135–146
23. Burt PJ, Adelson EH (1983) The Laplacian pyramid as a compact image code. IEEE Trans Commun 31(4):532–540
24. Burt PJ, Kolczynski RJ (1993) Enhanced image capture through fusion. In: Proceedings of the 4th IEEE international conference on computer vision (ICCV '93), pp 173–182
25. Toet A, Van Ruyven LJ, Valeton JM (1989) Merging thermal and visual images by a contrast pyramid. Opt Eng 28(7):789–792
26. Toet A (1989) Image fusion by a ratio of low-pass pyramid. Pattern Recogn Lett 9(4):245–253
27. Toet A (1989) A morphological pyramidal image decomposition. Pattern Recogn Lett 9 (4):255–261
28. Anderson CH (1998) Filter-subtract-decimate hierarchical pyramid signal analyzing and synthesizing technique. US Patent 4718104 A.
29. Li H, Manjunath BS, Mitra SK (1995) Multisensor image fusion using the wavelet transform. Graph Model Image Process 57(3):235–245
30. Mallat S (1999) A wavelet tour of signal processing. Academic Press/Elsevier, San Diego
31. Cheng S, He J, Lv Z (2008) Medical images of PET/CT weighted fusion based on wavelet transform. In: Proceedings of the 2nd international conference on bioinformatics and biomedical engineering (iCBBE), pp 2523–2525.
32. Piella G, Heijmans H (2002) Multiresolution image fusion guided by a multimodal segmentation. In: Proceedings of advanced concepts for intelligent vision systems, Ghent, Belgium, pp 175–182.
33. Zhang H, Liu L, Lin N (2007) A novel wavelet medical image fusion method. In: IEEE international conference on multimedia and ubiquitous engineering. IEEE, Seoul, pp 548–553
34. Vekkot S, Shukla P (2009) A novel architecture for wavelet based image fusion. World Acad Sci Eng Technol 57:372–377
35. Qu G, Zhang D, Yan P (2001) Medical image fusion by wavelet transform modulus maxima. Opt Express 9(4):184–190
36. Yang Y (2011) Multiresolution image fusion based on wavelet transform by using a novel technique for selection coefficients. J Multimed 6(1):91–98
37. Teng J, Wang X, Zhang J, Wang S, Huo P (2010) A multimodality medical image fusion algorithm based on wavelet transform. Proc Adv Swarm Intell, LNCS 6146:627–633
38. Yang Y (2010) Multimodal medical image fusion through a new DWT based technique. In: 4th IEEE international conference on bioinformatics and biomedical engineering (ICBBE), pp 1–4
39. Alfano B, Ciampi M, Pietro GD (2007) A wavelet-based algorithm for multimodal medical image fusion. Proc Semantic Multimedia, LNCS 4816:117–120
40. Sweldens W (1998) The lifting scheme: A construction of second generation wavelets. SIAM J Math Anal 29(2):511–546
41. Daubechies I, Sweldens W (1998) Factoring wavelet transforms into lifting steps. J Fourier Anal Appl 4(3):247–269

42. Kor S, Tiwary US (2004) Feature level fusion of multimodal medical images in lifting wavelet transform domain. In: 26th annual international conference of the IEEE engineering in medicine and biology society (EMBS '04), vol 1, pp 1479–1482
43. Xue-jun W, Ying M (2010) A medical image fusion algorithm based on lifting wavelet transform. IEEE Int Conf Artif Intell Comput Intell (AICI):474–476
44. Cotronei M, Montefusco LB, Puccio L (1998) Multiwavelet analysis and signal processing. IEEE Trans Circuits Syst II, Analog Digit Signal Process 45(8):970–987
45. Strela V, Heller PN, Strang G, Topiwala P, Heil C (1999) The application of multiwavelet filter banks to image processing. IEEE Trans Image Process 8(4):548–563
46. Wang H (2004) A new multiwavelet-based approach to image fusion. J Math Imaging Vision 21(2):177–192
47. Liu Y, Yang J, Sun J (2010) PET/CT medical image fusion algorithm based on multiwavelet transform. 2nd Int Conf Adv Comput Control (ICACC) 2:264–268
48. Cody MA (1994) The wavelet packet transform: extending the wavelet transform. Dr Dobb's J 19:44–46
49. Yang L, Liu X, Yao Y (2008) Medical image fusion based on wavelet packet transform and self-adaptive operator. 2nd IEEE Int Conf Bioinf Biomed Eng (ICBBE):2647–2650
50. Nason GP, Silverman BW (1995) The stationary wavelet transform and some statistical applications. Wavelets Stat Lecture Notes Statist 103:281–299
51. Fowler JE (2005) The redundant discrete wavelet transform and additive noise. IEEE Signal Process Lett 12(9):629–632
52. Chibani Y, Houacine A (2000) On the use of the redundant wavelet transform for multisensor image fusion. In: 7th IEEE International conference on electronics, circuits and systems (ICECS), pp 442–445.
53. Singh R, Vatsa M, Noore A (2009) Multimodal medical image fusion using redundant wavelet transform. In: 7th international conference on advances in pattern recognition, pp 232–235.
54. Kingsbury N (2001) Complex wavelets for shift invariant analysis and filtering of signals. Appl Comput Harmon Anal 10(3):234–253
55. Kingsbury NG (1998) The dual-tree complex wavelet transform: a new technique for shift invariance and directional filters. In: IEEE digital signal processing workshop, vol 86. Citeseer, Bryce Canyon, pp 120–131
56. Lina JM, Mayrand M (1995) Complex daubechies wavelets. Appl Comput Harmon Anal 2 (3):219–229
57. Lina JM (1998) Complex daubechies wavelets: filters design and applications. In: Inverse problems, tomography, and image processing. Springer, Boston, pp 95–112

Chapter 4
Integration of Wavelet Transforms for Single and Multiple Image Watermarking

Abstract Multimedia security has become challenging due to large amount of content generation and its distribution over network. Copyright protection and content authentication are the major key factor that avoids illegal distribution of digital data. However, due to availability of high bandwidth network, copyright violation is very common and many copies of data can be illegally distributed over network. Thus, to ensure multimedia security, image watermarking methods have been introduced which is a kind of information hiding technique. Watermarking provides an effective way to ensure copyright protection and content authentication and can be implemented in spatial and transform domain. The use of wavelet transforms in watermarking increases the embedding capacity and enhances the imperceptibility of the watermarked image. Being motivated from the use of wavelet transforms in image watermarking, in this chapter, a hybrid combination of the wavelet transforms have been discussed for single and multiple image watermarking. The transforms, combined in this chapter, are nonsubsampled contourlet transform (NSCT), discrete cosine transform (DCT) and multiresolution singular value decomposition (MSVD). This hybrid combination will take advantage of the characteristics and NSCT, DCT and MSVD to build a robust watermarking system in wavelet domain against signal processing and geometrical attacks.

Keywords Image watermarking · Wavelet transform · Singular value decomposition · Copyright protection · Hybrid wavelet domain image watermarking

4.1 Introduction

Multimedia content development has been influenced due to increase in the social network websites and easy availability of the handheld devices. This increase in multimedia data posed many challenges on the copyright protection and content authentication [1, 2]. In order to protect unauthorized use and access of the digital media, watermarking techniques have been used [3]. Digital watermarking uses secret message to be embedded into cover object to protect the copyright ownership. This embedding of secret message can address challenges like illegal copying and

© Springer Nature Switzerland AG 2020
R. Singh et al., *Intelligent Wavelet Based Techniques for Advanced Multimedia Applications*, https://doi.org/10.1007/978-3-030-31873-4_4

sharing, security, and confidentiality [4]. Image watermarking has also been explored for healthcare applications, particularly in the transfer of electronic patient record [5]. These applications of image watermarking demonstrate its importance in different research domains [6–9].

Watermarking techniques are categorized into spatial and transform domain [10, 11]. Spatial domain techniques are simple and embedding of watermark can be done by directly modify the intensity values of the cover media, whereas transform domain watermarking is a three step process. First step is forward transformation to obtain coefficients followed by embedding of watermark and the last step is inverse transformation that provides watermarked images. It has been found that spatial domain watermarking techniques lacks in providing robustness against signal processing and geometrical attacks [12]. However, it has been reported that spatial and transform domain techniques can be combined to reduce the computational complexity of transform domain methods [13]. These techniques should meet the key characteristics of any image watermarking systems, which are imperceptibility, robustness and capacity [1, 3]. Within the transform domain techniques, wavelet transform based methods have been extensively used and found better than discrete cosine transform (DCT) and other methods [14, 15]. Being motivated from these works, in this chapter, we present a study of the wavelet domain single and multiple image watermarking techniques. This chapter includes a new generation wavelet transform, nonsubsampled contourlet transform (NSCT) and multiresolution singular value decomposition (MSVD) which has been integrated with DCT. The results have been demonstrated to highlight the usefulness of the wavelet domain methods over others.

4.2   Related Work

In the early stage of transform domain watermarking, discrete Fourier transform (DFT) has been used [16]. It has been replaced with DCT domain methods [17] which provide better performance than DFT. It was realized that multiresolution analysis property of discrete wavelet transform (DWT) provides better representation of watermarked image and has a number of subbands that enables us the choice for embedding watermarks [18]. With these advantages, a number of DWT based watermarking techniques have been proposed in the literature [19–28]. A maximum-likelihood based image watermarking in DWT domain has been proposed in [19] which uses blind detection of watermark using statistical parameters mean and variance. This method was tested against JPEG compression, noise, and blur attacks. Singular value decomposition (SVD) has been widely used in DWT based image watermarking methods as it provides invariance against geometrical attack. An adaptive DWT-SVD based watermarking method has been proposed by Li et al. [20]. Li et al. used forward SVD decomposition for embedding and inverse SVD in reconstruction of the watermarked image. The methods discussed so far, are single image watermarking, i.e. they embed a single image watermark in DWT domain.

Multiple image watermarking has been introduced to take the advantage of different subbands produced after forward DWT decomposition. The central idea is to embed multiple watermarks into different subbands of the DWT [26–29]. These works have been extended and other transforms like DCT, integer wavelet transform (IWT) have been integrated with DWT to increase the security and robustness of image watermarking methods. A combined DWT-DCT based watermarking using SVD has been proposed to enhance the robustness of the watermarking method in [30]. This method has been implemented by dividing the cover image into non-overlapping regions. Singh et al. [31] have proposed a hybrid combination of DWT-DCT-SVD and watermark has been embedded into singular values of the DWT coefficients. Such hybrid combinations of DWT have been become very popular and many researchers proposed different combinations [32–34]. Though, DWT techniques have been very popular, yet shift sensitivity is its one of the major drawbacks. Shift invariance is highly desirable to obtain invariance against geometrical attacks. In order to develop shift invariant image watermarking, redundant discrete wavelet transform (RDWT) has been used [35–37]. RDWT enables shift invariance in the image watermarking process. Therefore, several researchers have proposed RDWT based hybrid combination for image watermarking. Roy and Pal introduced a RDWT based image watermarking method which integrates DCT and Arnold transform [35]. Similarly, SVD has been used for RDWT domain blind image watermarking in [36]. It has been also seen that multiple image watermarking can be done successfully using RDWT [37]. RDWT based methods provides shift invariance, however, these are computational costly. Therefore, integer wavelet transform (IWT) and lifting wavelet transform (LWT) based hybrid methods have been proposed to provide efficient and low cost image watermarking [38–41].

These wavelet transform domain methods provide spatial information into horizontal, vertical and diagonal directions. The directional information can be increased with the use of dual tree complex wavelet transform (DT-CWT), which is shift invariant as well. DT-CWT has also been used in image watermarking to take the advantage of shift invariance and better directional selectivity [42] and uses SVD as a mathematical tool for embedding watermark. It has been further realized that DT-CWT is not able to provide multiscale geometrical analysis and lacks to handle smoothness around contours. Experimentally, it was observed that new generation wavelet transforms such as curvelet transform (CVT), contourlet transform (CNT) and nonsubsampled contourlet transform (NSCT) provide multiscale geometrical analysis and smoothness around contours. Thus, in order to take the advantage of these properties, CVT, CNT and NSCT have been used for image watermarking [43–45]. These transforms are rich in directional information and enable better flexibility in the embedding of single and multiple image watermarks. Among these transforms, NSCT is shift invariant as it removes the downsampler in the implementation of CNT and found suitable for multiple image watermarking [8, 9]. Use of NSCT also provides geometrical invariance which can be increased by using it with SVD. Due to these reasons, we have been

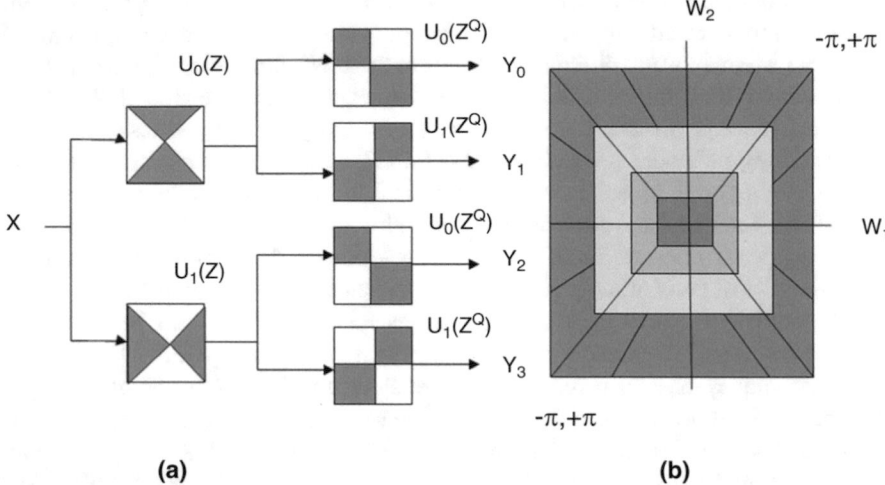

Fig. 4.1 Nonsubsampled contourlet transform. (**a**) Nonsubsampled directional filter bank, (**b**) The iterated frequency partitioning

motivated to present a study on the integration of wavelet domain methods for single and multiple image watermarking.

4.3   Theoretical Background

4.3.1   Nonsubsampled Contourlet Transform (NSCT)

NSCT is a redundant transform and provides high directionality than any other wavelet transform. It is also shift invariant and provides a number of subbands after decomposition which makes it suitable for watermarking. The details of NSCT implementation can be found in [46]. NSCT implementation includes two different filter banks which are shift invariant. First filter banks is nonsubsampled pyramid (NSP) and nonsubsampled directional filter banks (NSDFB) is the second filter bank. These have been shown in Fig. 4.1.

4.3.2   Discrete Cosine Transform (DCT)

Discrete cosine transform (DCT) [47] represent the cosine terms of the frequencies. It separates the given image into multiple frequency bands, called low, middle and high. This frequency division helps in the embedding of the watermark and provides robustness against compression. DCT transform is represented by the equation:

$$b(u,v) = c(u)c(v) \sum_{x=0}^{N-1} \sum_{y=0}^{N-1} a(x,y) \cos\left(\frac{\pi u(2y+1)}{2N}\right) \cos\left(\frac{\pi v(2y+1)}{2N}\right)$$

$$c(u) = \begin{cases} \dfrac{1}{\sqrt{N}}, & \text{if } u = 0 \\ \sqrt{\dfrac{2}{N}}, & \text{otherwise} \end{cases}$$

where (x,y) denotes the intensity values of an image and $b(u,v)$ are the DCT coefficients.

4.3.3 Multiresolution Singular Value Decomposition (MSVD)

SVD can be used like a transform in the wavelet domain image watermarking. It has been further extended to provide wavelet like multiresolution decomposition [48]. MSVD has less computation cost in comparison to the wavelet transforms. The main motivation behind the use of MSVD is to incorporate geometrical invariance in the image watermarking methods and to provide multilevel embedding of the watermarks. MSVD decomposition has been shown in Fig. 4.2.

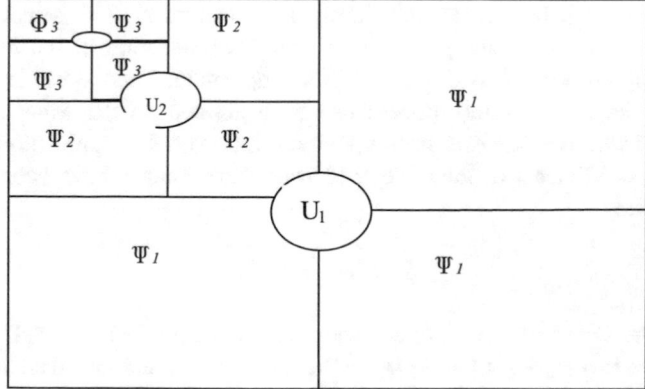

Fig. 4.2 MSVD decomposition

4.3.4   Arnold Transform

Arnold transform is a scrambling method and used in the image watermarking systems for the security enhancement. It provides the encrypted form of the image and after certain number of iterations, original image can be obtained. Thus, only a few iterations can be used for the scrambling, which is performed by following equation:

$$\begin{bmatrix} p' \\ q' \end{bmatrix} = \begin{bmatrix} 1 & 1 \\ 1 & 2 \end{bmatrix} \begin{bmatrix} p \\ q \end{bmatrix} (mod \ X)$$

where (p', q') are the scrambled values of (p, q) and X denotes the order of matrix such that $p, q \ \epsilon \ \{0, 1, 2, 3, \ldots \ldots \ldots, X - 1\}$.

4.4   Methodology and Comparative Analysis

On the basis of the reviewed literature, we have been influenced to propose a general framework for hybrid image watermarking system, which integrates multiple wavelet transforms and uses MSVD as an additional mathematical transform. This integration will take the advantage of all the transforms and incorporate the key characteristics of the watermarking i.e. imperceptibility and robustness in a better way. Embedding and extraction are the two steps of image watermarking systems. The proposed image watermarking framework can use different wavelet transforms together with SVD or MSVD. The embedding and extraction frameworks have been shown in Figs. 4.3 and 4.4. For embedding, two wavelet decompositions have been considered. In this study the first transform is NSCT and second is DCT. The first step of embedding is to divide the source image into non-overlapping image blocks and select the image blocks for embedding of the watermark. This selection may be based on the energy or entropy of the block. After selection of the block, apply NSCT decomposition followed by DCT decomposition. Then, SVD is applied on DCT coefficients. The same process has been applied on the watermark image i.e. two consecutive wavelet decomposition followed by application of SVD. Then, SVD coefficients of the cover and watermark images have been combined using following

$$S = S_C + \alpha * S_W$$

where S is the SVD coefficients of the watermarked image, S_C is the SVD coefficient of the source image, S_W is the SVD coefficient of the watermark data and α is the scaling parameter.

In order to obtain watermarked image, inverse SVD followed by two inverse transforms (NSCT and DCT) has been performed. For extraction of the image

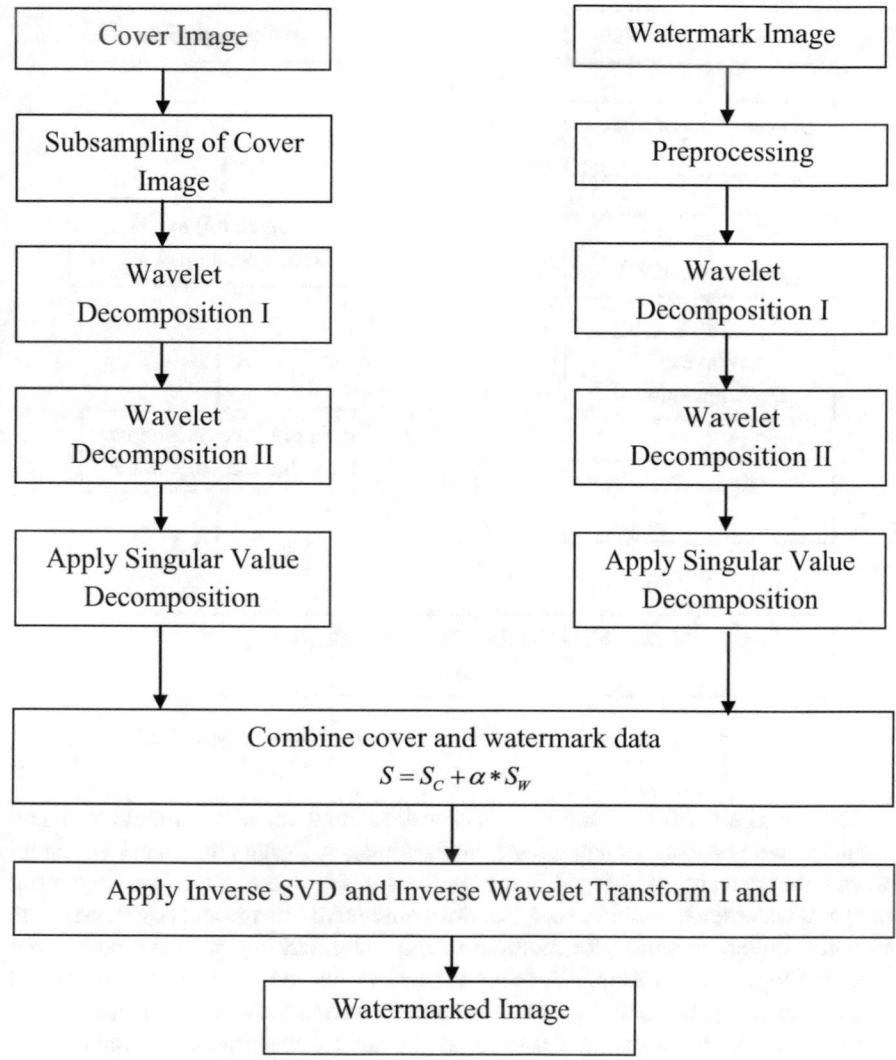

Fig. 4.3 A general framework of embedding process in image watermarking

watermark, reverse process of the embedding is performed and the singular values of the watermark will be extracted by using equation:

$$S_w = (S - S_c)/\alpha$$

The embedding and extraction methods, shown in the Figs. 4.3 and 4.4 show the use of single watermark only. However, this can be extended by adding one additional watermark in parallel way and then embedding the singular values of that watermark into different frequency subbands.

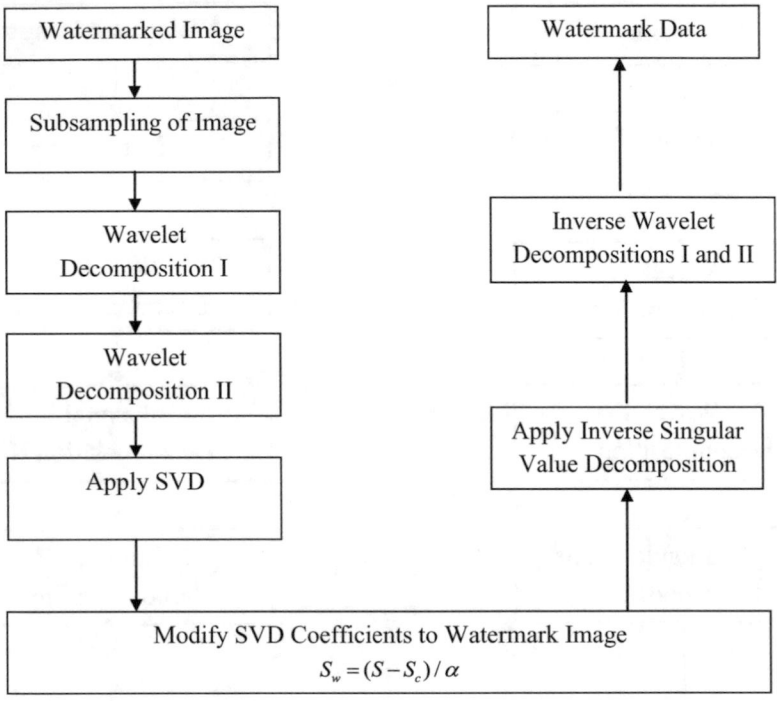

Fig. 4.4 A general framework of watermark extraction process in image watermarking

The results are shown here for single as well for dual image watermarking. These results include benchmark natural and medical images. Results for suggested framework have been shown in Fig. 4.5, which uses Lena image as cover and fingerprint image as watermark. It can be seen that the watermarked image and cover image are visually similar. Similarly for multiple image watermarking, we have considered dual and triple watermarking. For dual watermarking, the result for the suggested method has been shown in Fig. 4.6 which uses Lena and Cameraman image. Again, visual quality of the watermarked image and extracted watermarks are quite good. The concept of single and dual watermarking methods has been extended for triple watermarking to ensure the suitability of the NSCT based method. Results for triple image watermarking have been shown in Fig. 4.7, which uses medical image as cover image and three different watermarks. Two text and one image watermarks have been considered and one text watermark is scrambled before embedding. From Fig. 4.7, it is clear that the visual quality of the results have not been affected by the use of single, double or triple watermarks which validates the integration of the wavelet domain methods.

The qualitative evaluation of the image watermarking systems should be verified using quantitative analysis. For quantitative analysis of the image watermarking methods, peak signal to noise ratio (PSNR), correlation coefficient (CC) and bit error rate (BER) metrics have been used. The quantitative values for single and dual image

cover image

watermark image

watermarked image

recovered watermark image

Fig. 4.5   Single image watermarking in wavelet domain

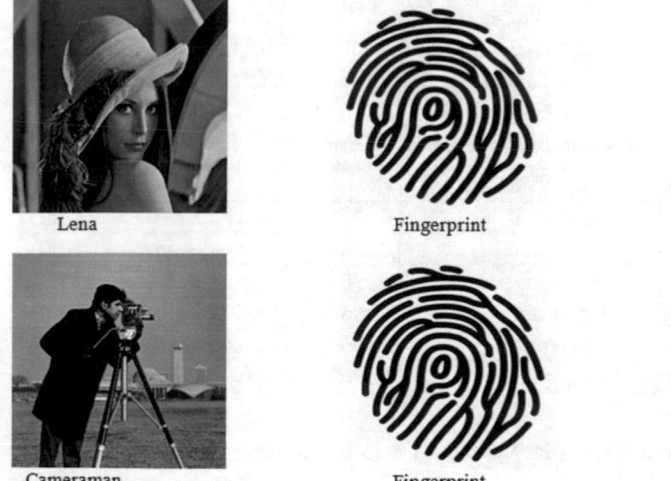

Lena   Fingerprint   Text Watermark

Cameraman   Fingerprint   Text Watermark

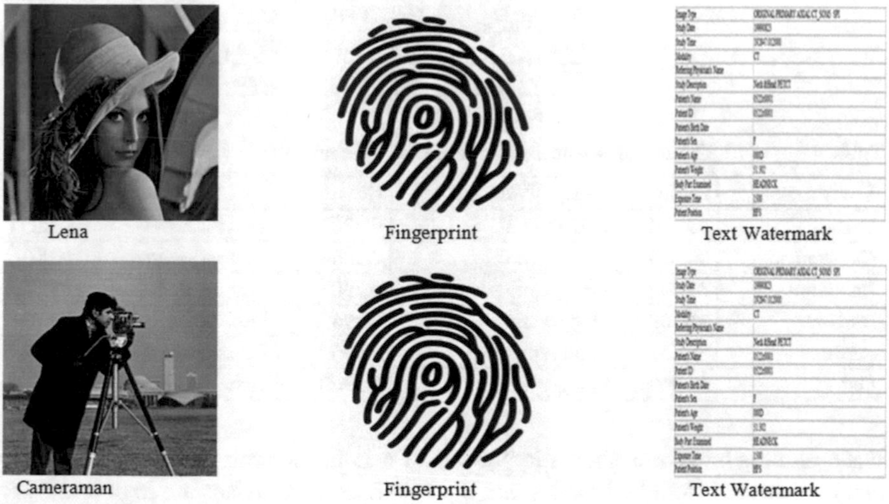

Fig. 4.6   Dual image watermarking in wavelet domain

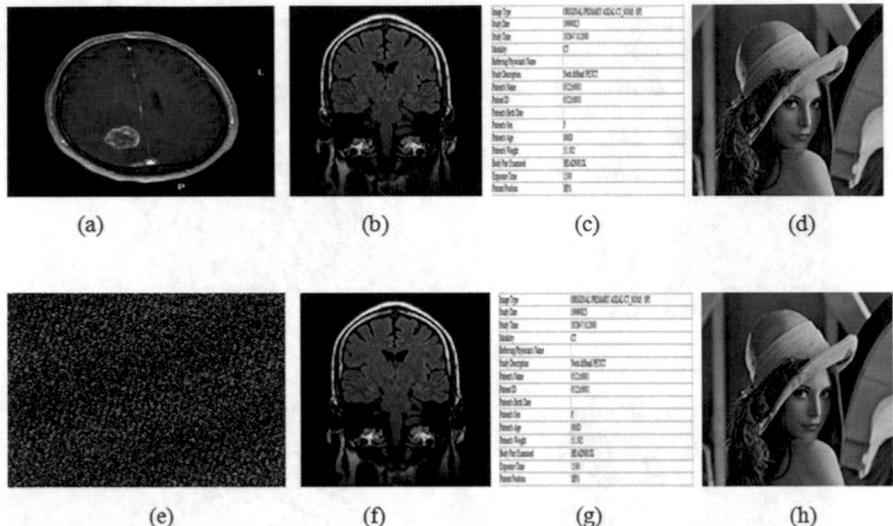

Fig. 4.7 (**a**) cover image, (**b**) image watermark 1, (**c**) text watermark 2, (**d**) image watermark 3, (**e**) scrambled text watermark 2, (**f**) recovered image watermark 1, (**g**) recovered watermark 2, (**h**) recovered watermark 3

Table 4.1 PSNR and CC values for single image watermarking in wavelet domain

Cover Image	PSNR	Image Watermark	CC
Lena	44.4023	Fingerprint	0.9962
Cameraman	44.7614	Fingerprint	0.9963
Baboon	42.0037	Fingerprint	0.9964
Barbara	38.8249	Fingerprint	0.9959
Pepper	46.7282	Fingerprint	0.9962
Girl	47.7556	Fingerprint	0.9962

Table 4.2 PSNR, CC and BER values for dual image watermarking in wavelet domain

Cover Image	PSNR	Image Watermark	CC	Text Watermark	BER
Lena	39.774	Fingerprint	0.9963	Text message	0.0037
Cameraman	39.619	Fingerprint	0.9964	Text message	0.0036
Baboon	32.492	Fingerprint	0.9965	Text message	0.0035
Barbara	35.189	Fingerprint	0.9965	Text message	0.0036
Pepper	39.031	Fingerprint	0.9962	Text message	0.0038
Girl	41.462	Fingerprint	0.9962	Text message	0.0039

watermarking have been shown in Tables 4.1 and 4.2 in terms of PSNR and CC. It can be observed from both tables that the PSNR and CC values are high and BER values are at lower side. Hence, we can conclude that the suggested method is well suitable for single and dual image watermarking. The robustness of the method should also be tested against various attacks for hybrid wavelet domain image watermarking method, given in Table 4.3. It has been found that the NSCT-DCT-

Table 4.3 Comparative evaluation of Hybrid wavelet domain image watermarking methods

Attacks	DWT + SVD	CNT + SVD	NSCT +SVD	(NSCT + DCT + MSVD)
JPEG compression	0.9992	0.9992	0.9992	0.9935
Histogram equalization	0.9537	0.8238	0.9722	0.9942
Median filtering	0.9602	0.9545	0.8636	0.9939
Salt and pepper noise	0.9458	0.9507	1.0000	0.9867
Weiner filtering	0.5727	0.7163	0.7794	0.9959
Gaussian noise	0.9755	0.8414	1.0000	0.9934
Cropping	0.9530	0.5101	0.9806	0.9935

MSVD method has the best performance against JPEG compression, Histogram equalization, Median filtering, Salt and pepper noise, Weiner filtering, Gaussian noise and Cropping. Thus, we can conclude that the hybrid wavelet domain image watermarking methods improves the performance and robustness and takes the advantages of all the transforms associated in its implementation.

4.5   Summary

In this chapter, we have provided a study on the use of multiple wavelet transforms for single and multiple image watermarking. This study includes NSCT, DCT and MSVD. We also provided a background and literature review of the hybrid wavelet domain single and multiple image watermarking methods. It can be easily observed that NSCT provides a number of subbands after decomposition which makes it suitable for embedding multiple watermarks. Further, using mathematical tools like MSVD increases the invariance against geometrical attacks. Thus, an invariant image watermarking system can be developed using hybrid combinations. This hybrid combination can be improved by using particle swarm optimization (PSO) or any soft computing techniques and more efficient methods should be investigated to reduce the computational complexity.

References

1. Cox IJ, Miller ML, Bloom JA, Honsinger C (2002) Digital watermarking, vol 53. Morgan Kaufmann, San Francisco
2. Katzenbeisser S, Petitcolas FAP (2000) Digital watermarking. Artech House, London
3. Potdar VM, Han S, Chang E (2005) A survey of digital image watermarking techniques. In: INDIN'05. 2005 3rd IEEE international conference on industrial informatics, 2005. IEEE, Perth, pp 709–716
4. Wang SH, Lin YP (2004) Wavelet tree quantization for copyright protection watermarking. IEEE Trans Image Process 13(2):154–165

5. Nyeem H, Boles W, Boyd C (2013) A review of medical image watermarking requirements for teleradiology. J Digit Imaging 26(2):326–343
6. Kumar C, Singh AK, Kumar P (2018) A recent survey on image watermarking techniques and its application in e-governance. Multimed Tools Appl 77(3):3597–3622
7. Agarwal N, Singh AK, Singh PK (2019) Survey of robust and imperceptible watermarking. Multimed Tools Appl 78(7):8603–8633
8. Singh S, Rathore VS, Singh R, Singh MK (2017) Hybrid semi-blind image watermarking in redundant wavelet domain. Multimed Tools Appl 76(18):19113–19137
9. Singh S, Rathore VS, Singh R (2017) Hybrid NSCT domain multiple watermarking for medical images. Multimed Tools Appl 76(3):3557–3575
10. Nikolaidis N, Pitas I (1998) Robust image watermarking in the spatial domain. Signal Process 66(3):385–403
11. Shieh CS, Huang HC, Wang FH, Pan JS (2004) Genetic watermarking based on transform-domain techniques. Pattern Recogn 37(3):555–565
12. Lai CC, Tsai CC (2010) Digital image watermarking using discrete wavelet transform and singular value decomposition. IEEE Trans Instrum Meas 59(11):3060–3063
13. Shih FY, Wu SY (2003) Combinational image watermarking in the spatial and frequency domains. Pattern Recogn 36(4):969–975
14. Bao P, Ma X (2005) Image adaptive watermarking using wavelet domain singular value decomposition. IEEE Trans Circuits Syst Video Technol 15(1):96–102
15. Wang S, Meng X, Yin Y, Wang Y, Yang X, Zhang X, Chen H (2019) Optical image watermarking based on singular value decomposition ghost imaging and lifting wavelet transform. Opt Lasers Eng 114:76–82
16. Solachidis V, Pitas L (2001) Circularly symmetric watermark embedding in 2-D DFT domain. IEEE Trans Image Process 10(11):1741–1753
17. Barni M, Bartolini F, Cappellini V, Piva A (1998) A DCT-domain system for robust image watermarking. Signal Process 66(3):357–372
18. Xia XG, Boncelet CG, Arce GR (1997) A multiresolution watermark for digital images. In: Proceedings of international conference on image processing, vol 1. IEEE, Santa Barbara, pp 548–551
19. Ng TM, Garg HK (2005) Maximum-likelihood detection in DWT domain image watermarking using Laplacian modeling. IEEE Signal Process Lett 12(4):285–288
20. Li Q, Yuan C, Zhong YZ (2007) Adaptive DWT-SVD domain image watermarking using human visual model. In: The 9th international conference on advanced communication technology, vol 3. IEEE, Okamoto, pp 1947–1951
21. Dawei Z, Guanrong C, Wenbo L (2004) A chaos-based robust wavelet-domain watermarking algorithm. Chaos, Solitons Fractals 22(1):47–54
22. Wang J, Liu G, Dai Y, Sun J, Wang Z, Lian S (2008) Locally optimum detection for Barni's multiplicative watermarking in DWT domain. Signal Process 88(1):117–130
23. He Z, Lu W, Sun W, Huang J (2012) Digital image splicing detection based on Markov features in DCT and DWT domain. Pattern Recogn 45(12):4292–4299
24. Sverdlov A, Dexter S, Eskicioglu AM (2005) Robust DCT-SVD domain image watermarking for copyright protection: Embedding data in all frequencies. In: 2005 13th European signal processing conference. IEEE, Antalya, pp 1–4
25. Ansari IA, Pant M (2017) Multipurpose image watermarking in the domain of DWT based on SVD and ABC. Pattern Recogn Lett 94:228–236
26. Wang J, Lian S, Shi YQ (2017) Hybrid multiplicative multi-watermarking in DWT domain. Multidim Syst Sign Process 28(2):617–636
27. Gao Y, Wang J, Shi YQ (2019) Dynamic multi-watermarking and detecting in DWT domain. J Real-Time Image Proc 16:1–12
28. Liu J, Huang J, Luo Y, Cao L, Yang S, Wei D, Zhou R (2019) An optimized image watermarking method based on HD and SVD in DWT domain. IEEE Access 7:80849

29. Singh AK, Dave M, Mohan A (2015) Robust and secure multiple watermarking in wavelet domain. J Med Imaging Health Inf 5(2):406–414
30. Fazli S, Moeini M (2016) A robust image watermarking method based on DWT, DCT, and SVD using a new technique for correction of main geometric attacks. Optik-Int J Light Electron Opt 127(2):964–972
31. Singh AK, Dave M, Mohan A (2014) Hybrid technique for robust and imperceptible image watermarking in DWT–DCT–SVD domain. Natl Acad Sci Lett 37(4):351–358
32. Kasmani SA, Naghsh-Nilchi A (2008, November) A new robust digital image watermarking technique based on joint DWT-DCT transformation. In: 2008 third international conference on convergence and hybrid information technology, vol 2. IEEE, Piscataway, pp 539–544
33. Huang F, Guan ZH (2004) A hybrid SVD-DCT watermarking method based on LPSNR. Pattern Recogn Lett 25(15):1769–1775
34. Rastegar S, Namazi F, Yaghmaie K, Aliabadian A (2011) Hybrid watermarking algorithm based on singular value decomposition and radon transform. AEU-Int J Electron Commun 65 (7):658–663
35. Roy S, Pal AK (2017) A robust blind hybrid image watermarking scheme in RDWT-DCT domain using Arnold scrambling. Multimed Tools Appl 76(3):3577–3616
36. Makbol NM, Khoo BE (2013) Robust blind image watermarking scheme based on redundant discrete wavelet transform and singular value decomposition. AEU-Int J Electron Commun 67 (2):102–112
37. Hien TD, Nakao Z, Chen YW (2006) Robust multi-logo watermarking by RDWT and ICA. Signal Process 86(10):2981–2993
38. Makbol NM, Khoo BE (2014) A new robust and secure digital image watermarking scheme based on the integer wavelet transform and singular value decomposition. Digital Signal Process 33:134–147
39. Ansari IA, Pant M, Ahn CW (2016) Robust and false positive free watermarking in IWT domain using SVD and ABC. Eng Appl Artif Intell 49:114–125
40. Verma VS, Jha RK (2015) Improved watermarking technique based on significant difference of lifting wavelet coefficients. SIViP 9(6):1443–1450
41. Verma VS, Jha RK, Ojha A (2015) Significant region based robust watermarking scheme in lifting wavelet transform domain. Expert Syst Appl 42(21):8184–8197
42. Mansouri A, Aznaveh AM, Azar FT (2009) SVD-based digital image watermarking using complex wavelet transform. Sadhana 34(3):393–406
43. Zhang C, Cheng LL, Qiu Z, Cheng LM (2008) Multipurpose watermarking based on multiscale curvelet transform. IEEE Trans Inf Forensics Secur 3(4):611–619
44. Jayalakshmi M, Merchant SN, Desai UB (2006, August) Digital watermarking in contourlet domain. In: 18th international conference on pattern recognition (ICPR'06), vol 3. IEEE, Hong Kong, pp 861–864
45. Niu PP, Wang XY, Yang YP, Lu MY (2011) A novel color image watermarking scheme in nonsampled contourlet-domain. Expert Syst Appl 38(3):2081–2098
46. Da Cunha AL, Zhou J, Do MN (2006) The nonsubsampled contourlet transform: Theory, design, and applications. IEEE Trans Image Process 15(10):3089–3101
47. Ahmed N, Natarajan T, Rao KR (1974) Discrete cosine transform. IEEE Trans Comput 100 (1):90–93
48. Kakarala R, Ogunbona PO (2001) Signal analysis using a multiresolution form of the singular value decomposition. IEEE Trans Image Process 10(5):724–735

Chapter 5
On Wavelet Domain Video Watermarking Techniques

Abstract The large availability and access of video data for education, entertainment such as games and movies poses several challenges of copyright violation and illegal distribution of data. More specifically, pirated video distribution has been a key threat for such copyright violation. To handle these challenges, watermarking techniques can be used to provide copyright protection. The wide application of wavelet transform in the implementation of image watermarking techniques compelled to discuss wavelet domain video watermarking techniques in this chapter. The present chapter provides an overview of video watermarking techniques in wavelet domain and discusses various methods used for embedding and extraction of watermark. It also provides the description of various attacks and key characteristics of video watermarking techniques with comparative analysis of results for evaluation of the existing methods.

Keywords Video watermarking · Watermark embedding · Watermark extraction · Copyright protection · Geometric attacks · Wavelet transforms

5.1 Introduction

In the modern age of computing, huge amount of video data generation can be seen everywhere such as movies, games, social media. The content can be illegally copied, tampered and can be distributed easily over internet [1]. One such example is video piracy which has violated copyright protection of the owners [2, 3]. Video piracy can be defined as an act of illegal production and distribution the copy of digital media without permission of the owner. This can be observed in Fig. 5.1 which shows the process creation of pirated video from copyright material using camcorder and making it available over internet for public [1]. This problem is not limited to a single country, it is a worldwide issue that is not still being solved or resolved. For example, many cases have been reported for pirated copies of Bollywood (Indian) and Hollywood movies. The pirated downloads of Indian movies have been grown by more than 100% in countries like Tanzania, Ireland etc., as reported by Tecxipio, a German data analytics company [4]. Indian

© Springer Nature Switzerland AG 2020   65
R. Singh et al., *Intelligent Wavelet Based Techniques for Advanced Multimedia Applications*, https://doi.org/10.1007/978-3-030-31873-4_5

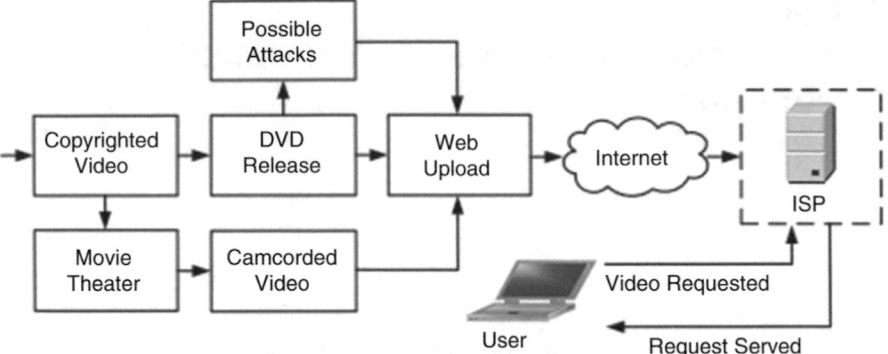

Fig. 5.1 Copyright violation and distribution of pirated data through Internet [1]

government has introduced a bill in its parliament to stop such piracy by taking strict legal actions for unauthorized use of camcorders for duplication and distribution of movies [5]. The same incident can be seen for the Batman series movie 'The Dark Knight' whose seven million copies have been downloaded in the first 6 months. However, the producers of the film Warner Brothers has well planned antipiracy campaign [6] to stop the duplication of the movie. Thus, we can conclude that neither any bill nor any campaign is able to stop such violation of copyright. Due to this, a great loss of revenue may happen to the producers consequently government and may introduce unemployability or any other business loss. Since, no control mechanism is able to stop such kind of piracy; therefore, we need some robust information security techniques to prevent duplication and distribution of movies or any other copy protected contents. Watermarking techniques are capable of providing copyright protection and ensure protection of digital media content against any kind of tampering and illegal distribution [7]. The concept of image watermarking, discussed in previous chapter can be extended to video watermarking. Primary goal of video watermarking will be to stop violation of copyright and illegal distribution of digital media over Internet by means of a secret message [8]. Success of wavelet domain methods in image watermarking made us to explore and provide a study of wavelet domain video watermarking techniques [9]. This chapter will discuss the video watermarking techniques, their applications, major characteristics, embedding and extraction methodologies and evaluation strategies.

5.2   Video Watermarking: An Overview of Applications and Characteristics

Watermarking for video data is more complex than image watermarking. However, the concept of embedding and extraction process remains the same. In video watermarking, watermark should be embedded and extracted by the system or

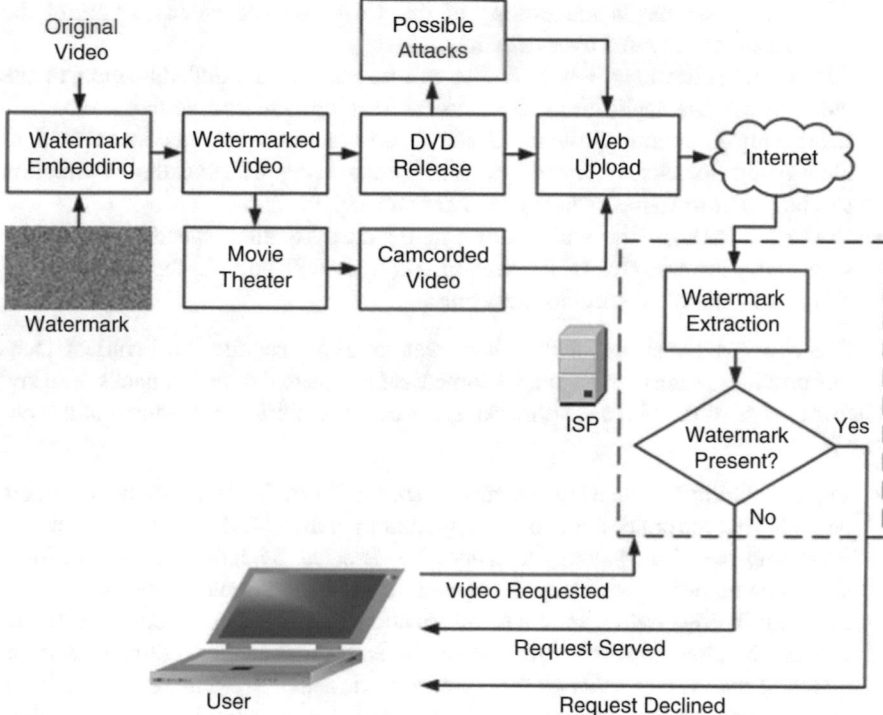

Fig. 5.2 A general video watermarking system

Internet Service Provider (ISP) to stop downloading of illegal data. This can be achieved by with the help of secret message that may have the information of copyright owner or similar message. A general video watermarking procedure has been shown in Fig. 5.2, taken from [1].

Video watermarking algorithms can be classified into spatial and transform domain [9]. Transform domain methods have been found better than spatial domain video watermarking methods in terms of robustness against different attacks [10, 11]. On the basis of available literature video watermarking applications can be found in following.

- Copyright Protection: The embedded watermark can be used to protect digital video against illegal distribution. But, it should be robust against attacks as attempts can be made to remove watermark information from the digital video. This can be further enhanced to prevent making illegal copies of the video.
- Broadcast Monitoring: Video watermarking enables the monitoring of the commercial advertisements that have been broadcasted over the network. Thus, a video watermarking can act as a broadcast monitoring system.
- Copy Control: Digital media can be protected by using a watermark to restrict devices for making illegal copies of a DVD. On the detection of the watermark,

device may decline to make copy of the video file and can also control the
distribution of the same over network.
- Video Authentication: Watermarking can be used in the authentication of the
  video data in the applications like medical imaging, video surveillance etc.
- Identifying Location of Illegal User: Video watermarking can be utilized to
  identify the location of the illegal distributors using ISP and the information
  can be provided to the owners of the data for legal action.
- Content Filtering: The watermark can be used to filter specific content by
  identifying the message of the watermark. This will provide the access of the
  digital content to the specific users only.

The above applications of the video watermarking require the invariant techniques providing robustness against geometrical and spatial domain attacks. The key
characteristics of the video watermarking are imperceptibility, robustness and security [1, 7].

- Imperceptibility: Embedded watermark should be invisible in the cover media
  and must not introduce any kind of degradation in the visual quality of the media.
  Ideal imperceptible watermark cannot be detected by human eyes, i.e. there
  should be no difference between original video and watermarked video.
- Payload: It refers to the amount of information embedded in the cover object. In
  general, it is the number of bits that can be embedded as the watermark without
  affecting the visual quality of the watermarked media. Watermark granularity is
  another term related with video watermarking and can be defined as the data
  required to embed one unit of the watermark.
- Robustness: It refers to the invariance of the watermark against attacks performed
  by general users that includes signal processing and geometrical attacks. Signal
  processing attacks include addition of noise, filtering, compression (MPEG,
  H.264) etc. to remove or tamper the watermark from media. Similarly, geometrical attacks include cropping, resizing, rotation, shearing to remove the watermark information for illegal use of the media.
- Security: It is the one of the important and major concern of video watermarking.
  In the case of embedding and extraction method is known to the unauthorized
  users, it must remain secure and cannot be detected and removed.

5.3   Video Watermarking in Wavelet Domain: Literature Review

Video watermarking in wavelet domain has been influenced from image
watermarking. A joint image and video watermarking method has been proposed
using discrete wavelet transform (DWT) [9] using multiresolution analysis. In this
method, watermark has embedded into high frequency subbands of the DWT
coefficients for multilevel DWT and used non-linear insertion methodology. Set

partitioning in hierarchical tree (SPIHT) compression scheme has been adopted for video sequence. This method considers only compression attack for video watermarking using simple DWT decomposition.

A hybrid combination of DWT and singular value decomposition (SVD) has been explored to utilize the advantages of DWT and SVD [12]. This work has reported the performance of a number of spatial and wavelet domain watermarking methods against various attacks such as JPEG compression, cropping, resize, noise, filtering etc. On the basis of this study, embedding has been done by making groups of several frames together and transforming the color space from RGB to YC_bC_r followed by 2-level DWT decomposition. After DWT decomposition, SVD is applied to middle and high frequency subbands for watermark embedding. Watermark has been divided into many sequences and then embedded into video frames. To obtain watermarked video frame Inverse DWT has been taken. Results have been shown for scaling and cropping, rotation, H.264 compression attacks, measured in terms of peak signal to noise ratio (PSNR) and bit error rate (BER) and found better than existing simple DWT based methods. A spread spectrum based DWT video watermarking scheme has been introduced in [10] for video copyright protection. This research used error correction code for binary watermark image and spread spectrum with a secret key for watermark embedding. The secret key has been used in watermark extraction as well. Three video sequences – Stefan, Forman and Bus have been used for experiments. These experiments have been performed in two categories. First set of experiments have been shown using no error correction whereas hamming code has been used for second set of experiments. The authors have considered different quantization size, noise, filtering and other attacks to validate their video watermarking method.

Another quantization based video watermarking method has been proposed using spatial and temporal redundancy and color space conversion from RGB to YC_bC_r [13]. Compression attacks such as JPEG (Quality factor = 80), MPEG (at different bit rates) with and without error correction codes have been exploited to show the goodness of the algorithm. Perceptual masking based video watermarking has been proposed by Campisi and Neeri [14]. In this work, apart from DWT decomposition, a perceptual mask has been considered by calculating contrast sensitive function, image brightness and eye sensitivity to noise. Video quality metric (VQM) has been chosen to evaluate the performance of this approach. An entropy based non-blind video watermarking has been proposed by Rasti et al. [15]. This method uses entropy based watermark embedding, DWT and SVD decomposition. Blocks with low entropy values have been selected for watermark embedding. The results have shown comparative analysis with existing methods considering different signal processing and geometrical attacks.

A hybrid color video watermarking technique has been introduced in [16]. This method uses a number of transforms such as DWT, contourlet transform (CT) and SVD for video watermarking. Thus, it can be observed that hybrid combination of the various transforms will increase the performance of the video watermarking. Motion activity analysis based video watermarking is another method that can be utilized for watermarking of video media [17]. This includes motion estimation and embedding watermarks to the fast motion areas that increases the imperceptibility of the watermarked video. Number theoretic functions have also been exploited for video watermarking. Fibonacci sequence based video watermarking using DWT and SVD has been proposed by Sathya and Ramakrishnan [18]. The sequence has been used to identify the key video frames for video watermarking followed by DWT and SVD decomposition. This method has shown improved PSNR values against existing methods, which motivates the use of other number theoretic functions for video watermarking. Other than DWT, many other wavelet transforms have been explored for video watermarking. Integer wavelet transform (IWT) based video watermarking using chaotic map has been introduced to increase the security of the embedded watermark [19]. The method has been evaluated in terms of PSNR and structural similarity index metric (SSIM). Lifting wavelet transform (LWT) based video watermarking has been proposed by Bhardwaj et al. [20] which is based on coefficient differencing. This method used a three level LWT decomposition and a frame selection method for watermark embedding.

A comparative evaluation of the DWT based video watermarking method can be found in [21] which summarizes the performance of the existing methods and evaluation parameters. In order to introduce invariance against rotation, a DWT based video watermarking has been proposed by Singh [22]. In this work, watermark has been embedded into the high frequency subbands (HH) of the DWT after applying encryption. Another invariant video watermarking has been proposed by Serdean et al. [23] which use HVS based embedding.

These discussed methods are based on DWT and other wavelet transforms which provide real valued wavelet coefficients. A new family of wavelet transforms, called complex wavelet transforms has been also explored for video watermarking. Dual tree complex wavelet transform (DT-CWT) introduced by Kingsbury [24] which is better than DWT as it provides shift invariance and high directional information. These properties have been found useful in the implementation of invariant video watermarking [25]. DT-CWT based video watermarking provides invariance against rotation, scaling, cropping and compression attacks. Similarly, another DT-CWT based blind video watermarking technique has been introduced by Esfahani et al. [26]. This method uses low frequency wavelet coefficients for watermark embedding. This method improves the perceptual quality and performs better against geometrical and signal processing attacks.

5.4   Methodology and Evaluation Strategies

Based on the literature review, in this section, we discuss a general framework for video watermarking in wavelet domain and performance evaluation parameters. Like image watermarking, video watermarking consists of two steps, i.e. embedding and extraction of watermark. The framework presented here is motivated from the different models of video watermarking in wavelet domain. Embedding and extraction procedures have been shown in Figs. 5.3 and 5.4. In

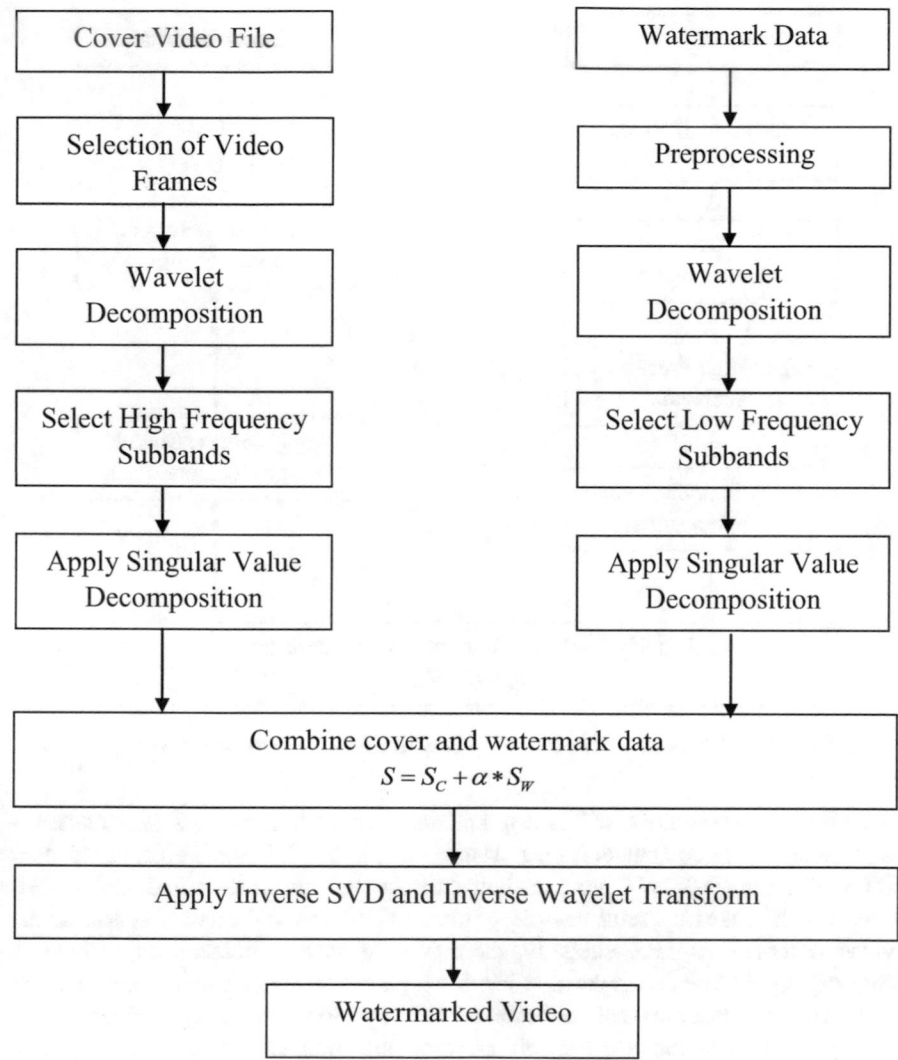

Fig. 5.3 A general framework of embedding process in video watermarking

the embedding process, we require cover video file (color or gray) and then we have
to select appropriate video frames for watermark embedding. The selection process
of video frames can be based on entropy, energy or on some other parameters. In
literatures, it has been found that entropy has been used for selection of blocks and
frames for the cases of image and video watermarking respectively. After frame
selection, wavelet decomposition is performed on video frames. The wavelet transform can be DWT, IWT, DT-CWT as the method discussed here provides a general
framework. However, the choice of wavelet transform and decomposition level
should be experimentally chosen. DWT and IWT are non-redundant wavelet

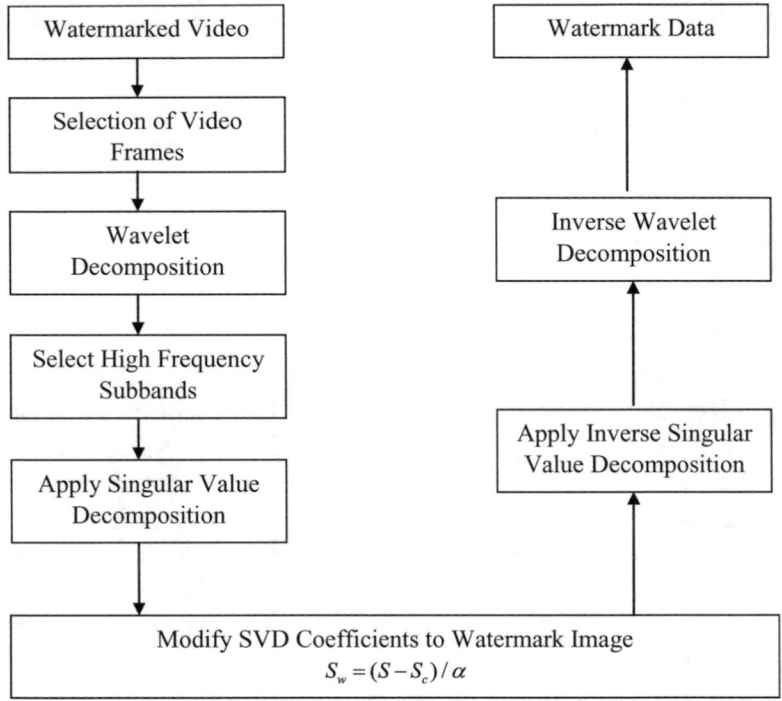

Fig. 5.4 A general framework of watermark extraction process in video watermarking

transforms whereas DT-CWT is a redundant wavelet transform. The redundancy will increase the computation cost. Hence, DWT or IWT can be preferred over DT-CWT. But, DT-CWT provides better directional information and shift invariance which makes it useful against geometrical attacks and reconstruction of the video watermarked data. Similarly, the choice of wavelet decomposition level is challenging. At low decomposition level, we have less high frequency information and vice-versa. For practical applications, decomposition level may vary from level 2 to level 4 to maintain a tradeoff between low frequency and high frequency information. High frequency subband is selected for watermark embedding and then SVD decomposition is performed. Similarly, watermark image has to be processed for resizing or any other requirement. Then, wavelet decomposition should be performed followed by SVD decomposition. Once, we have obtained the SVD coefficients for cover and watermark data, we have to combine them by following equation:

$$S = S_C + \alpha * S_W$$

where S is the SVD coefficients of the watermarked data, S_C is the SVD coefficient of the cover media, S_W is the SVD coefficient of the watermark data and α is the scaling parameter.

(a)   (b)   (c)

Fig. 5.5 Sample images from Akiyo, Foreman and Bus video datasets

Inverse SVD and inverse wavelet transform on S will be taken to obtain the watermarked video. Extraction of the watermark can be done by performing the reverse of the embedding process. Initially, watermarked video will be decomposed using wavelet transform and SVD decomposition has been performed. Then, the singular values of the watermark will be obtained by the relation:

$$S_w = (S - S_c)/\alpha$$

where symbols have the same meaning as explained for the watermark embedding process.

The most commonly used datasets for video watermarking are 'Akiyo', 'Bus' and 'Foreman' [27]. Sample test images of these datasets are given in Fig. 5.5. The watermark image can be any gray scale, binary or color image. Here, we provide a comparative study of different video watermarking method in wavelet domain in terms of correlation coefficient (CC). The watermark image to perform experiments is the benchmark cameraman image. The methods compared for this study is [15, 28–30] which considered a number of geometrical and signal processing attacks. These attacks are Flipping, Histogram equalization, Cropping, JPEG, Blurring, Contrast enhancement, Salt and pepper noise, Gaussian noise, Sharpening, Gamma correction, Scaling. Comparisons of the wavelet domain video watermarking methods have been shown in Tables 5.1 and 5.2 in terms of CC values. It can be easily observed from the Table 5.1 that Rasti et al. [15] method is better than others as it uses entropy based QR decomposition in wavelet domain. A very similar analysis can be found in Table 5.2.

5.5 Summary

In this chapter, we have provided an overview of video watermarking methods in wavelet domain and discussed the importance and key characteristics. A detailed literature review of the existing wavelet domain methods have been discussed in brief. Based on the existing literature review, we have suggested a general method

Table 5.1 Comparative evaluation of wavelet domain methods in terms of CC for Bus video sequence

Attacks	Rasti et al. [15]	Lai et al. [28]	Agoyi et al. [29]	Hamad et al. [30]
Flipping	1	0.9641	0.0422	0.7954
Histogram equalization	0.9979	0.8658	0.6808	0.8337
Cropping	0.9854	0.8552	0.2961	0.8432
JPEG	0.9396	0.9194	0.0612	0.9828
Blurring	0.9336	0.1880	0.7051	0.6145
Contrast enhancement	0.9671	0.9149	0.1394	0.8174
Salt & pepper noise	0.9979	0.9103	0.5300	0.5028
Gaussian noise	0.9454	0.7777	0.5199	0.4763
Sharpening	0.9979	0.7570	0.8561	0.8675
Gamma correction	0.9854	0.9476	0.0998	0.7613
Scaling	0.8732	0.2414	0.7047	0.5965

Table 5.2 Comparative evaluation of wavelet domain methods in terms of CC for Akiyo video sequence

Attacks	Rasti et al. [15]	Lai et al. [28]	Agoyi et al. [29]	Hamad et al. [30]
Flipping	0.9875	0.9363	0.8855	0.6420
Histogram equalization	0.9572	0.9470	0.8324	0.9539
Cropping	0.9096	0.9470	0.5490	0.7711
JPEG	0.9937	0.9587	0.9644	0.8169
Blurring	0.9301	0.3148	0.6975	0.6127
Contrast enhancement	0.8372	0.9506	0.9604	0.7433
Salt & pepper noise	0.9452	0.8676	0.6050	0.5290
Gaussian noise	0.8229	0.6761	0.5506	0.4919
Sharpening	1	0.8610	0.9567	0.8396
Gamma correction	0.9471	0.9469	0.7574	0.7593
Scaling	1	0.3250	0.6942	0.6163

for video watermarking in wavelet domain that considers singular value decomposition as a mathematical tool to enhance the performance of the watermarking method against geometrical and signals processing attacks, Comparative analysis of the wavelet methods clearly indicated the goodness of these algorithms. However, existing wavelet domain methods should be improved and analyzed in terms of new generation wavelet transforms such as curvelet transform (CVT), contourlet transform (CNT) etc.

References

1. Asikuzzaman M, Pickering MR (2017) An overview of digital video watermarking. IEEE Trans Circuits Syst Video Technol 28(9):2131–2153
2. Barni M, Bartolini F (2004) Data hiding for fighting piracy. IEEE Signal Process Mag 21 (2):28–39
3. Bloom JA, Cox IJ, Kalker T, Linnartz JP, Miller ML, Traw CBS (1999) Copy protection for DVD video. Proc IEEE 87(7):1267–1276
4. https://www.thehindu.com/entertainment/movies/bollywoods-biggest-piracy-khiladis/arti cle24333045.ece
5. https://www.thehindu.com/news/national/government-introduces-bill-in-rajya-sabha-to-amend-cinematograph-act-jail-term-fine-for-film-piracy/article26249683.ece
6. https://www.nytimes.com/2009/02/05/business/media/05piracy.html
7. Langelaar GC, Setyawan I, Lagendijk RL (2000) Watermarking digital image and video data. A state-of-the-art overview. IEEE Signal Process Mag 17(5):20–46
8. Haitsma J, Kalker T (2001) A watermarking scheme for digital cinema. In: Proceedings 2001 international conference on image processing (Cat. No. 01CH37205), vol 2. IEEE, pp 487–489
9. Zhu W, Xiong Z, Zhang YQ (1999) Multiresolution watermarking for images and video. IEEE Trans Circuits Syst Video Technol 9(4):545–550
10. Preda RO, Vizireanu DN (2010) A robust digital watermarking scheme for video copyright protection in the wavelet domain. Measurement 43(10):1720–1726
11. Doerr G, Dugelay JL (2003) A guide tour of video watermarking. Signal Process Image Commun 18(4):263–282
12. Faragallah OS (2013) Efficient video watermarking based on singular value decomposition in the discrete wavelet transform domain. AEU-Int J Electron Commun 67(3):189–196
13. Preda RO, Vizireanu ND (2011) Quantisation-based video watermarking in the wavelet domain with spatial and temporal redundancy. Int J Electron 98(3):393–405
14. Campisi P, Neri A (2005) Video watermarking in the 3D-DWT domain using perceptual masking. In: IEEE International conference on image processing 2005, vol 1. IEEE, pp I–997
15. Rasti P, Samiei S, Agoyi M, Escalera S, Anbarjafari G (2016) Robust non-blind color video watermarking using QR decomposition and entropy analysis. J Visual Commun Image Represent 38:838–847
16. Agilandeeswari L, Ganesan K (2016) A robust color video watermarking scheme based on hybrid embedding techniques. Multimed Tools Appl 75(14):8745–8780
17. El'Arbi M, Koubaa M, Charfeddine M, Amar CB (2011) A dynamic video watermarking algorithm in fast motion areas in the wavelet domain. Multimed Tools Appl 55(3):579–600
18. Alias Sathya SP, Ramakrishnan S (2018) Fibonacci based key frame selection and scrambling for video watermarking in DWT–SVD domain. Wirel Pers Commun 102(2):2011–2031
19. Farri E, Ayubi P (2018) A blind and robust video watermarking based on IWT and new 3D generalized chaotic sine map. Nonlinear Dyn 93(4):1875–1897
20. Bhardwaj A, Verma VS, Jha RK (2018) Robust video watermarking using significant frame selection based on coefficient difference of lifting wavelet transform. Multimed Tools Appl 77 (15):19659–19678
21. Shukla D, Sharma M (2018) Robust scene-based digital video watermarking scheme using level-3 DWT: approach, evaluation, and experimentation. Radioelectron Commun Syst 61 (1):1–12
22. Singh KM (2018) A robust rotation resilient video watermarking scheme based on the SIFT. Multimed Tools Appl 77(13):16419–16444
23. Serdean CV, Ambroze MA, Tomlinson M, Wade JG (2003) DWT-based high-capacity blind video watermarking, invariant to geometrical attacks. IEE Proc Vis Image Signal Process 150 (1):51–58
24. Kingsbury N (2001) Complex wavelets for shift invariant analysis and filtering of signals. Appl Comput Harmon Anal 10(3):234–253

25. Coria LE, Pickering MR, Nasiopoulos P, Ward RK (2008) A video watermarking scheme based on the dual-tree complex wavelet transform. IEEE Trans Inf Forensics Secu 3(3):466–474
26. Esfahani R, Akhaee MA, Norouzi Z (2019) A fast video watermarking algorithm using dual tree complex wavelet transform. Multimed Tools Appl 78(12):16159–16175
27. http://trace.kom.aau.dk/yuv/index.html
28. Lai CC, Tsai CC (2010) Digital image watermarking using discrete wavelet transform and singular value decomposition. IEEE Trans Instrum Meas 59(11):3060–3063
29. Agoyi M, Çelebi E, Anbarjafari G (2015) A watermarking algorithm based on chirp z-transform, discrete wavelet transform, and singular value decomposition. Signal Image Video Process 9(3):735–745
30. Hamad S, Khalifa A (2015) Non-blind data hiding for RGB images using DCT-based fusion and H. 264 compression concepts. Adv Comput Sci Int J 4(3):97–103

Chapter 6
Object Tracking

Abstract Object tracking is core probelm in computer vision for effective video surveillance. Wavelet based tracking techniques have emerged as a powerful tool. We have exploited newly emerged curvelet transform coefficients for video object tracking. Unlike existing methods, wavelet based tracking computes only wavelet coefficients and do not get affected by variations in object's shape, size or color. However, we assumed that size of object does not change significantly in consecutive frames. A small change is permissible only. If we take long frame range, we see that object's shape and size changes significantly. Experimentation demonstrates that curvelet transform is capable of tracking of single object as well as multiple objects. It is found superior when compared qualitatively and quantitatively with existing tracking methods.

Keywords Tracking · Random motion · Multiple objects · Complex environment

6.1 Introduction

In video object tracking, an object's movement and displacement is captured with respect to time. It depicts an association between target object in sequential frames. Tracking is foundation of several applications viz. human protection and security, medical field, biometrics, scene analysis, crime investigations, etc. [1, 2].

Video object tracking is not easy, complications arise because of certain factors such as:

 (i) Real-world requirements
 (ii) Object's scale variations in different frames
(iii) Full or partial occlusion
(iv) Noisy or blurred video
 (v) Light illumination variations in the scene
(vi) Random motion of object

Aforementioned challenges clearly state that, video object tracking has always been a critical issue. In order to handle such challenges, various adaptive tracking

© Springer Nature Switzerland AG 2020

R. Singh et al., *Intelligent Wavelet Based Techniques for Advanced Multimedia Applications*, https://doi.org/10.1007/978-3-030-31873-4_6

algorithms are proposed in recent years [3]. These algorithms analyze consecutive frames of a video and output the trajectory locating the target object in those frames.

For handling above challenges, we have explored curvelet transform which is one step ahead of classical wavelet transforms. Wavelet transforms are best for detecting point discontinuities, and ridgelet transforms perform better for line discontinuities. But curvelet is superior when compared to both of these since it can compute curve discontinuities as well. We have explored this property in present chapter and performed experimentation on four single object and multiple objects video sequences. Results have shown that curvelet is much accurate as compared to existing methods.

Remaining chapter is organized as: literature review is provided in Sect. 6.2, Significance of curvelet for tracking of object is provided in Sect. 6.3, detailed experimentation and results are given in Sect. 6.4, and a conclusion of the study is provided in Sect. 6.5.

6.2   Literature Analysis

Nowadays, sensors and cameras are used for video object tracking. Based on location of these devices, tracking systems are classified in four categories. These categories are described here one by one.

6.2.1   Sensors Based Systems

Sensors based systems are incorporated with the help of body sensors that are attached on human body. These body sensors extract information of movement of different human body parts. These sensors are broadly classified into five categories (i) inertia sensors (ii) mechanical sensors (iii) acoustic sensors (iv) magnetic sensors and (v) radio or microwave sensors. Accelerometer sensors are extensively used as an inertia sensor that convert input acceleration signal into output signal. Accelerometer sensors are further divided into three categories [4–6]. Piezo-electric sensors explore the piezoelectric effect when quartz crystals produce an electric charge between two terminals. Piezo-resistive sensors measure resistance of a mechanically deformed fine wire. Variable capacitive sensors explore variations in capacitance that changes with acceleration or deceleration. However, each kind of sensors has limitations also. The performance of these sensors depends on different models, measurements and circumstances. These limitations accordingly affect the application of these sensors in various environments. Some of these sensors have a small sensing capability. Hence these sensors can monitor only small movements like finger or toe movement [7]. In addition, response capability increases with the increase in computing power. Furthermore, interface circuitry limits the resolution and signal bandwidth.

6.2.2   Marker Based Vision Systems

Since, even a small body part of humans moves in so many directions in a fully three dimensional space, hence those body parts frequently comes under partial or full occlusion situation with respect to the camera position. It results in unreliable and inaccurate tracking. Marker based vision systems overcome the limitations of sensor based systems. These systems use body sensors along with camera and place markers to track the movement of human body [8]. An important approach for tracking of full human body efficiently is presented in [9]. This approach is not based on old conventional assumptions about movements, view angle or the position of markers. Instead, it used modified particle filtering techniques for tracking purpose. A cheap, efficient and robust human tracking technique that tracked edges for varying video situations is provided in [10]. The main drawback of using marker based vision systems is that it is difficult to accurately measure joint rotations with them. This makes difficult to create a real-time 3 dimensional model of these measured objects.

6.2.3   Marker-Less Vision Systems

In the previous section, we have discussed the attributes of marker based vision systems. However, applicability of these systems is limited because of the presence of markers. Marker-less vision systems alleviate this shortcoming. Capture of movement is less restrictive in these systems. They take care of only human body features or boundaries and hence capable of handling mutual occlusion. This active and promising approach considers human motion in an image plane, although sometimes a 3D structure is intended to project into its image plane for tracking purposes.

To handle the problem of occlusion and drift, Guan et al. [11] developed an event-triggered tracking approach for efficient object tracking. This was a real time approach which effectively handled the problem arises due to fast movement and occlusion. It consists of an event-triggered module as its core component. Other modules included a short-term tracking module, tracker updating module, occlusion and drift detection module, target re-identification module and an on-line discriminative learning module. Each module was coordinated with a defined event which was triggered on fulfillment of a specific condition. This system effectively handled occlusion and model drift problem.

Since deep learning approaches have been widely popular, hence Chen and Tao [12] presented a convolution based approach. However, they proved that a single convolution layer can be used to form a large regression model for tracking purpose. They fully explored a large number of background images as a training set to form a strong regression model. Their holistic approach was capable of determining object location, size and texture accurately.

Using color histogram is popular form of object tracking and combination of corrected background weighted histogram with mean shift tracking is its enhanced version [13]. A very complicated situation in visual tracking is tracking of multiple objects in a traffic scene. Approaches proposed for this purpose mostly failed in presence of noise or occlusion. To handle this difficulty, Tian et al. [14] presented an approach that used both structural and temporal information. Their method consists of 3 phases. In the first phase, object detection is performed using object affinity based small tracklets. In the second phase, all tracklets are associated using motion patterns between them. In the third phase, temporal information is added to accurately localize the object. This approach was very effective while taking less processing time.

Kim et al. [15] alleviated problem aroused due to large camera or object motion. They presented a coarse-to-fine approach and provided a method based on superpixels. First, they extracted superpixels in the area of interest and then applied sampling and other processes on these superpixels. This approach showed high efficiency and robustness in local minima towards several deformations, occlusion and rotation. Color and texture are used to obtain better results in [16].

Combination of two adaptive Kernels based approach for object tracking was proposed by Chen et al. [17]. In first phase of this approach, a Linear Kernel and a Gaussian Kernel were used to measure the response of adjusting weights of the Kernels. In the second phase, updation is done for the maximum response. This approach provided minimum risk with high accuracy. Covariance based tracking method has gained importance since it is invariant against several complexities such as noise, illumination, etc. [18].

Spatio-temporal relationships among target templates are considered by Li et al. [19]. These templates which depend on different time frames can represent a better object model from different viewing angles. Inverse representation of collective templates can provide information regarding the spatial structure of target objects. This approach provided a stable tracking system. New forms of tracking that use curvelet transform coefficients are presented in [20, 21].

6.2.4   Robot-Guided Systems

Robot guided systems are extensively used today as they provide interaction between a human and a robot in indoor as well as outdoor in different real-world scenarios. These systems take advantage of sensors to discriminate between static and dynamic movements. They retrieve object's location by processing of images captured by the cameras placed inside them. Their main objective is to accurately identify and track the object and get its position, pose, and velocity. These robot guided systems use available sensors efficiently to explore the information for decision making, planning, and human interaction. However, these stems are bidi-rectional as robot watches human subject and vice-versa and can affect human decision-making [22].

6.3 Significance of Curvelet in Tracking

Curvelet transform is very useful in object tracking due to its following properties:

  (i) It provides multiscale analysis.
 (ii) It has limited or no redundancy.
(iii) It represents curve points in an efficient manner.

6.4 Experimentation and Results

This section provides experiments and results of curvelet based object tracking method. Here, we present results for single object tracking and multiple object tracking scenarios using four representative object tracking videos – Child video, Soccer video, Own video and Challenge video. Experiments are performed in Matlab R2013a environment on an Intel® Core™ i3 2.27 GHz machine.

Four case studies of Child video, Soccer video, Own video and Challenge video are discussed here one by one. In case of Child video and Soccer video, we have compared wavelet based tracking with other existing methods. These methods are corrected background weighted histogram (CBWH) method [13], joint color-texture histogram method (JCTH) [16] and the covariance tracking (CT) method [18].

6.4.1 Single Object Tracking: Child Video Results

The Child video sequence consists of 458 frames of size 352×288. In Fig. 6.1 we provide results of frames 1–440 by jumping 20 frames each time for the sake of space.

One can observe in Fig. 6.1, Child video consists of random motion of a child who moves very fast in 360° direction. In the first frame child object is inside the bounding box and moves outside of the box from frame 20 to frame 100. Child object moves backward from frame 120 to frame 200. Child object's movement becomes very slow after frame 200 and posture position also changes from frame 240 to frame 420. Also, child object's size varies with respect to distance from the camera position from frame 320 to 440. Background is also complex as well as slightly moving. Despite of such uncommon behavior, we see that curvelet based tracking method is suitable for tracking of the child object.

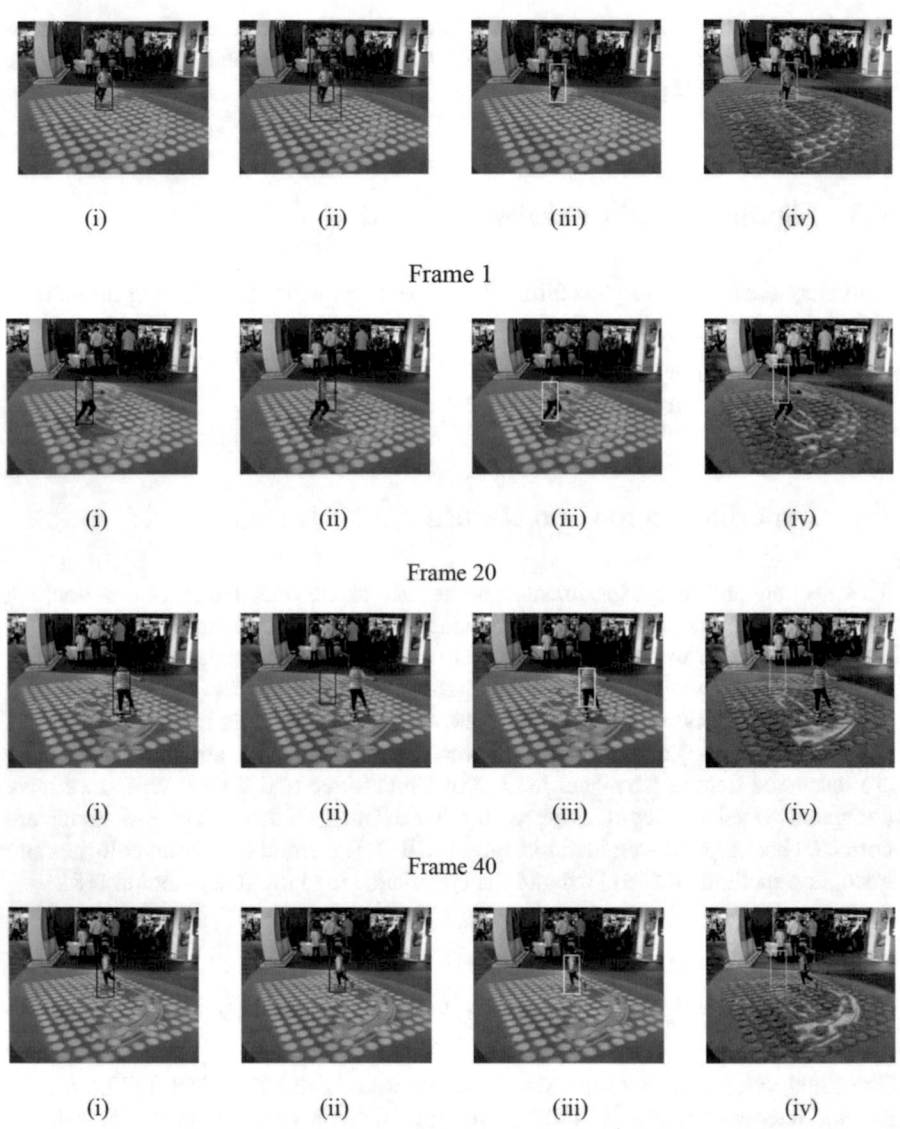

(i)   (ii)   (iii)   (iv)

Frame 1

(i)   (ii)   (iii)   (iv)

Frame 20

(i)   (ii)   (iii)   (iv)

Frame 40

(i)   (ii)   (iii)   (iv)

Frame 60

Fig. 6.1 Single object tracking: child video visual results (i) Curvelet tracking method (ii) CBWH tracking method [13] (iii) JCTH tracking method [16] (iv) CT tracking method [18]

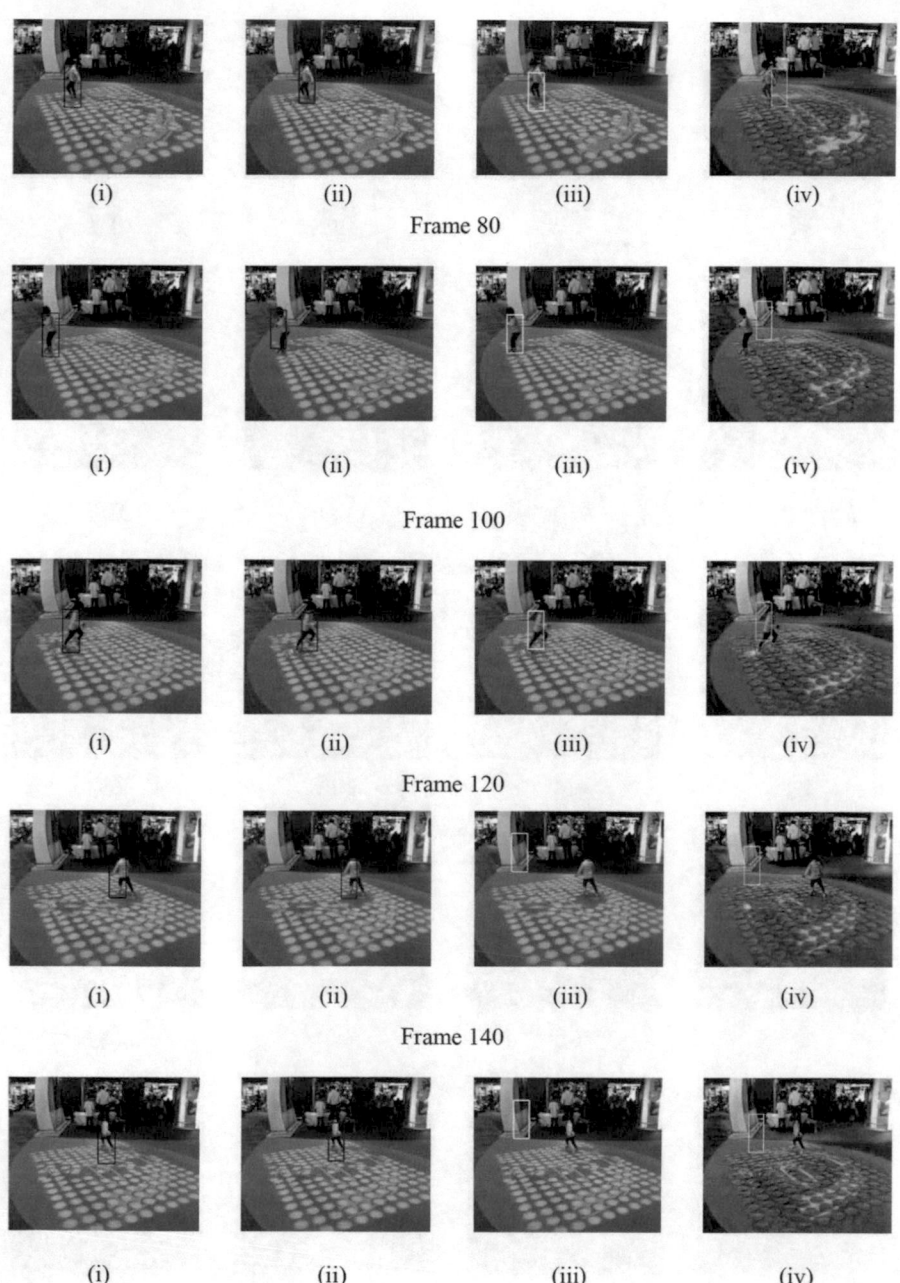

(i)   (ii)   (iii)   (iv)

Frame 80

(i)   (ii)   (iii)   (iv)

Frame 100

(i)   (ii)   (iii)   (iv)

Frame 120

(i)   (ii)   (iii)   (iv)

Frame 140

(i)   (ii)   (iii)   (iv)

Frame 160

Fig. 6.1 (continued)

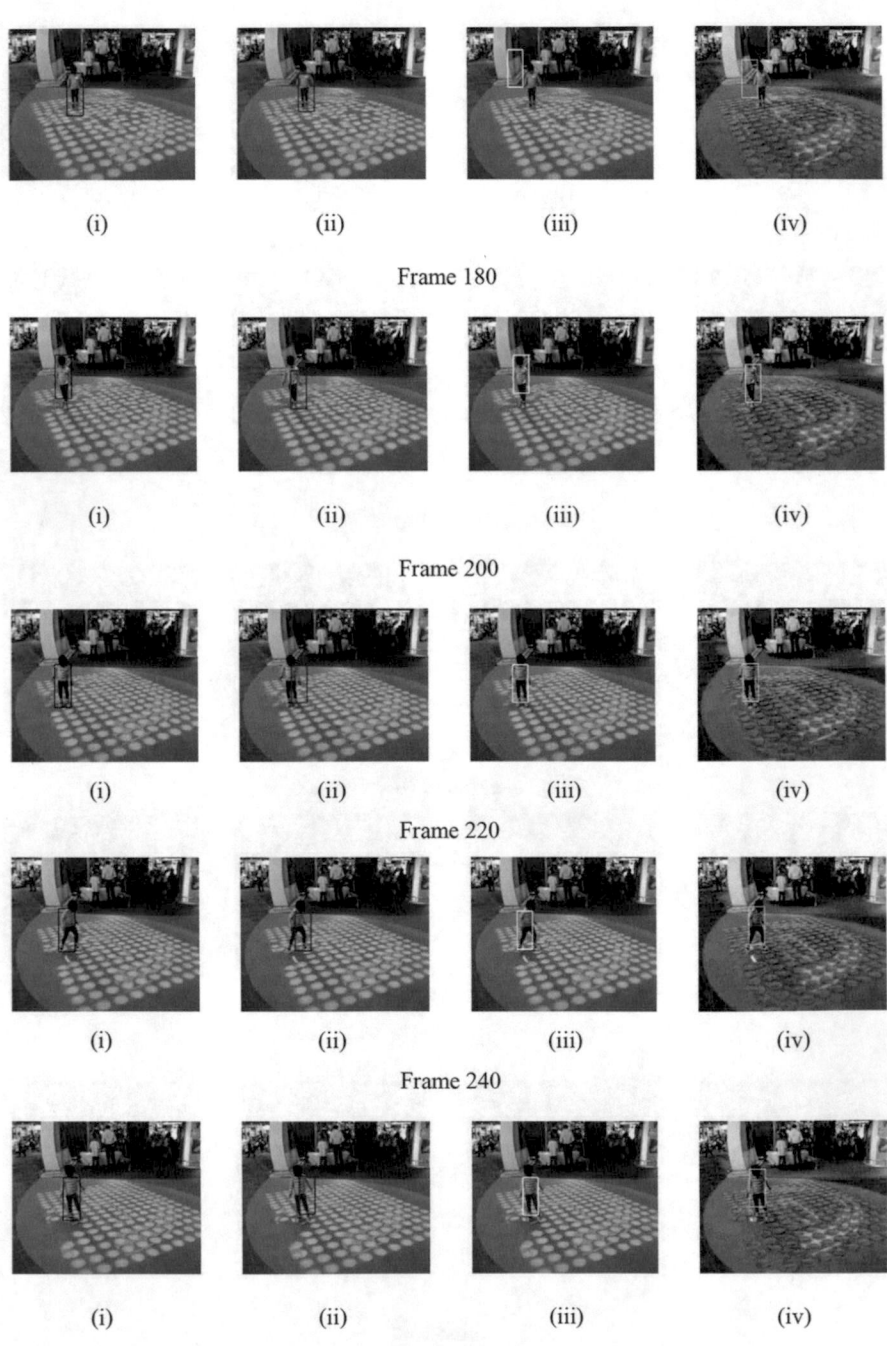

(i)   (ii)   (iii)   (iv)

Frame 180

(i)   (ii)   (iii)   (iv)

Frame 200

(i)   (ii)   (iii)   (iv)

Frame 220

(i)   (ii)   (iii)   (iv)

Frame 240

(i)   (ii)   (iii)   (iv)

Frame 260

Fig. 6.1 (continued)

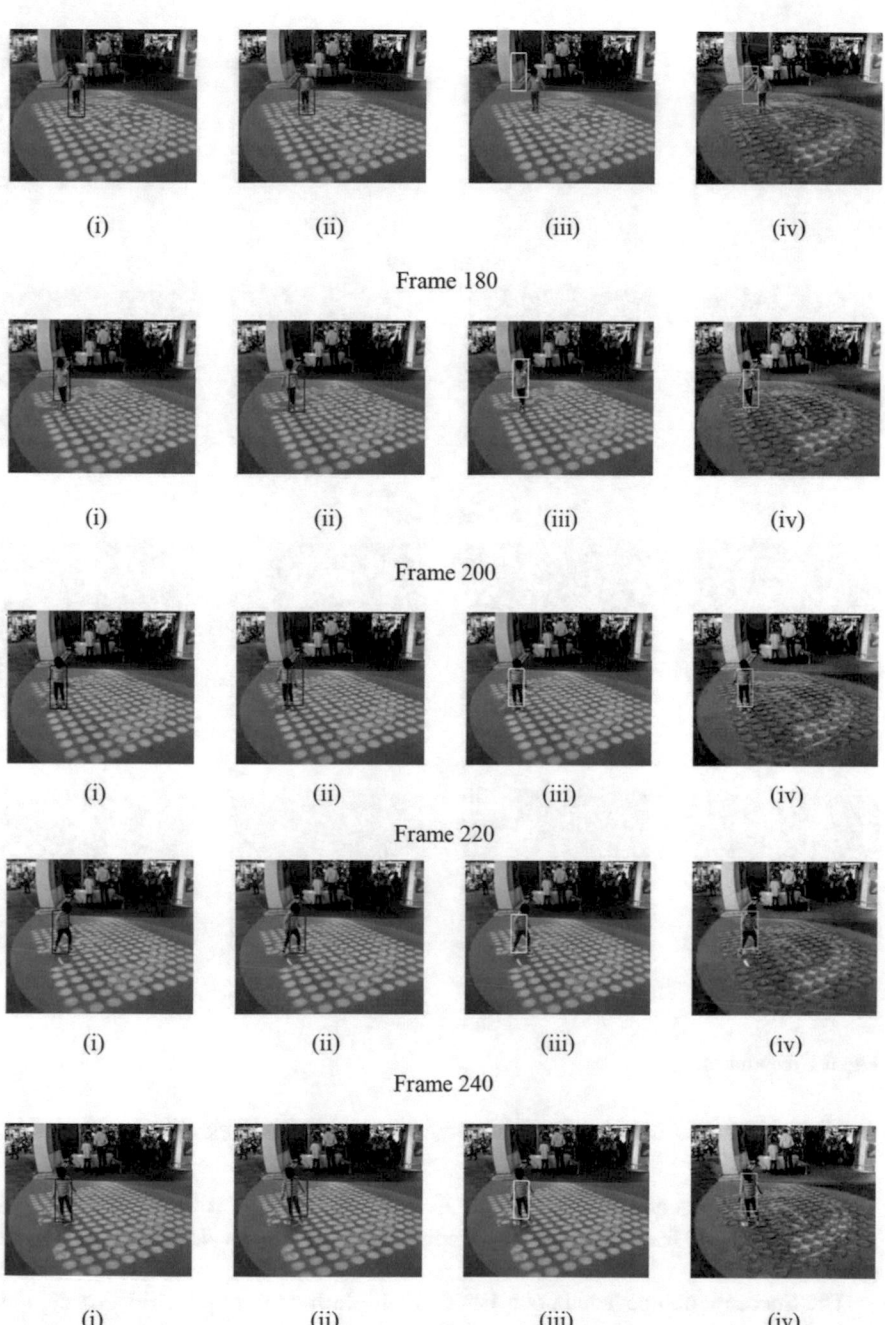

(i)   (ii)   (iii)   (iv)

Frame 180

(i)   (ii)   (iii)   (iv)

Frame 200

(i)   (ii)   (iii)   (iv)

Frame 220

(i)   (ii)   (iii)   (iv)

Frame 240

(i)   (ii)   (iii)   (iv)

Frame 260

Fig. 6.1 (continued)

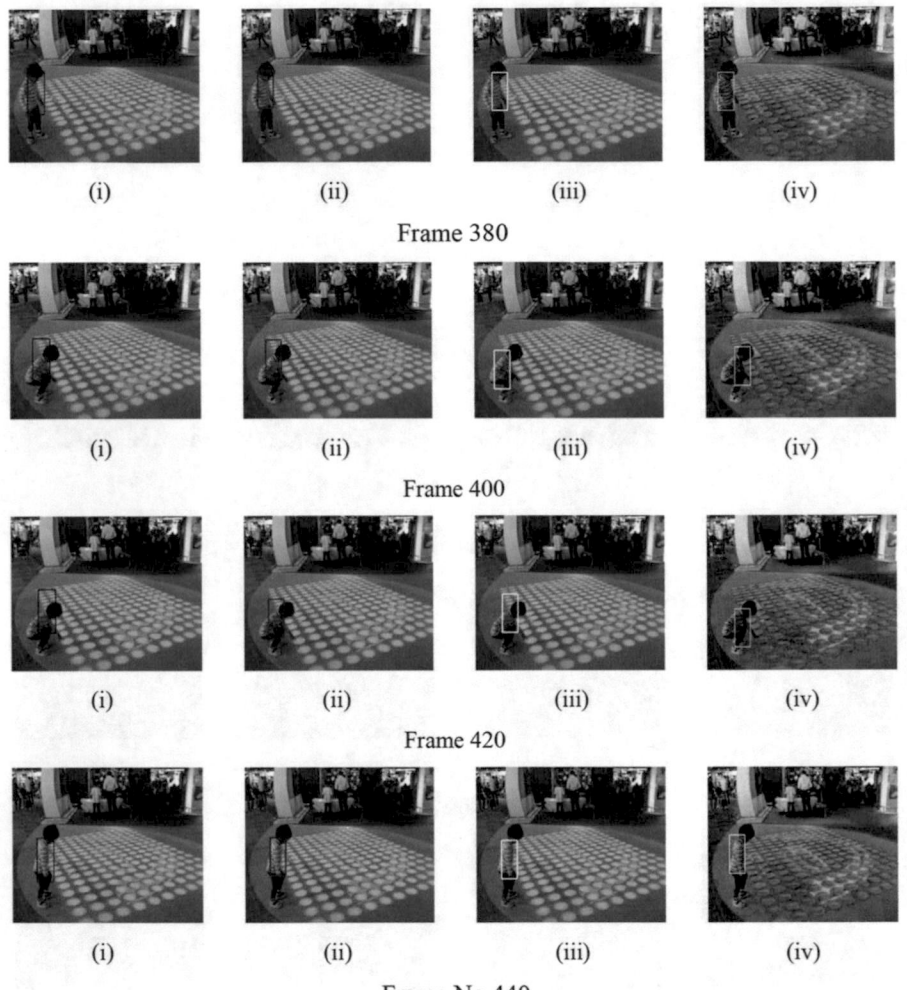

Fig. 6.1 (continued)

6.4.2   Multiple Object Tracking: Soccer Video Results

The Soccer video sequence consists of 329 frames of size 352×288. In Fig. 6.2 we provide results of frames 1–320 by jumping 20 frames each time for the sake of space.

The Soccer video sequence consists of multiple human objects since it depicts scenario of two teams playing soccer against each other. We have selected one of the player as target object. This target human object is covered inside the bounding box from frame 1 to 60. Partial occlusion occurs when another player comes inside the bounding box of target player. This happens from frame 100 to 200. Full occlusion occurs from frame 200 to 300 when another player comes inside the bounding box fully. Background is complex and dynamic. Size of players is very small. Curvelet based tracking is capable of handling such real world complexities and occlusion situation.

6.4.3 Multiple Object Tracking: Own Video Results

Here we show experimental results of our own captured video. It contains total 708 frames of size 320 × 240. In Fig. 6.3. we show visual results of frames 1–665 by jumping 35 frames each time for the sake of space.

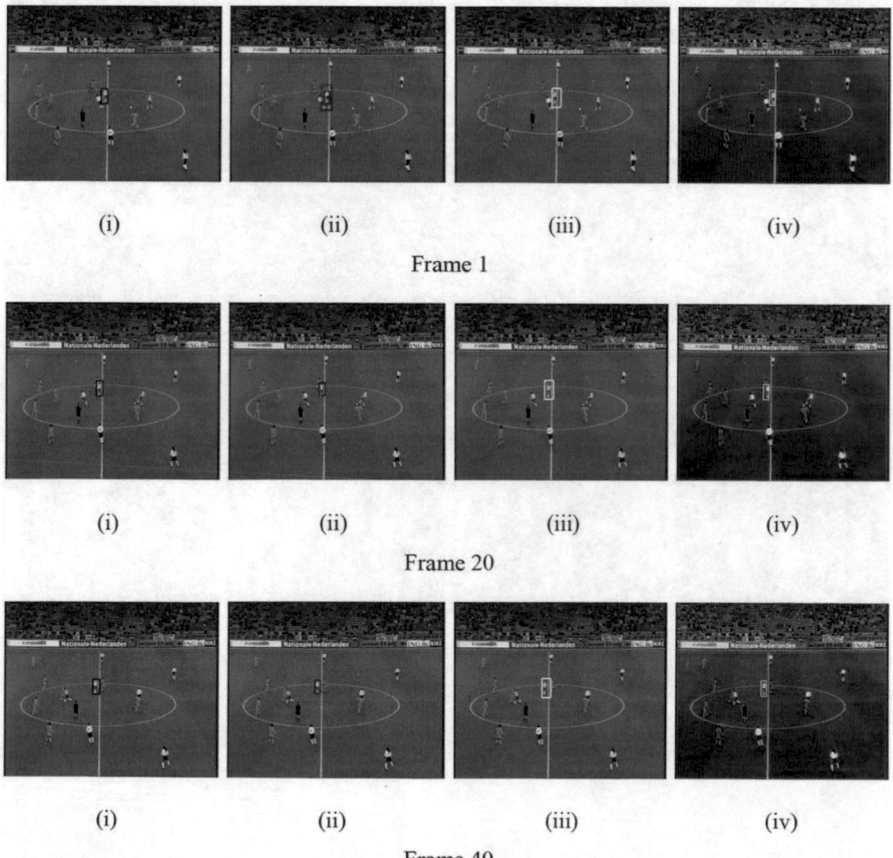

(i)   (ii)   (iii)   (iv)

Frame 1

(i)   (ii)   (iii)   (iv)

Frame 20

(i)   (ii)   (iii)   (iv)

Frame 40

Fig. 6.2 Multiple object tracking: soccer video visual results (i) Curvelet tracking method (ii) CBWH tracking method [13] (iii) JCTH tracking method [16] (iv) CT tracking method [18]

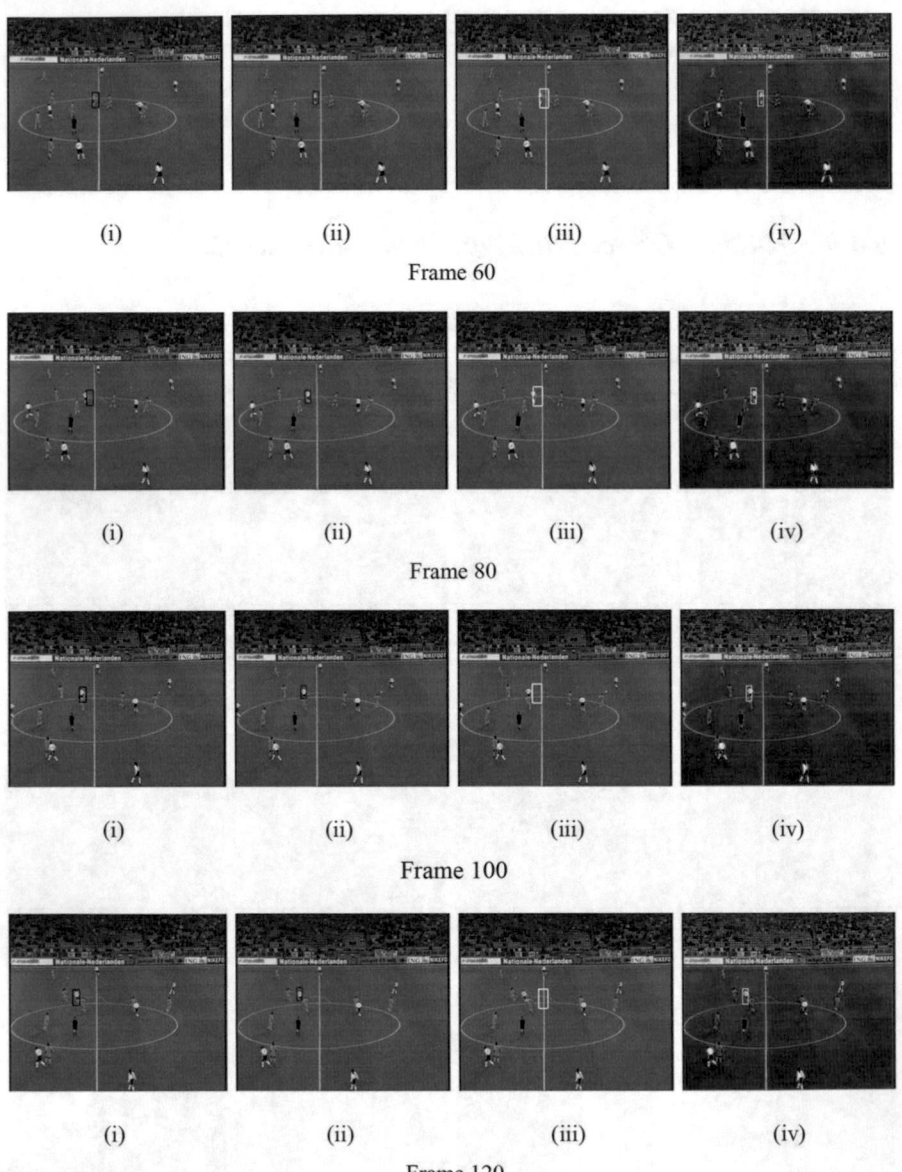

(i)   (ii)   (iii)   (iv)

Frame 60

(i)   (ii)   (iii)   (iv)

Frame 80

(i)   (ii)   (iii)   (iv)

Frame 100

(i)   (ii)   (iii)   (iv)

Frame 120

Fig. 6.2 (continued)

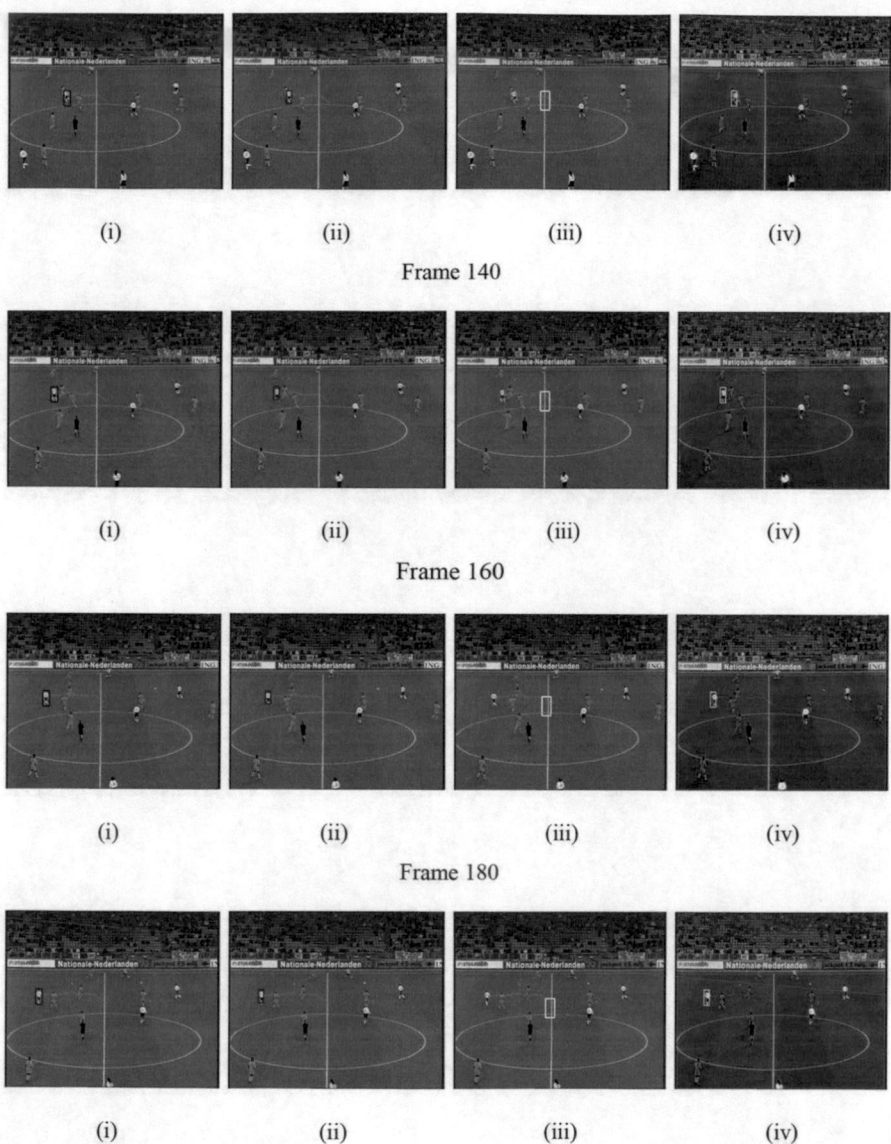

Fig. 6.2 (continued)

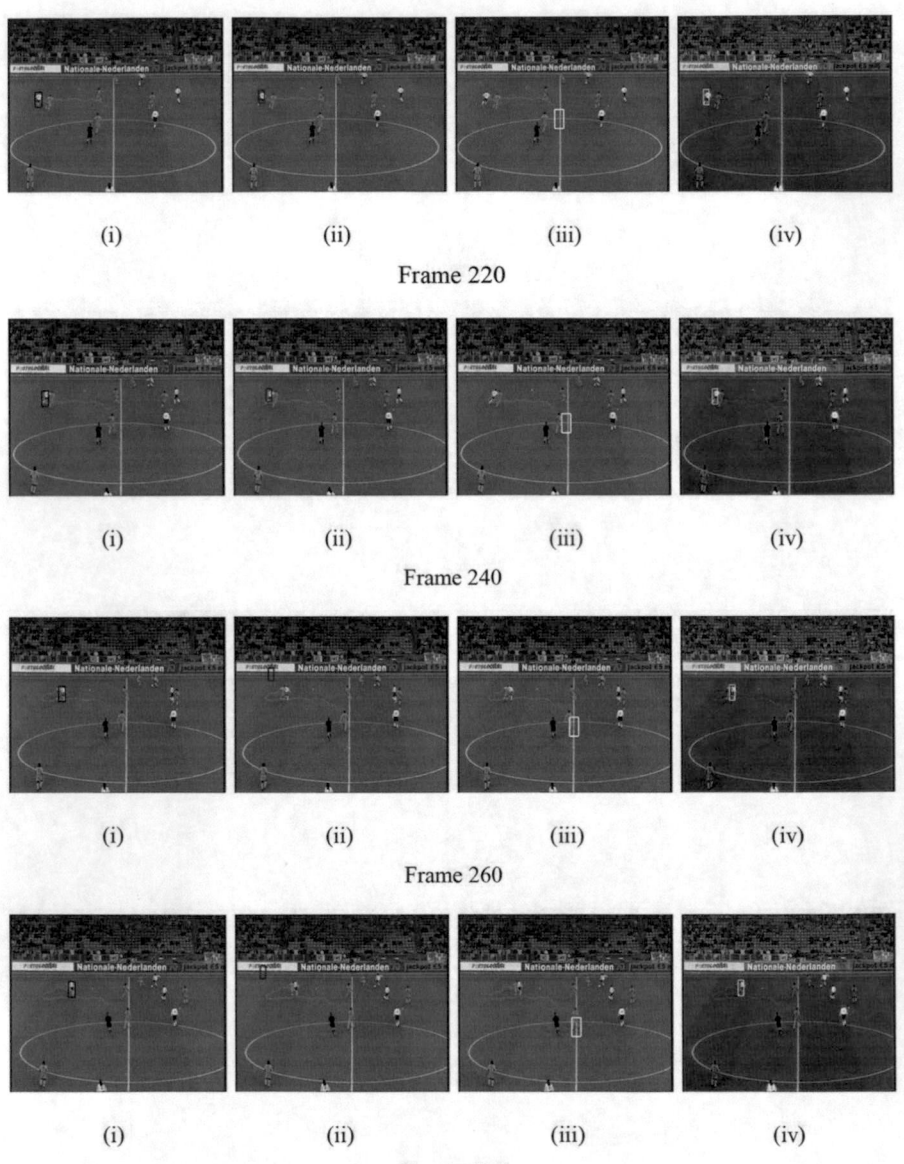

(i)   (ii)   (iii)   (iv)

Frame 220

(i)   (ii)   (iii)   (iv)

Frame 240

(i)   (ii)   (iii)   (iv)

Frame 260

(i)   (ii)   (iii)   (iv)

Frame 280

Fig. 6.2 (continued)

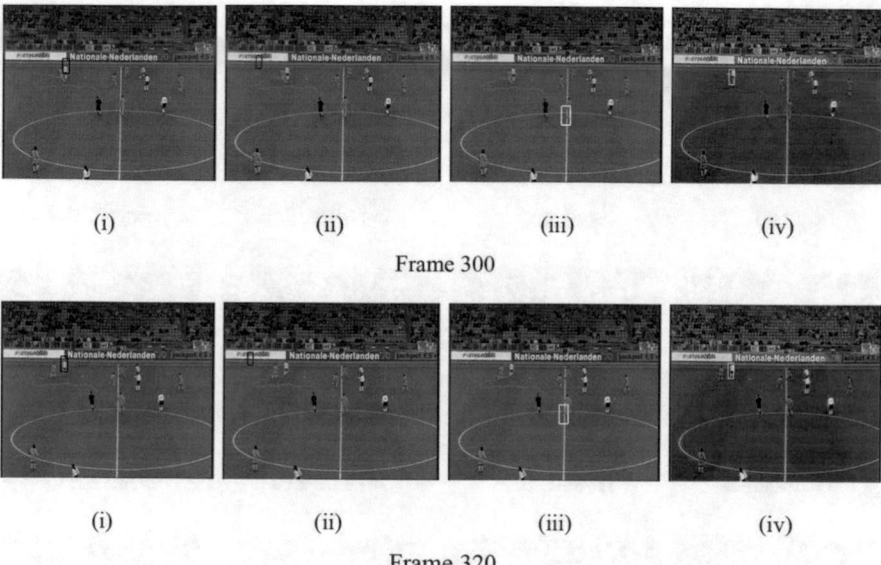

(i)   (ii)   (iii)   (iv)

Frame 300

(i)   (ii)   (iii)   (iv)

Frame 320

Fig. 6.2 (continued)

From the results in Fig. 6.3, we see that our own captured video consists of multiple human objects moving here and there. We have tried to track the central human object. The human objects are big in size and they are clearly visible. In the first frame, target object is covered inside the bounding box. Upto frame 175, there are present three human objects in the video and central human object has been tracked accurately. In frame 210–280, suddenly a human object enters into the video and passes through very nearly to the central object. In this situation, the central human object has been tracked clearly. In frame 315 another human object enters into the video. Both these objects entered in the middle of the video, walk and remain until the end of the video. But the accuracy of the proposed method was not affected by this and the central human object was tracked accurately from starting to end.

6.4.4 Multiple Object Tracking: Challenge Video Results

In case study 4, experimental results for challenge video are shown. This video clip contains total 225 frames of frame size 320 × 240, and here we show results for frame number 1–225 with difference of 25 frames, in Fig. 6.4.

In Fig. 6.4, we see that that Challenge video includes two human subjects crossing each other while a vehicle is coming. We have tried to track the human object on the right. The human objects were standing apart in the starting in frame 1. From frame 1–125, both human objects are approaching towards each other. In

Fig. 6.3 Multiple object tracking: own video visual results

that case, the proposed method clearly tracked the human object. In frame 150, both humans just crossed each other and were positioned in the same bounding box. In frame 175, they are again separate moving in different directions. By this typical

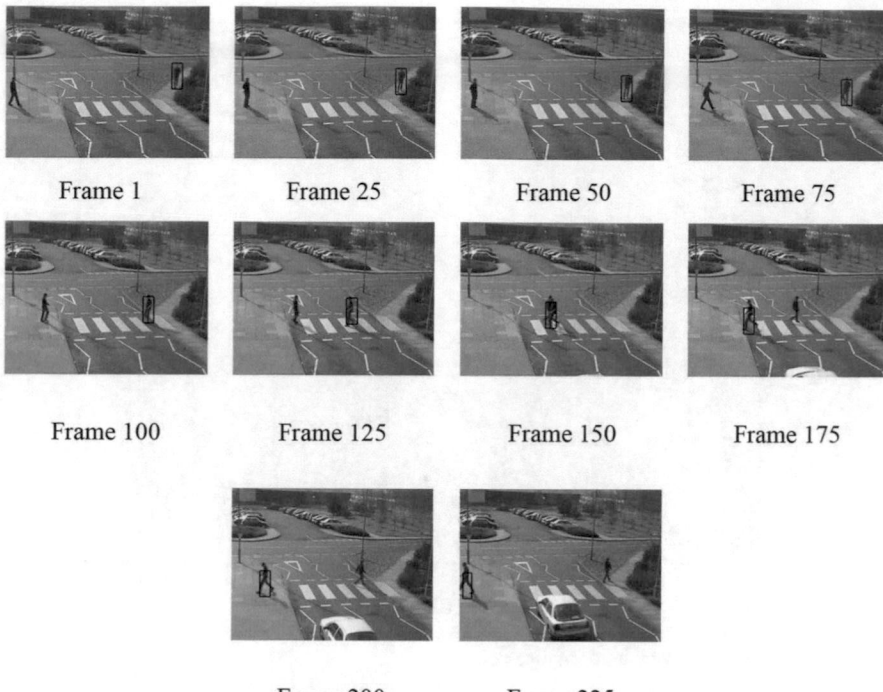

Frame 1	Frame 25	Frame 50	Frame 75

Frame 100   Frame 125   Frame 150   Frame 175

Frame 200   Frame 225

Fig. 6.4 Multiple object tracking: challenge video visual results

situation, the proposed method did not get affected and tracked the human object accurately from starting to end.

6.4.5   Performance Evaluation

Objective performance of curvelet based tracking is evaluated by comparing it with method CBWH [13], method JCTH [16] and method CT [18]. Here, we have shown comparison results only for Child video sequence. For quantitative investigation of the curvelet based tracking, we incorporated two parameters.

(i) **The Euclidean Distance**

The Euclidean distance of the tracked object is calculated using following formula:

$$ED = \sqrt{(x_A - x_c)^2 + (y_A - y_c)^2} \tag{6.1}$$

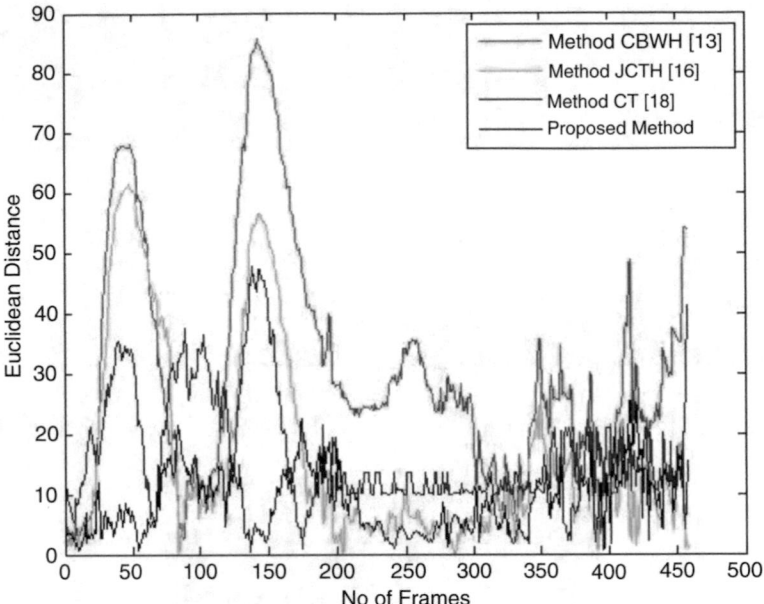

Fig. 6.5 No of frames vs Euclidean distance

where (x_A, y_A) is actual centroid value and (x_C, y_C) is calculated value. Figure 6.5 depicts Euclidean distance of four methods that are method CBWH [13], method JCTH [16], method CT [18] and proposed curvelet based tracking method. Figure 6.5 shows superior value of Euclidean distance for curvelet based tracking method.

(ii) **The Bhattacharyya Distance**

The Bhattacharyya distance is used to compute difference between actual object position and tracked object position. For two classes of actual and tracked values, it is given by

$$BD = \frac{1}{8}(mean_c - mean_a)^T \left[\frac{cov_a + cov_c}{2}\right]^{-1}(mean_c - mean_a)$$
$$+ \frac{1}{2}\ln\frac{|(cov_a + cov_c)/2|}{|cov_a|^{1/2}|cov_c|^{1/2}} \tag{6.2}$$

where

$mean_a$ = mean vector for actual object position
$mean_c$ = mean vector for tracked object position
cov_a = covariance matrix for actual object position
cov_c = covariance matrix for tracked object position

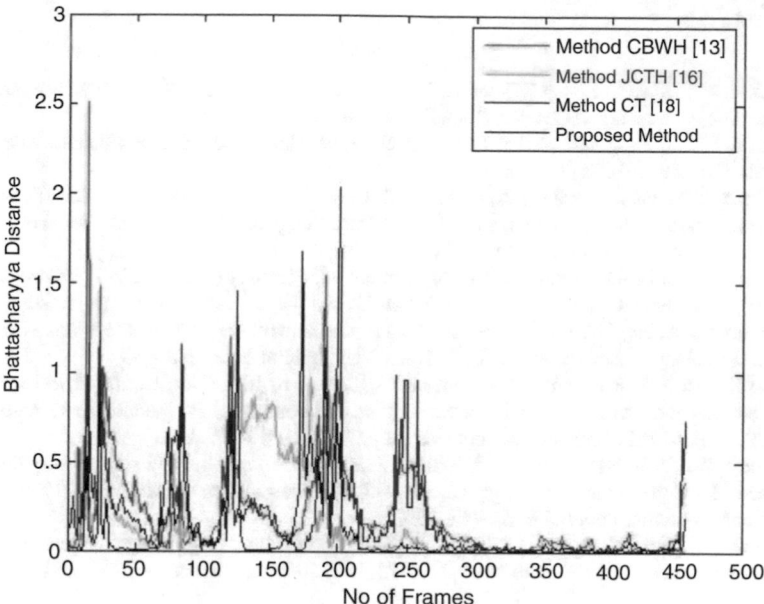

Fig. 6.6 No of frames vs Bhattacharyya distance

Figure 6.6 depicts Bhattacharyya distance of four methods that are method CBWH [13], method JCTH [16], method CT [18] and proposed curvelet based tracking method. Figure 6.6 shows superior value of Bhattacharyya distance for curvelet based tracking method.

6.5 Summary

In this chapter, we have developed and demonstrated a new algorithm for tracking of moving human objects in video. This algorithm exploited curvelet transform coefficients for real world single as well as multiple object tracking. From experimentation it is clear that curvelet based tracking performed well. Curvelet based tracking approach allowed to accurately track the target object in different frames. Also it is capable of handling several real world complexities such as partial or full occlusion. Experimental results show that Curvelet based tracking method is better when compared to existing tracking methods such as method CBWH [13], method JCTH [16], method CT [18].

References

1. Li X, Hu W, Shen C, Zhang Z, Dick A, Hengel AVD (2013) A survey of appearance models in visual object tracking. ACM Trans Intell Syst Technol 4(4):58
2. Wu Y, Lim J, Yang MH (2015) Object tracking benchmark. IEEE Trans Pattern Anal Mach Intell 37(9):1834–1848
3. Kristan M, Matas J, Leonardis A, Felsberg M, Cehovin L, Fernandez G et al (2015) The visual object tracking vot2015 challenge results. In: Proceedings of the IEEE international conference on computer vision workshops, pp 1–23
4. Viani F, Lizzi L, Rocca P, Benedetti M, Donelli M, Massa A (2008) Object tracking through RSSI measurements in wireless sensor networks, vol 44. University of Trento, p 653
5. Samarah S, Al-Hajri M, Boukerche A (2011) A predictive energy-efficient technique to support object-tracking sensor networks. IEEE Trans Veh Technol 60(2):656–663
6. Cho H, Seo YW, Kumar BV, Rajkumar RR (2014) A multi-sensor fusion system for moving object detection and tracking in urban driving environments. In: Robotics and automation (ICRA), 2014 IEEE international conference on. IEEE, pp 1836–1843
7. Raheja JL, Chaudhary A, Singal K (2011) Tracking of fingertips and centers of palm using kinect. In: Computational intelligence, modelling and simulation (CIMSiM), 2011 third international conference on. IEEE, pp 248–252
8. Kendrick L, Bzostek A, Doerr VJ (2015) System and method for tracking positions of uniform marker geometries. U.S. Patent No. 9,220,573. U.S. Patent and Trademark Office, Washington, DC
9. Tang X, Sharp GC, Jiang SB (2007) Fluoroscopic tracking of multiple implanted fiducial markers using multiple object tracking. Phys Med Biol 52(14):4081–4098
10. Maharbiz MM, Morichau-Beauchant T (2013) Intelligent board game system with visual marker based object tracking and identification. U.S. Patent Application 13/294,071, filed May 16, 2013
11. Guan M, Wen C, Shan M, Ng CL, Zou Y (2019) Real-time event-triggered object tracking in the presence of model drift and occlusion. IEEE Trans Ind Electron 66(3):2054–2065
12. Chen K, Tao W (2019) Learning linear regression via single-convolutional layer for visual object tracking. IEEE Trans Multimed 21(1):86–97
13. Ning J, Zhang L, Zhang D, Wu C (2012) Robust mean-shift tracking with corrected background-weighted histogram. IET Comput Vis 6(1):62–69
14. Tian W, Lauer M, Chen L (2019) Online multi-object tracking using joint domain information in traffic scenarios. IEEE Trans Intell Transp Syst:1–11
15. Kim C, Song D, Kim CS, Park SK (2019) Object tracking under large motion: combining coarse-to-fine search with superpixels. Inf Sci 480:194–210
16. Ning J, Zhang L, Zhang D, Wu C (2009) Robust object tracking using joint color-texture histogram. Int J Pattern Recogn Artif Intell 23(7):1245–1263
17. Chen Y, Wang J, Xia R, Zhang Q, Cao Z, Yang K (2019) The visual object tracking algorithm research based on adaptive combination kernel. J Ambient Intell Humaniz Comput:1–13
18. Porikli F, Tuzelq O, Meer P (2006) Covariance tracking using model update based on lie algebra. Proc IEEE Conf Comput Vision Pattern Recog USA:728–735
19. Li M, Peng Z, Chen Y, Wang X, Peng L, Wang Z et al (2019) A novel reverse sparse model utilizing the spatio-temporal relationship of target templates for object tracking. Neurocomputing 323:319–334
20. Nigam S, Khare A (2010) Curvelet transform based object tracking. In: IEEE international conference on computer and communication technology, pp 230–235
21. Nigam S, Khare A (2012) Curvelet transform-based technique for tracking of moving objects. IET Comput Vis 6(3):231–251
22. Heinrich S, Springstübe P, Knöppler T, Kerzel M, Wermter S (2019) Continuous convolutional object tracking in developmental robot scenarios. Neurocomputing 342:137–144

Chapter 7
Camouflaged Person Identification

Abstract This chapter proposes a new method of camouflaged person identification that combines discrete wavelet coefficients with support vector machine (SVM) classifier. Multiresolution property of wavelet transform provides invariant person identification against camouflaged scenes and do not get affected by similar foreground and background objects. Flexibility of wavelet and SVM makes the proposed method robust while providing better efficiency. For evaluation of the proposed method, we have experimented it over CAMO_UOW dataset. From objective evaluation it is clear that proposed approach outperforms existing camouflaged person identification approaches. The proposed methodology is simple and does not depend on a specific special resolution. It is suitable for detecting camouflaged persons in the images or videos where foreground and background are almost similar.

Keywords Person detection · Camouflaged data · Ambiguous background · F-measure

7.1 Introduction

Person identification is the key step in foundation of a smart visual surveillance system [1, 2]. It can be defined as identifying a person in a scene and to recognize it from previously trained data. It includes labelling of human objects in an image or video that have been modelled before irrespective of their orientation or scale. Many approaches have been developed for person identification and most of them depend on local silhouette features. Considering the importance of local silhouette features, major issues involved in selection and creation of features for their implication on a real time ground truth data are discussed in [3]. Different scenes in different images vary in lighting condition, brightness, and contrast, etc. These variations make real-world object detection problem difficult and computationally costly. Major challenges that should be addressed while incorporating a person identification method are

(i) Variability in number of persons

© Springer Nature Switzerland AG 2020
R. Singh et al., *Intelligent Wavelet Based Techniques for Advanced Multimedia Applications*, https://doi.org/10.1007/978-3-030-31873-4_7

 (ii) Inter-class and intra-class variations in human postures
(iii) Diversity in appearance
 (iv) Background clutter
  (v) Poor illumination, etc.

Considering the above challenges, an effective method should be capable of handling above challenges while maintaining computational efficiency. To incorporate automatic person identification efficient features as well as classifiers are needed. Work done in this field can be classified in two categories: region and boundary based methods. Fourier descriptor [4] has been extensively used as a boundary. However, region based approaches are a better choice as they extract information from boundary internal pixels both. Hence, they have been used more widely in literature for general shape representation. Geometrical moment is a popular example of it [5]. Moment invariant [6] is used for invariant detection against linear transformations [7, 8]. Blur and affine invariance is achieved in a method proposed by Suk and Flusser [9]. Zernike moment is used to get rotation invariance [10] and Legendre moment [11] is used to get translation and scale invariance in person identification.

Person identification in real world is a complex problem since people appear in different clothes, poses and illumination conditions. Histogram of Oriented Gradients (HOG) feature was used to handle these problems and unambiguous person identification in real scenes [12, 13]. They combined HOG features along with linear SVM classifier and achieved good results. Further modifications in HOG feature include [14]. Variations of HOG include Related HOG [15], compressed HOG (CHOG) [16], Pyramidal HOG (PHOG) [17], Circular HOG (CirHOG) [18] and spherical HOG (SHOG) [19] and hybrid HOG [20].

Local binary pattern (LBP) is more effective and simple when compared to HOG like gradient features. Discriminating power of LBP is used as a window based descriptor in object detection in [21, 37]. This method was robust against multiple viewpoints even in different poses and real environment. A fast person identification method was proposed using center symmetric LBP in wavelet domain in [22]. Modified strategies of HOG and LBP were used in [23–25] for robust person identification in real world scenarios.

However these features lack in providing robustness against variable number of persons, e.g. one or more number of persons present in a scene. Further problems like change in pose, appearance, background and illumination cannot be handled separately by these features. Therefore, to facilitate more accurate and invariant person identification, we propose a new approach which incorporates discrete wavelet transform. Linear SVM [26, 27] is used for classification of person and other objects. Since, wavelet is shift invariant and multi-resolution analysis provides description of different orientations of objects, the proposed approach is appropriate for identification of persons present in various pose, appearance, background as well as under different illumination conditions. To demonstrate the effectiveness of the proposed approach, we have tested it for camouflaged person objects. Experimentation has been done on CAMO_UOW dataset [28] which contains camouflaged person objects. The results have been evaluated with parameters F-measure. Compared with Methods 1–8 [29–36], the proposed approach achieves better accuracy.

This chapter is structured in 5 sections. Section 7.2 describes properties of wavelet transform useful in person identification; a general activity recognition algorithm is described in Sect. 7.3. Experimentation and objective evaluations are performed in Sect. 7.4. Finally, Sect. 7.5 is the conclusion of this study.

7.2   Wavelet for Person Identification

There are many variants of wavelet. We have used the discrete wavelet transform. Following useful and invariant properties of discrete wavelet have been exploited in this work.

(i) Directional selectivity
(ii) Multi-resolution analysis

7.3   A General Algorithm

A robust general algorithm for camouflaged person identification is shown in Fig. 7.1. It is a multi-resolution approach which is shift invariant.

Algorithmic Steps:

Step 1: Representation of camouflaged person objects in real scenarios

Step 2: Two step preprocessing of images

> *Scale normalization*

> *Color normalization*

Step 3: Extraction of multi-resolution wavelet coefficients

Step 4: Wavelet coefficients classification

Fig. 7.1 Algorithmic steps for person identification

The algorithm explained in detail as follows:

7.3.1   Representation of Camouflaged Person Objects in Real Scenarios

Camouflaged person objects in real scenarios are represented as a 2D gray level function $f(x,y)$ of size $M \times N$.

7.3.2   Two Step Preprocessing of Images

This step consists of scale and color normalization processes.

(i) **Normalization of image size**

The input image $f(x,y)$ is scale normalized and converted from $M \times N$ to 256×256 size.

(ii) **Normalization of color space**

Now the image is transformed into gray scale so that images of different color formats become homogeneous.

7.3.3   Extraction of Multi-Resolution Wavelet Coefficients

In this step wavelet coefficients in four subbands LL, LH, HL and HH are computed. A sample image and its corresponding wavelet bands are shown in Figs. 7.2 and 7.3, respectively.

Fig. 7.2 Sample camouflaged human object

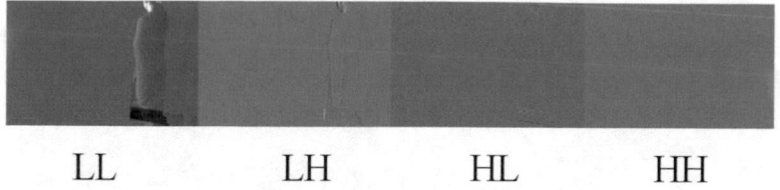

$$\text{LL} \qquad\qquad \text{LH} \qquad\qquad \text{HL} \qquad\qquad \text{HH}$$

Fig. 7.3 Wavelet coefficients in wavelet subbands

Fig. 7.4 Samples of CAMO_UOW dataset

7.3.4   Wavelet Coefficients Classification

A support vector machine classifier is used for classification of feature data. It has Gaussian radial basis function (RBF) kernel with default scaling factor of 1.

7.4   Results and Discussion

This section discusses and demonstrates experimentation and results of the method which collectively applies wavelet coefficients with SVM classifier. The experimentation is done on an Windows 7 Matlab 8.1 (R2014a) environment and Intel® Core™ i5 350 M CPU (2.27 GHz) machine. We tested the proposed person identification method on several datasets. Here, we present results for camouflaged person identification dataset the CAMO_UOW video dataset [28]. It is a real-world dataset that includes 10 videos from indoor as well as outdoor environment both. Foreground persons wear clothes same as background. All frames are labelled in CAMO_UOW dataset. Few sample images of the 10 videos from CAMO_UOW datasets are shown in Fig. 7.4.

Now the performance of the Wavelet based method is shown objectively. Eight existing methods are selected for objective comparison. These are Method 1 [29], Method 2 [30], Method 3 [31], Method 4 [32], Method 5 [33], Method 6 [34],

Method 7 [35] and Method 8 [36]. These results are presented without using morphological processing.

Objective evaluation of all methods is performed using F-measure parameter. This parameters is computed using following equation

$$F - measure = 2 \cdot \frac{precision \cdot recall}{precision + recall} \qquad (7.1)$$

Obtained results for representative frames are shown in Figs. 7.5, 7.6, 7.7, 7.8, 7.9, 7.10, 7.11, 7.12, 7.13 and 7.14. It can be observed that Wavelet demonstrates better performance when compared to existing methods [29–36]. It has an average F-measure value of 0.87 which is higher than other methods.

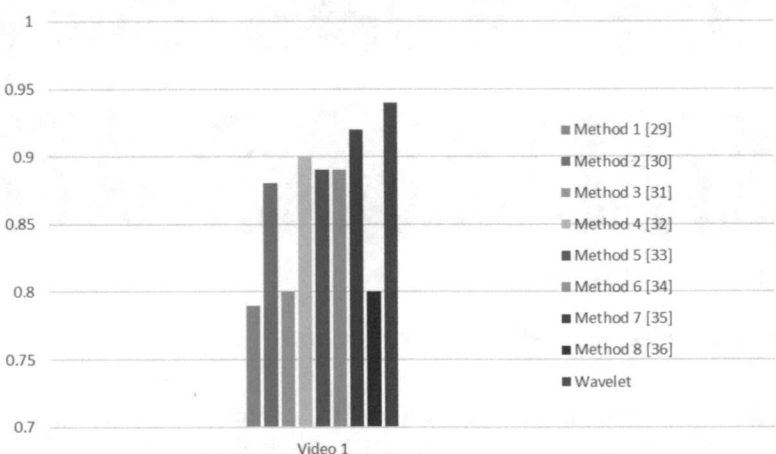

Fig. 7.5 Performance comparison of different methods in terms of F-measure for Video 1

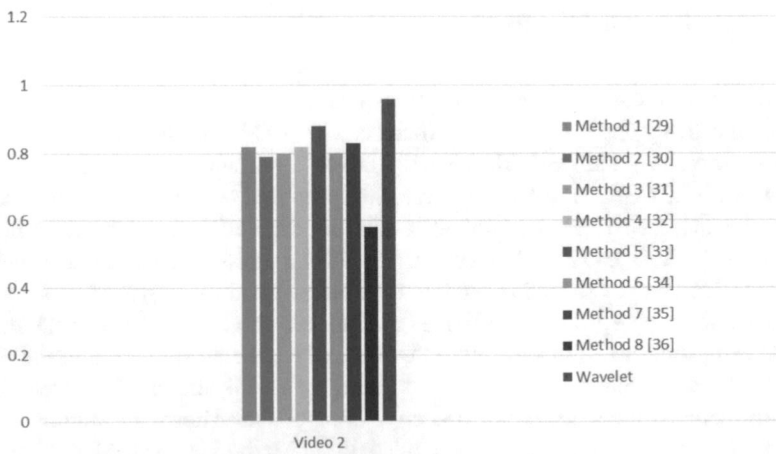

Fig. 7.6 Performance comparison of different methods in terms of F-measure for Video 2

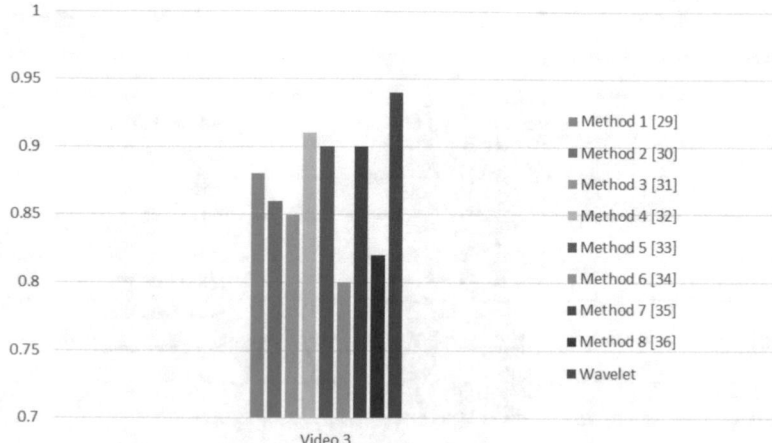

Fig. 7.7 Performance comparison of different methods in terms of F-measure for Video 3

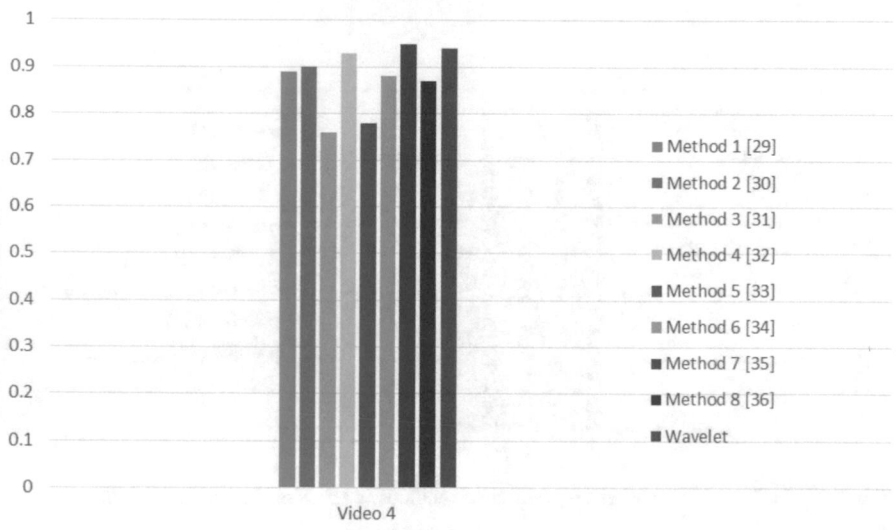

Fig. 7.8 Performance comparison of different methods in terms of F-measure for Video 4

7.5   Summary

This chapter presents a camouflaged person identification method which integrates discrete wavelet coefficients with support vector machine classifier. The multi-resolution nature of wavelet transform provides invariant person identification against camouflaged scenes and do not get affected by similar background and foreground objects. Flexibility of wavelet and SVM makes this method accurate resulting in better efficiency. For objective evaluation of this method, CAMO_UOW video dataset is used. This evaluation shows that wavelet outperforms Method

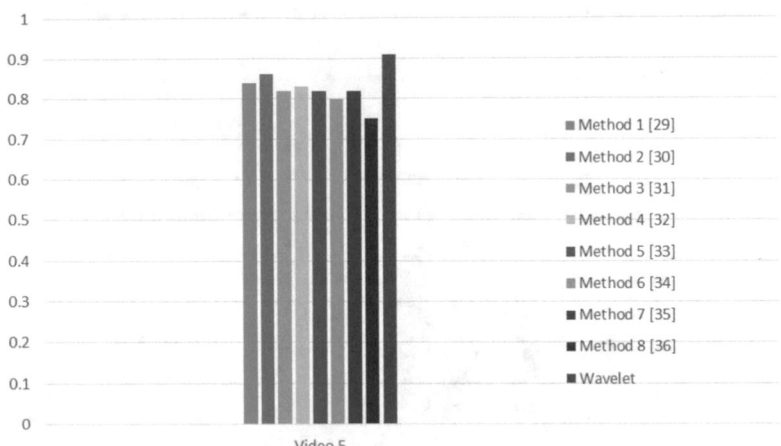

Fig. 7.9   Performance comparison of different methods in terms of F-measure for Video 5

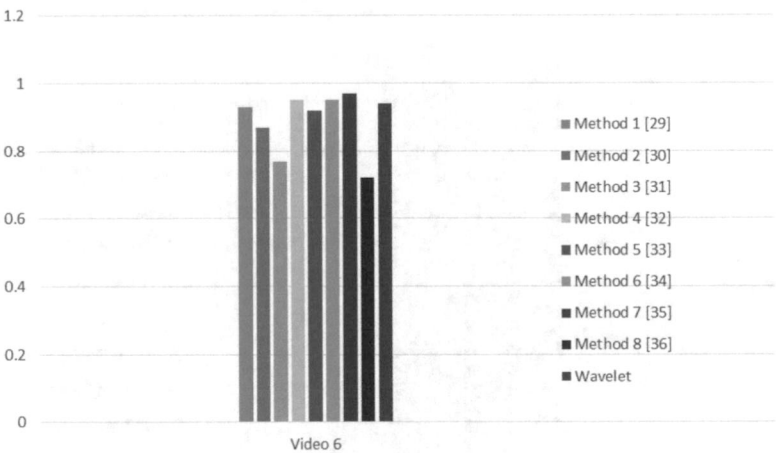

Fig. 7.10   Performance comparison of different methods in terms of F-measure for Video 6

1 [29], Method 2 [30], Method 3 [31], Method 4 [32], Method 5 [33], Method 6 [34], Method 7 [35] and Method 8 [36] camouflaged person identification approaches. This objective evaluation demonstrates high performance of this method. This method is capable of handling background and foregrounds ambiguity for camouflaged persons.

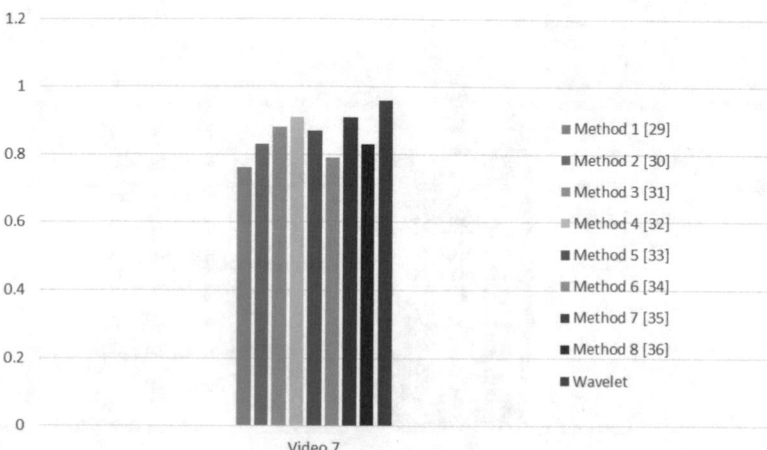

Fig. 7.11 Performance comparison of different methods in terms of F-measure for Video 7

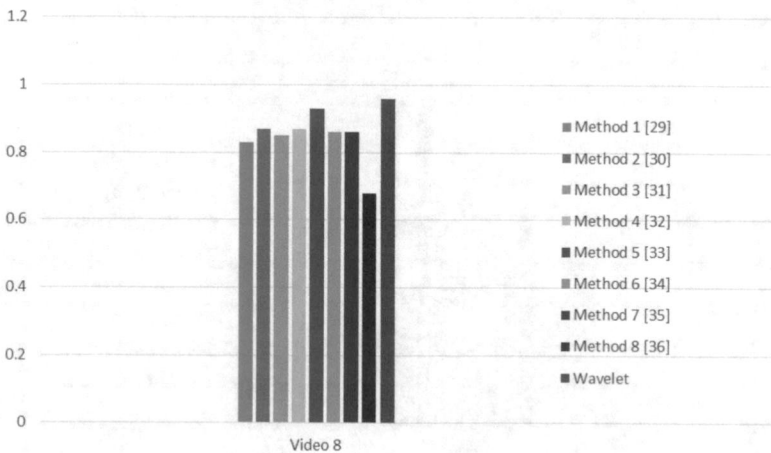

Fig. 7.12 Performance comparison of different methods in terms of F-measure for Video 8

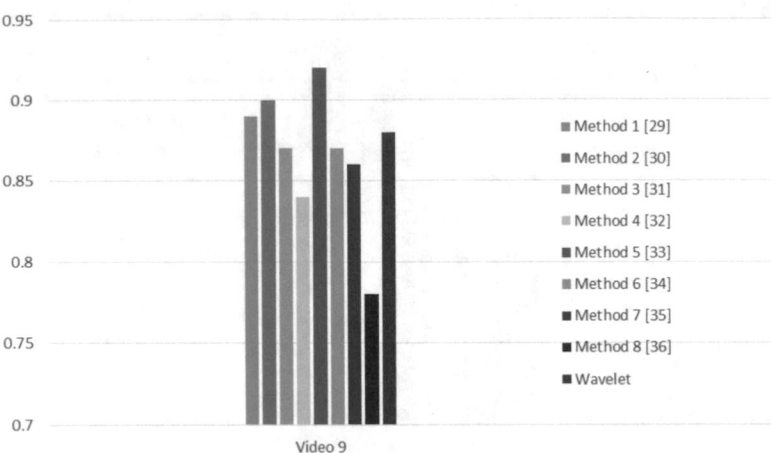

Fig. 7.13 Performance comparison of different methods in terms of F-measure for Video 9

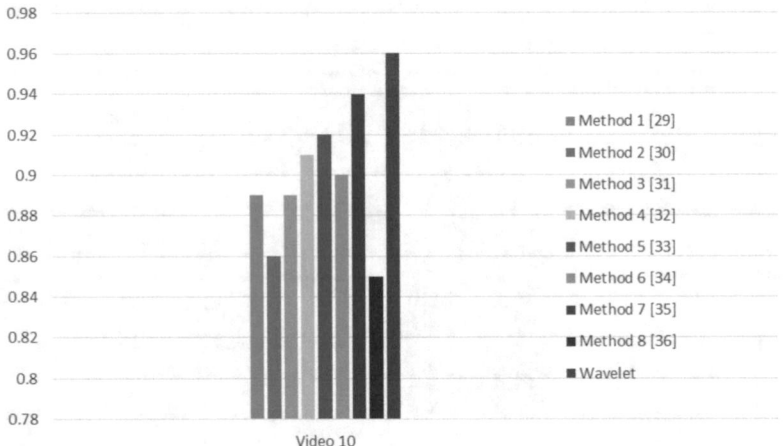

Fig. 7.14 Performance comparison of different methods in terms of F-measure for Video 10

References

1. Sharma L, Garg PK (2019) From visual surveillance to internet of things: technology and applications. Taylor and Francis, New York
2. Kavalionak H, Gennaro C, Amato G, Vairo C, Perciante C, Meghini C, Falchi F (2019) Distributed video surveillance using smart cameras. J Grid Comput 17(1):59–77
3. Anderson NW, Turner CD, Le DM, Vollmar U, Davis TJ (2019) U.S. Patent Application No. 10/183,667
4. Zhao Y, Belkasim S (2012) Multiresolution Fourier descriptors for multiresolution shape analysis. IEEE Signal Process Lett 19(10):692–695
5. Flusser J, Suk T, Zitova B (2009) Moments and moment invariants in pattern recognition. Wiley, Chichester

6. Hu M (1962) Visual pattern recognition by moment invariants. IRE Trans Inf Theory 8:179–187
7. Guo L, Zhao J (2008) Specific human detection from surveillance video based on color invariant moments. Int Symp Intell Inf Technol Appl 2:331–335
8. Nigam S, Deb K, Khare A (2013) Moment invariants based object recognition for different pose and appearances in real scenes. In: 2013 international conference on informatics, electronics and vision (ICIEV). IEEE, pp 1–5
9. Suk T, Flusser J (2003) Combined blur and affine moment invariants and their use in pattern recognition. Pattern Recogn 36(12):2895–2907
10. Chen BJ, Shu HZ, Zhang H, Chen G, Toumoulin C, Dillenseger JL, Luo LM (2012) Quaternion Zernike moments and their invariants for color image analysis and object recognition. Signal Process 92:308–318
11. Hosny KM (2010) Refined translation and scale Legendre moment invariants. Pattern Recogn Lett 31:533–538
12. Dalal N, Triggs B (2005) Histogram of oriented gradients for human detection. IEEE Int Conf Comput Vis Pattern Recogn:886–893
13. Soler JD, Beuther H, Rugel M, Wang Y, Clark PC, Glover SCO et al (2019) Histogram of oriented gradients: a technique for the study of molecular cloud formation. Astron Astrophys 622:A166
14. Pang Y, Yuan Y, Li X, Pan J (2011) Efficient HOG human detection. Signal Process 91:773–781
15. Liu H, Xu T, Wang X, Qian Y (2013) Related HOG features for human detection using cascaded Adaboost and SVM classifiers. Int Multimed Model Conf (MMM) LNCS 7733 (2):345–355
16. Chandrasekhar V, Takacs G, Chen D, Tsai S, Grzeszczuk R, Girod B (2009) CHoG: compressed histogram of gradients A low bit-rate feature descriptor. IEEE Int Conf Comput Vis Pattern Recogn:2504–2511
17. Bosch A, Zisserman A, Munoz X (2007) Representing shape with a spatial pyramid kernel. ACM Int Conf Image Video Retr:401–408
18. Skibbe H, Reisert M, Schmidt T, Brox T (2012) Fast rotation invariant 3D feature computation utilizing efficient local neighborhood operators. IEEE Trans Pattern Anal Mach Intell 34 (8):1563–1575
19. Skibbe H, Reisert M, Burkhardt H (2011) SHOG – spherical HOG descriptors for rotation invariant 3D object detection. Int Conf Pattern Recogn:142–151
20. Nigam S, Khare M, Srivastava RK, Khare A (2013) An effective local feature descriptor for object detection in real scenes. In: 2013 IEEE conference on information & communication technologies. IEEE, pp 244–248
21. Nguyen DT, Ogunbona PO, Li W (2013) A novel shape-based non-redundant local binary pattern descriptor for object detection. Pattern Recogn 46:1485–1500
22. Ko BC, Kim DY, Jung JH, Nam JY (2013) Three-level cascade of random forests for rapid human detection. Opt Eng 52(2):027204
23. Zhang JG, Huang KQ, Yu YN, Tan TN (2011) Boosted local structured HOG-LBP for object localization. IEEE Int Conf Comput Vis Pattern Recogn:1393–1400
24. Shen J, Yang W, Sun C (2012) Real-time human detection based on gentle MILBoost with variable granularity HOG-CSLBP. Neural Comput Applic. https://doi.org/10.1007/s00521-012-1153-5. ISNN 2012
25. Zhou S, Liu Q, Guo J, Jiang Y (2012) ROI-HOG and LBP based human detection via shape part-templates matching. Int Conf Neural Inf Process LNCS 7667(5):109–115
26. Malisiewicz T, Gupta A, Efros AA (2011) Ensemble of exemplar-svms for object detection and beyond. IEEE Int Conf Comput Vis:89–96
27. Burges CJC (1998) A tutorial on support vector machines for pattern recognition. Data Min Knowl Disc 2(2):121–167

28. Li S, Florencio D, Li W, Zhao Y, Cook C (2018) A fusion framework for camouflaged moving foreground detection in the wavelet domain. IEEE Trans Image Process 27(8):3918–3930
29. Zivkovic Z, Van Der Heijden F (2006) Efficient adaptive density estimation per image pixel for the task of background subtraction. Pattern Recogn Lett 27(7):773–780
30. El Baf F, Bouwmans T, Vachon B (2008) Fuzzy integral for moving object detection. In: 2008 IEEE international conference on fuzzy systems (IEEE world congress on computational intelligence). IEEE, pp 1729–1736
31. Maddalena L, Petrosino A (2008) A self-organizing approach to background subtraction for visual surveillance applications. IEEE Trans Image Process 17(7):1168–1177
32. Hofmann M, Tiefenbacher P, Rigoll G (2012) Background segmentation with feedback: the pixel-based adaptive segmenter. In: 2012 IEEE computer society conference on computer vision and pattern recognition workshops. IEEE, pp 38–43
33. St-Charles PL, Bilodeau GA, Bergevin R (2014) Subsense: a universal change detection method with local adaptive sensitivity. IEEE Trans Image Process 24(1):359–373
34. Yao J, Odobez JM (2007) Multi-layer background subtraction based on color and texture. In: 2007 IEEE conference on computer vision and pattern recognition. IEEE, pp 1–8
35. Zhou X, Yang C, Yu W (2012) Moving object detection by detecting contiguous outliers in the low-rank representation. IEEE Trans Pattern Anal Mach Intell 35(3):597–610
36. Shakeri M, Zhang H (2016) COROLA: a sequential solution to moving object detection using low-rank approximation. Comput Vis Image Underst 146:27–39
37. Nigam S, Khare A (2015) Multiresolution approach for multiple human detection using moments and local binary patterns. Multimed Tools Appl 74(17):7037–7062

Chapter 8
Wavelets for Activity Recognition

Abstract This chapter analyses real world human activity recognition problem. It uses discrete wavelet transform and multiclass support vector machine (SVM) classifier for recognition. The experiments are done using Weizmann and KTH action datasets. Objective evaluation is done for nine activities walk, run, bend, gallop sideways, jumping jack, one handwave, two handwave, jump in place and skip from Weizmann dataset. Six activities that are considered from KTH dataset are handwaving, running, walking, boxing, jogging and handclapping. Results are shown qualitatively as well as quantitatively on two publicly available dataset Weizmann and KTH. Quantitative evaluations demonstrate better performance of the proposed method in comparison to the existing methods.

Keywords Behavior recognition · Action · Interaction · Abnormal activities

8.1 Introduction

Recently interest is increasing for automatic detection of human behavior. A method for determining human behavior is comprised of detection and tracking of objects of interest for generating motion descriptors followed by activity recognition [1, 2]. It is a core element in the development of a visual surveillance system. Unlike human operator based security systems where it is difficult to monitor a number of scenes simultaneously as well as human operator's concentration may drop suddenly; these systems reduce dependence on human operator and enhance the performance of systems in detection of security breaches [3]. These systems have potential applications in security and surveillance, biometric applications, human-robot interaction, medical analysis, education and sports.

Activity recognition can be defined as a stochastic sequence of simple actions. In other words, recognition of activities can be performed by finding out correspondence between time-varying feature data of a group of labeled reference. This correspondence is done by using a holistic feature vector that consists of various local motion descriptors. These feature vectors are fed into a pattern classifier for recognition of activities. This classifier should be such that it can differentiate

© Springer Nature Switzerland AG 2020
R. Singh et al., *Intelligent Wavelet Based Techniques for Advanced Multimedia Applications*, https://doi.org/10.1007/978-3-030-31873-4_8

between inter-class and intra-class variations. Final recognition is done by matching and searching an upcoming activity in the image feature database representing previously seen actions or activities. This whole task is very complex due to several challenges. Robustness against environment variations, actor's movement variations, variations in activities and insufficient amount of training videos are a few of them.

Human behavior is performed at several levels of understandings semantically such as analysis of activity, gesture or emotion [4]. However, efficiency and robustness of the algorithm is compromised when analysis is performed at various levels of understanding. Therefore, existing approaches have focused on only one level of understanding depending on application [5]. This study also focuses on human behavior understanding with the help of one level of understanding i.e. through activity recognition for visual surveillance. This fact is worthwhile to mention that an efficient surveillance system is human behavior centric. It considers motion information regarding human objects that interact in a holistic manner [6, 7].

Human activities are divided into four categories. First category involves single human which is called human actions, second category involves two humans and called human-human interactions, third category involves human and object and called human-object interactions and fourth category involves multiple humans which is group activities [8, 9]. However, activity recognition is a challenging task because of several challenges that exist in its practical implication. Environment variations, inter-class variations, intra-class variations, and insufficient amount of training videos are few to mention [10, 11].

To deal with the above challenges, this study takes advantage of frequency domain wavelet transform feature. Advantage of using this feature is that it is suitable to discriminate different aspects of an activity. This feature is supplied to radial basis function (RBF) SVM classifier. Experimentation is done over two real-world, publicly available video datasets Weizmann and KTH. Analysis shows that discussed approach outperforms existing approaches.

Rest of the chapter is organized as follows: Section 8.2 provides a brief literature review, Section 8.3 discusses wavelet based activity recognition algorithm, Section 8.4 performs experimentation and Sect. 8.5 concludes this study.

8.2   Literature Review

Since, this work analyses holistic feature based activity recognition approach. This section reviews representative papers on feature based activity recognition approaches. Among several features, Histogram of oriented gradients is a prominent feature for this purpose. Bibi et al. [14] retrieved trajectory information for multi-person activity recognition. For this, they labeled individual activities with the help of Histogram of Oriented Gradients (HOG) and median compound Local Binary Pattern (CLBP) feature. Circular HOG [15] and hybrid HOG [16] are one of the few variants of HOG. HOG was used for abnormal activity recognition in [17].

A hierarchical model is proposed by Kong and Fu [18] for interaction analysis. It maps spatiotemporal patches with set of hidden variables to represent region of interest. Correspondence between local and global motion pattern is exploited in [19]. It applied combination of different features to analyze complex activities of humans. Scale invariant feature transform (SIFT) as well as its several variants SIFT Flow [20] and 3D SIFT [21] are also successfully used for this purpose. In an approach by Slimani et al. [22], a combination of 3D SIFT and K-nearest neighbor (KNN) classifier is successfully used. A combination of seven moment invariants and uniform LBP is used in [23] for activity recognition in real world scenario. Invariance property of moment invariants and high discriminating power of LBP made this made this feature to shows a high recognition rate.

Clearly, above mentioned features show significant performance and can be efficiently used in activity recognition. However, in comparison to handcrafted feature descriptors deep learning based methods demonstrated better recognition accuracy for activity recognition. Various methods have been proposed to use deep learning based approaches for feature learning from different modalities such as RGB images, depth images, and skeleton data. Deep learning based methods can retrieve such data from a unimodal network as well as multimodal network. Few multimodal networks based deep feature learning methods for RGB images are [24–27]. These methods take into consideration appearance, optical flow and skeleton data. Since appearance and optical flow data retrieval is easier, therefore most deep learning techniques take advantage of RGB images. Whereas, depth and skeleton data are comparatively harder to retrieve, therefore techniques based on them are fewer. However, recently skeleton data based deep learning methods have shown high efficiency in multiple human interaction analysis [28–30].

8.3   Activity Framework

This section provides methodology for activity recognition system whose block diagram is given in Fig. 8.1.

Activity recognition methodology is described below.

8.3.1   Input Video

Input training video is a sequence of frames varying from $1 \ldots n$.

Fig. 8.1 Block diagram of the activity recognition system

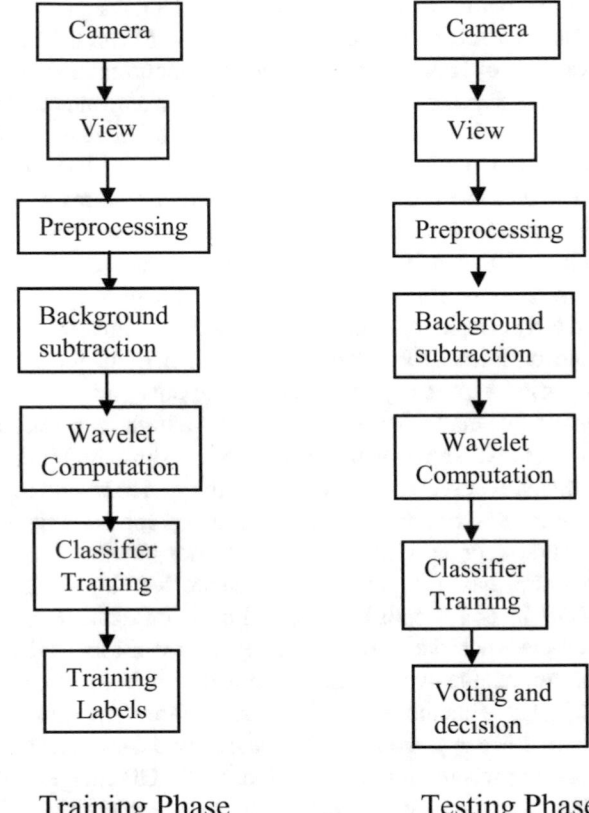

Training Phase   Testing Phase

8.3.2   Preprocessing

Scale normalization and color normalization steps are performed in preprocessing phase.

8.3.3   Motion Segmentation

After preprocessing, motion segmentation is done. The goal of motion segmentation is to detect all the foreground objects in a given video. Segmenting moving objects helps to provide important information about activities of moving foreground objects and discard any additional effect of background. However, change in illumination, change in motion and change in background geometry make this process difficult. Several motion segmentation approaches have been proposed for this purpose. Background subtraction approach is the most popular for its simplicity and effectiveness [31]. Frame differencing is a basic method for background subtraction while Gaussians, kernel density and mean shift are some other methods for background subtraction [31]. We have adopted simple frame differencing method for our approach. Algorithm for background subtraction using frame difference method is given below.

Algorithm for Background Subtraction:

input: input video file|V|
output: background subtracted video file|V_{bs}|
threshold ← t
background ← first video frame|F_1|
for frame_number ← 2 to |F_n|

frame ← current_frame|F_i|
frame_difference ← frame − background i.e. |F_i| − |F_1|
if frame_difference ≥ threshold

then pixel is foreground pixel
otherwise pixel is background pixel

end
background is reinitialized with previous frame i.e. |F_1| = |F_i|

end

Threshold value should be chosen according to application. We have selected different threshold values in case of different datasets to achieve better result. Few results have been shown in Fig. 8.2.

8.3.4 Wavelet Feature Extraction

Now, wavelet feature is computed from the background segmented video. Features are extracted from each frame through whole activity sequence.

(a)   (b)   (c)   (d)

Fig. 8.2 (a) and (c) Original images, and (b) and (d) background subtracted images

8.3.5   Classifier Training and Testing

For classification of wavelet based features, SVM pattern classifier is used as

$$
V \in \begin{cases}
activity_1 & iff \quad V \in class_1 \\
activity_2 & iff \quad V \in class_2 \\
\dots\dots\dots\dots\dots\dots\dots\dots\dots\dots\dots\dots \\
activity_n & iff \quad V \in class_n
\end{cases}
\tag{8.1}
$$

8.4   Results and Discussion

In the implementation of activity recognition framework, Weizmann [12] and KTH [13] benchmark datasets are used. To demonstrate performance of the method, confusion matrix is used as an objective evaluation parameter. Confusion matrix demonstrates performance of an algorithm in tabular form. In this table, diagonal values show performance of the method that how many instances have been recognized accurately. Non-diagonal elements show that how many instances have been recognized inaccurately.

8.4.1   Results over Weizmann Dataset

Weizmann dataset [12] is one of the most widely used activity datasets. In consists of 90 videos of 10 action classes that are run, jump, walk, bend, gallop sideways, jump in place, jumping jack, skip, one-hand wave and two-hands wave. Resolution of the videos is 180 × 144 pixels and captured by a static camera in homogeneous background condition. Visual results are shown in Fig. 8.3 and confusion matrix is shown in Table 8.1. Accuracy of this method and other existing methods [32–38] is shown in Fig. 8.4. From Fig. 8.4, it can be observed that the proposed method achieves the highest values for parameters Accuracy which is 97%.

8.4.2   Results over KTH Dataset

Now, experimentation is done on KTH dataset [13]. It includes 6 different activities walking, handwaving, handclapping, running, boxing, and jogging. Figure 8.5 visu-ally shows results for few representative frames. From Fig. 8.5, it is seen that discussed method recognizes different pair of activities accurately. These activities

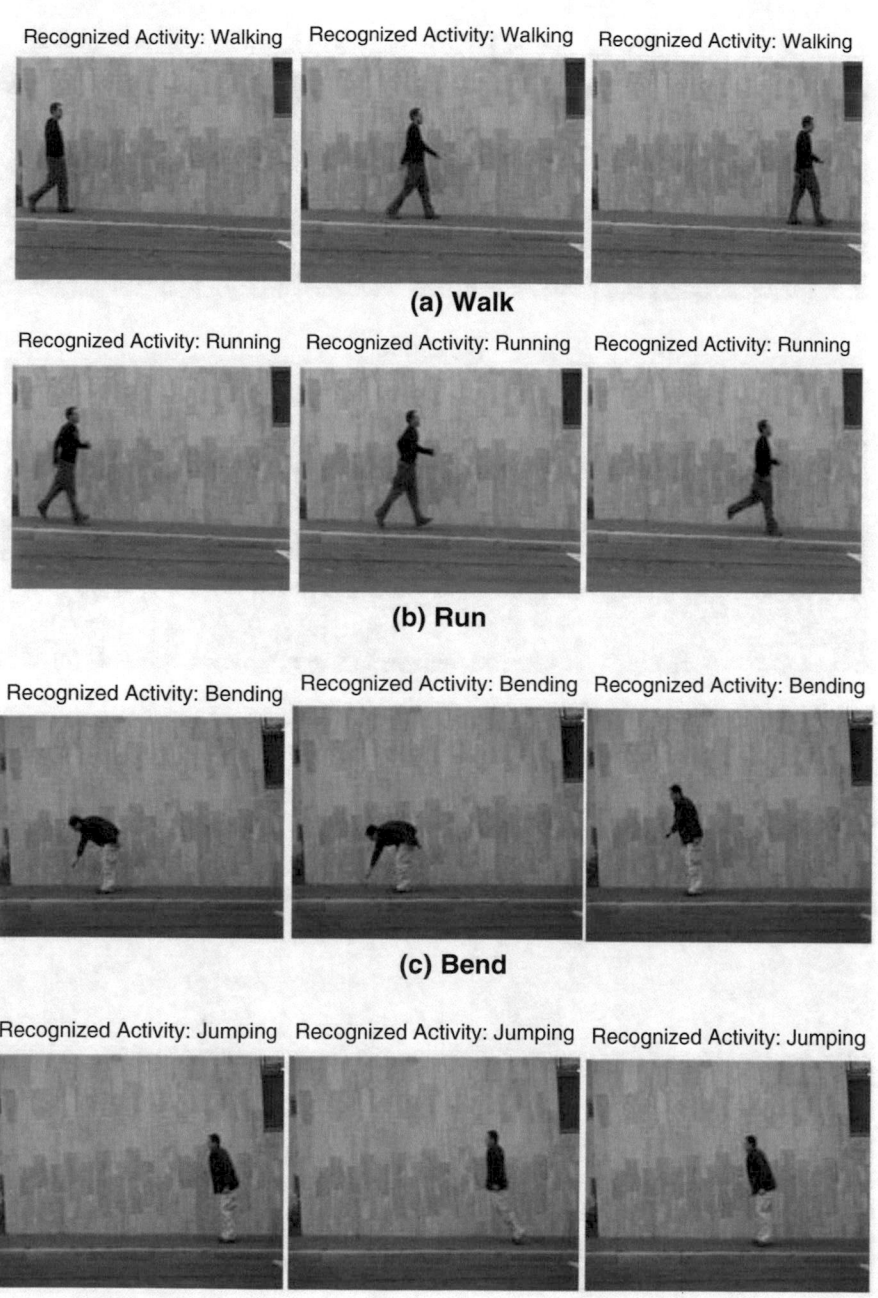

Fig. 8.3 Visual results of Weizmann dataset [12]

(e) Jack

(f) Skip

Fig. 8.3 (continued)

Table 8.1 Confusion matrix for Weizmann dataset [12]

Activities	Walk	Run	Gallop sideways	Bend	One-hand wave	Two-hands wave	Jump in place	Jumping jack	Skip
Walk	97	0	1	1	0	0	1	0	0
Run	1	96	0	0	0	0	0	2	1
Gallop sideways	1	1	97	0	0	0	0	1	0
Bend	1	0	1	97	0	0	0	1	0
One-hand wave	0	2	0	0	96	0	0	0	2
Two-hands wave	0	0	1	0	0	97	0	1	0
Jump in place	0	1	0	0	0	0	98	0	1
Jumping jack	0	1	0	0	0	0	0	98	1
Skip	0	0	0	0	0	0	2	0	98

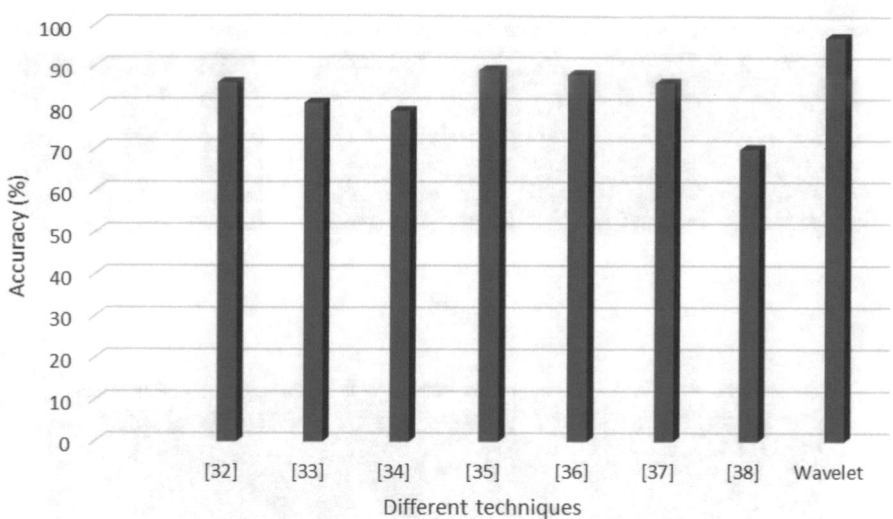

Fig. 8.4 Recognition accuracies of different techniques

are hand-waving, boxing, handclapping, walking, running, and jogging. Confusion matrix of this method is shown in Table 8.2. Average recognition rate of the method is 97%.

8.5 Summary

This chapter analyzed classification based human activity recognition. It used wavelet transform and multiclass SVM classifier for this. The experiments are done on Weizmann and KTH video datasets. Nine activities considered for objective evaluations from Weizmann dataset are walk, run, bend, gallop sideways, jumping jack, one handwave, two handwave, jump in place and skip. Six activities that have been considered from KTH dataset are handwaving, walking, running, boxing, handclapping and jogging. Performance is discussed visually and analytically both which show that wavelet outperforms other existing methods [32–38].

Recognized Activity: Handwaving   Recognized Activity: Handwaving   Recognized Activity: Handwaving

(a)

Recognized Activity: Walking   Recognized Activity: Walking   Recognized Activity: Walking

(b)

Recognized Activity: Running   Recognized Activity: Running   Recognized Activity: Running

(c)

Recognized Activity: Boxing   Recognized Activity: Boxing   Recognized Activity: Boxing

(d)

Fig. 8.5 Visual results of KTH dataset [13]

Recognized Activity: Handclapping Recognized Activity: Handclapping Recognized Activity: Handclapping

(e)

Recognized Activity: Jogging Recognized Activity: Jogging Recognized Activity: Jogging

(f)

Fig. 8.5 (continued)

Table 8.2 Confusion matrix for KTH dataset [13]

Activities	Handwaving	Walking	Running	Boxing	Handclapping	Jogging
Handwaving	97	0	2	2	0	1
Walking	0	98	0	0	0	0
Running	0	2	97	0	1	0
Boxing	0	0	0	99	0	0
Handclapping	0	0	0	4	96	0
Jogging	0	2	0	2	0	96

References

1. Borges PVK, Conci N, Cavallaro A (2013) Video-based human behavior understanding: a survey. IEEE Trans Circuits Syst Video Technol 23(11):1993–2008
2. Gonzàlez J, Moeslund TB, Wang L (2012) Semantic understanding of human behaviors in image sequences: from video-surveillance to video-hermeneutics. Comput Vis Image Underst 116(3):305–306
3. Wiliem A, Madasu V, Boles W, Yarlagadda P (2012) A suspicious behaviour detection using a context space model for smart surveillance systems. Comput Vis Image Underst 116 (2):194–209
4. Nigam S, Singh R, Misra AK (2018) A review of computational approaches for human behavior detection. Arch Comput Methods Eng:1–33

5. Tran C, Doshi A, Trivedi MM (2012) Modeling and prediction of driver behavior by foot gesture analysis. Comput Vis Image Underst 116(3):435–445
6. Vishwakarma S, Agrawal A (2013) A survey on activity recognition and behavior understanding in video surveillance. Vis Comput 29(10):983–1009
7. Nigam S, Singh R, Misra AK (2019) Towards intelligent human behavior detection for video surveillance. In: Censorship, surveillance, and privacy: concepts, methodologies, tools, and applications. IGI Global, Hershey, pp 884–917
8. Ziaeefard M, Bergevin R (2015) Semantic human activity recognition: a literature review. Pattern Recogn 48(8):2329–2345
9. Aggarwal JK, Xia L (2014) Human activity recognition from 3d data: a review. Pattern Recogn Lett 48:70–80
10. Yanan L, Kun JL, Yu YW (2014) Capturing human motion based on modified hidden markov model in multi-view image sequences. J Multimed 9(1):92–99
11. Binh NT, Nigam S, Khare A (2013) Towards classification based human activity recognition in video sequences. In: International conference on context-aware systems and applications. Springer, Cham, pp 209–218
12. Gorelick L, Blank M, Shechtman E, Irani M, Basri R (2007) Actions as space-time shapes. IEEE Trans Pattern Anal Mach Intell 29(12):2247–2253
13. Laptev I, Caputo B (2004) Recognizing human actions: a local SVM approach. In: null. IEEE, pp 32–36
14. Bibi S, Anjum N, Sher M (2018) Automated multi-feature human interaction recognition in complex environment. Comput Ind 99:282–293
15. Skibbe H, Reisert M, Schmidt T, Brox T, Ronneberger O, Burkhardt H (2012) Fast rotation invariant 3D feature computation utilizing efficient local neighborhood operators. IEEE Trans Pattern Anal Machine Intell 34(8):1563–1575
16. Nigam S, Khare M, Srivastava RK, Khare A (2013) An effective local feature descriptor for object detection in real scenes. In: 2013 IEEE conference on information & communication technologies. IEEE, pp 244–248
17. Yussiff AL, Yong SP, Baharudin BB (2014) Detecting people using histogram of oriented gradients: a step towards abnormal human activity detection. In: Advances in computer science and its applications. Springer, Berlin/Heidelberg, pp 1145–1150
18. Kong Y, Fu Y (2016) Close human interaction recognition using patch-aware models. IEEE Trans Image Process 25(1):167–178
19. Cho NG, Park SH, Park JS, Park U, Lee SW (2017) Compositional interaction descriptor for human interaction recognition. Neurocomputing 267:169–181
20. Liu C, Yuen J, Torralba A (2011) Sift flow: dense correspondence across scenes and its applications. IEEE Trans Pattern Anal Mach Intell 33(5):978–994
21. Scovanner P, Ali S, Shah M (2007) A 3-dimensional sift descriptor and its application to action recognition. In: Proceedings of the 15th ACM international conference on multimedia. ACM, pp 357–360
22. Slimani KNEH, Benezeth Y, Souami F (2014) Human interaction recognition based on the co-occurence of visual words. In: IEEE CVPR CMSI workshop, pp 455–460
23. Nigam S, Khare A (2016) Integration of moment invariants and uniform local binary patterns for human activity recognition in video sequences. Multimed Tools Appl 75(24):17303–17332
24. Simonyan K, Zisserman A (2014) Two-stream convolutional networks for action recognition in videos. In: Advances in neural information processing systems, pp 568–576
25. Tran D, Bourdev L, Fergus R, Torresani L, Paluri M (2015) Learning spatiotemporal features with 3d convolutional networks. In: Proceedings of the IEEE international conference on computer vision, pp 4489–4497
26. Liu J, Shahroudy A, Xu D, Wang G (2016) Spatio-temporal LSTM with trust gates for 3D human action recognition. In: European conference on computer vision. Springer, Cham, pp 816–833

27. Wang L, Qiao Y, Tang X (2015) Action recognition with trajectory-pooled deep-convolutional descriptors. In: Proceedings of the IEEE conference on computer vision and pattern recognition, pp 4305–4314
28. Alp Güler R, Neverova N, Kokkinos I (2018) Densepose: dense human pose estimation in the wild. In: Proceedings of the IEEE conference on computer vision and pattern recognition, pp 7297–7306
29. Cao Z, Simon T, Wei SE, Sheikh Y (2017) Realtime multi-person 2d pose estimation using part affinity fields. In: Proceedings of the IEEE conference on computer vision and pattern recognition, pp 7291–7299
30. Yan S, Xiong Y, Lin D (2018) Spatial temporal graph convolutional networks for skeleton-based action recognition. In: Thirty-second AAAI conference on artificial intelligence
31. Piccardi M (2004) Background subtraction techniques: a review. In: 2004 IEEE international conference on systems, man and cybernetics (IEEE Cat. No. 04CH37583), vol 4. IEEE, pp 3099–3104
32. Uddin MZ, Lee JJ, Kim TS (2010) Independent shape component-based human activity recognition via Hidden Markov Model. Appl Intell 33(2):193–206
33. Roshtkhari MJ, Levine MD (2012) A multi-scale hierarchical codebook method for human action recognition in videos using a single example. In: 2012 ninth conference on computer and robot vision. IEEE, pp 182–189
34. Ballan L, Bertini M, Del Bimbo A, Seidenari L, Serra G (2009) Human action recognition and localization using spatio-temporal descriptors and tracking. In: Proceedings of the workshop on pattern recognition and artificial intelligence for human behaviour analysis, Reggio Emilia, Italy, pp 1–8
35. Goudelis G, Karpouzis K, Kollias S (2013) Exploring trace transform for robust human action recognition. Pattern Recogn 46(12):3238–3248
36. Roshtkhari MJ, Levine MD (2013) Human activity recognition in videos using a single example. Image Vis Comput 31(11):864–876
37. Gupta JP, Singh N, Dixit P, Semwal VB, Dubey SR (2013) Human activity recognition using gait pattern. Int J Comput Vis Image Process 3(3):31–53
38. Arunnehru J, Geetha MK (2013) Motion intensity code for action recognition in video using PCA and SVM. In: Mining intelligence and knowledge exploration. Springer, Cham, pp 70–81

Chapter 9
Biometric Recognition of Emotions Using Wavelets

Abstract This study demonstrates analysis of an advanced technique that enhances performance of facial expression recognition method. Face preprocessing is conducted by face cropping. These cropped faces are rescaled by using bilinear interpolation. Multi-scale wavelet is used for extraction of facial patterns. Extracted features are down-sampled using principal component analysis (PCA) to reduce execution time as well as misclassification. The approach reduced the image dimensions and preserved the perceptual quality of the original images. Downsampled features are classified using multiclass support vector machine (SVM) that has a one versus all architecture. This system is trained with benchmark JAFFE and CK+ facial expression datasets. Performance of wavelet is compared with other existing frequency domain techniques and wavelets are found better in terms of recognition rate.

Keywords Emotion recognition · Facial expressions · Abnormal behavior detection · Face detection

9.1 Introduction

Emotion is a form of nonverbal communication by humans. Facial expression is the best way to represent human emotions. It evolves on contraction of the muscular patterns of a face. Different facial muscle movement corresponds to different emotional states. Hence, facial expression recognition (FER) is an interesting topic of research in computer vision area. It has great impact in biometrics, security, surveillance, human-computer interaction, animations, etc. [1]. There are two categories of each expression: spontaneous and induced. Spontaneous expressions are those which arise naturally and induced expressions are those which arise intentionally. There are six basic facial expressions whether spontaneous or induced. These are angry, disgust, fear, happy, sad, surprised and one additional neutral expression. These seven expressions are benchmark to every human. There may be more complex expressions dependent on person's behavior [2]. A more complex class of facial expressions is micro-expressions. These are expressions depicted using a

© Springer Nature Switzerland AG 2020
R. Singh et al., *Intelligent Wavelet Based Techniques for Advanced Multimedia Applications*, https://doi.org/10.1007/978-3-030-31873-4_9

little movement within facial area. They often arise when a person intentionally attempts to conceal his natural expression.

There are several challenges for FER. It is possible that a person may not be facing the camera in his frontal position. In this case, it is difficult to recognize his expression by exploring a part of his face. Also, it is possible that same expression is displayed by different people differently. In that case it is difficult to analyze same expression in different people. A facial expression recognition algorithm should be robust towards these challenges. It should be hard enough so that it is capable of discriminating between different facial expressions and soft enough so that slight variations in the same class of expressions should not be judged under different class. Since emotions are represented with a small portion of human body i.e. facial area, therefore the technique must be quite efficient [3].

Although, most of the techniques developed so far are quite efficient and show high recognition accuracy, however correct emotion recognition and to infer a person's intention from their expressions is still a challenging task. It faces several problems such as different lighting conditions, occlusions, involvement of single or multiple humans in a scene, a person's real or fake expressions, etc. therefore, in this work, we have provided an emotion prediction technique which is based on facial expression recognition since expressions are the most authentic way to analyze a person's emotion. We presented here an efficient wavelet based technique which show better performance than existing one in terms of recognition accuracy.

Rest of the chapter is structured as follows: a literature review is provided in Sect. 9.2, facial expression recognition framework is provided in Sect. 9.3, results and discussion are shown in Sect. 9.4 and conclusions are given in Sect. 9.5.

9.2   Literature Review

Numerous approaches have been developed for FER recently. Few surveys on expression analysis have been provided that presented possible solutions for various challenges [4]. Based on these reviews, FER techniques are divided in three classes (i) Basic FER techniques, (ii) Micro FER techniques (iii) 3D FER techniques. Here we describe each category one by one.

9.2.1   Basic FER Techniques

Most of the techniques developed so far have dealt with 6 basic expressions i.e. angry, fear, disgust, happy, sad, surprised and neutral defined by Ekman [5]. Depending on feature representation FER methods are divided in four classes. These are (i) geometric features (ii) appearance (iii) motion features (iv) action unit based approaches.

Geometric features based methods use geometric relationships between facial components like perimeter, compactness, eccentricity, shape, scale space, etc. [6]. Appearance-based methods apply filters to retrieve global information from an image. Some commonly used appearance based methods apply Pixel intensity [7], Gabor texture [8], local binary patterns (LBP) [9, 10], and histogram of oriented gradients (HOG) [11] feature. Motion features take into account temporal correlations of consecutive frames of a video. Few popular motion features are motion history images (MHI) [12], and optical flow [13]. Different facial expressions evolve due to different facial muscle movements which are called action units (AU). Since a facial expression can be decomposed into multiple AU, therefore these AU are extensively used in expression analysis as facial action coding systems (FACS) [14].

Recently, deep learning approaches based on convolutional neural network (CNN) have gained much attention due to their high success rate. Their accuracy rate is high because of various factors such as kernel size and filter count [15]. Twelve convolutional and pooling layers are used for efficient performance by Tang et al. [16]. Each video frame was retrieved by VGG16 network followed by four one dimensional CNN networks in [17]. Finally, 2 fully connected (FC) layers are used for expression classification. Occlusion problem is handled in [18].

9.2.2   Micro FER Techniques

As compared to normal facial expressions, micro expressions (ME) are more likely to represent a person's deepest emotions. Therefore, interest is increasing to develop ME recognition approaches. Temporal interpolation method (TIM) is used in [19, 20] for MER. It handles the problem of varying size of videos by normalizing them into a fixed size of video. Video of larger size are down-sampled and videos of smaller size are up-sampled to convert them into fixed size video. Liong et al. [21, 22] developed systems which use only the apex frame for MER. Apex frame is that frame which contains maximum intensity of a specific expression.

Local binary patterns (LBP) possess high discrimination power and low computation cost that has been used efficiently in expression recognition. Its several variants like spatio-temporal completed local quantization patterns (STCLQP) [23], LBP with six intersection points (LBP-SIP) [24], LBP with mean orthogonal planes (LBP-MOP) [25] are used in expression analysis. Another popular technique is optical flow that captures small face motion. Variants such as fuzzy histogram of oriented optical flow (FHOOF) [26], optical strain feature (OSF) [27], optical strain weight (OSW) [28], bi-weighted oriented optical flow (Bi-WOOF) [29] and main directional mean optical flow (MDMO) [30] are successfully implemented for MER.

As deep learning approaches are growing interest, an initial attempt was performed using convolutional neural network (CNN) in [31]. But this method did not show high recognition accuracy when compared to traditional methods due to over-fitting. In another approach [32], a VGGNet was applied on apex frame of each video. After that it fine-tuned network weights with small scale data. Wang et al. [33]

provided a system using CNN and Long short term memory (LSTM). A three-stream CNN based system is developed in [34] in which each CNN stream is applied over grayscale frame and horizontal-vertical optical flow field. Very few works performed cross-dataset validation on CASME II, SMIC, SAMM datasets [35, 36].

However, when we compare recognition accuracy of micro-expressions with normal expressions, we find it very less which is less than 70% for ME and almost 100% for normal expressions. This is because of the reason that duration of normal expression varies between 0.75 s and 2 s whereas duration of micro-expression varies between 0.04 s and 0.2 s. Due to small time duration, ME are captured with high speed cameras (i.e., >100fps). Because of high speed of cameras several replicative frames exist. Hence, it is difficult to remove interference from unrelated data and to enhance significant characteristics of ME.

9.2.3 3D FER Techniques

3D imaging systems provide a more accurate way of capturing facial expressions as compared to simple imaging systems since they capture information from different viewing angles. For this reason, 3D FER has become a significant field of research. Methods proposed in [37, 38] used 2D as well as 3D facial data for enhanced performance. Nowadays, deep learning based methods have shown highly improved performance for 3D FER, hence several deep methods have been developed recently for this purpose. A combination of two convolution neural networks (CNN) is used by Huynh et al. [39] for expression recognition in 3D BU-3DFE database. Hinton et al. [40] developed a method based on Deep Belief Networks (DBNs). They used a greedy algorithm for fast learning of each layer of a generative model. Multiple learning stages were developed by Fathallah et al. [41] for understanding of face and facial parts. This method used a sliding window mechanism to extract histogram of oriented gradients (HOG) feature from facial area and a DBN as a hierarchical detector for expression recognition. Its shortcoming is that it did not clearly mention which facial area corresponds to which expression.

In a recent work, Zhong et al. [42] divided facial area into three categories of small non-overlapping patches. These categories are common, specific and remaining facial patches. Facial expressions are determined based on these patches. However, including a large number of patches involves that make recognition task difficult. Li et al. [43] presented deep CNNs to learn from region of interest (ROI) of face parts. These ROI are then used to recognize expressions from facial movements and action units (AU). In the most recent works by Jan et al. [44], accurate facial parts are determined and expression recognition is performed depending on deep feature fusion of these facial patches. These mentioned approaches look deeper into the facial movement and provide better recognition of different facial expressions.

9.3 FER Framework

We present a scheme containing four modules that are face detection and normalization, discrete wavelet coefficient extraction, feature selection and multiclass SVM classifier. Here, we demonstrate a wavelet based technique that extracts information from different scales. The extracted features have been reduced with the help of PCA. In last step, a multiclass SVM is applied for expression recognition. The results are tested on two benchmark datasets that are the JAFFE [45] and the CK+ [46] facial expression databases. Objective evaluation of wavelets and existing methods in terms of percentage recognition rate demonstrate superiority of wavelet over other methods.

9.3.1 Face Detection and Normalization

The facial expression recognition scheme involves a three step preprocessing phase. First step of face detection is carried out by applying Viola-Jones method. It extracts haar like features and classifies them with the help of Adaboost classifier to find out location of face in an image [47]. Figure 9.1 depicts sample face detection by Viola-Jones method. Now, detected face part is cropped in order to reduce region of interest. Finally, size of an image is scaled to 50×50 pixels. Many approaches used bilinear interpolation to incorporate scaling. We also used similar approach. This down sampling reduces feature extraction area and enhances execution time. Figure 9.2 shows few sample cropped and scale normalized face images.

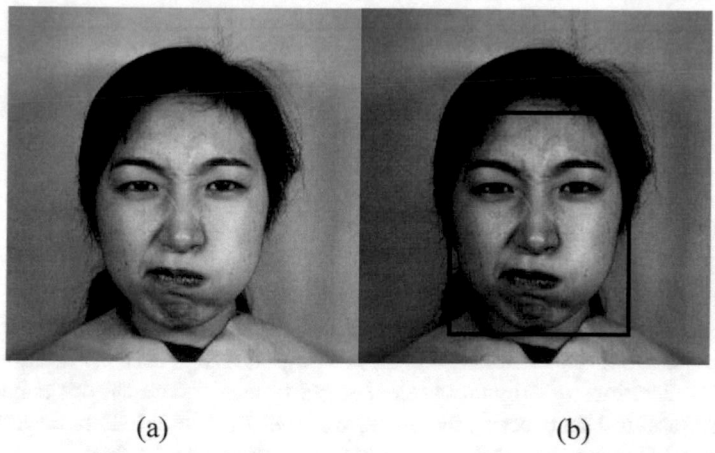

(a)   (b)

Fig. 9.1 (a) Original image (b) detected face

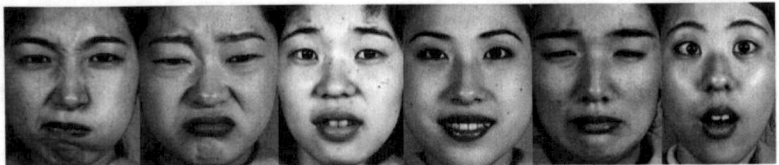

Fig. 9.2 Samples of cropped and scale normalized face images from JAFFE database

Fig. 9.3 LL subband
coefficents

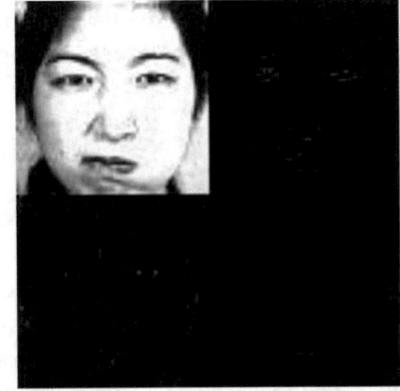

9.3.2   Discrete Wavelet Coefficient Extraction

Performance of discrete wavelet transform is high by providing multi-scaling, and more image features can be represented under different conditions. In general, wavelet features at various scales are retrieved and their histograms are concatenated to make a high dimensional feature vector. Figure 9.3 depicts corresponding discrete wavelet LL subband coefficients of cropped and scale normalized image.

9.3.3   Feature Selection

Since, extracted features are high dimensional and due to their large size, it is not practically possible to use all of them as an input to the classifier because it may result in misclassification and possible system crash. Principal component analysis (PCA) is a popular feature selection technique [48]. High dimensionality of features is reduced to lower dimensionality features using PCA. It is used for finding the best projection directions of original data using least mean-square [48]. It enhances the speed of classification process, therefore, we used PCA as a feature selection tool. The selected features represent samples motion patterns of the face.

9.3.4 Multiclass SVM Classifier

Support vector machine (SVM) was developed by Cortes and Vapnik in 1995 [49]. Recently, it has shown high performance in several vision problems [50–52]. It has been a significant tool in activity recognition also. General SVM classifier deals with binary classification problem. The basic facial expressions for a given video sequence are classified using multiclass SVM classifier in following manner:

$$
Expression\ (E) \in
\begin{cases}
angry & iff\ \ E \in class_1 \\
disgust & iff\ \ E \in class_2 \\
fear & iff\ \ E \in class_3 \\
happy & iff\ \ E \in class_4 \\
neutral & iff\ \ E \in class_5 \\
sad & iff\ \ E \in class_6 \\
surprised & iff\ \ E \in class_7
\end{cases}
\tag{9.1}
$$

9.4 Results and Discussion

This section presents experimentation and results analysis. Facial expression recognition framework is tested on several datasets. Results are shown for two most extensively used datasets – Japanese Female Facial Expression (JAFFE) dataset [45], and extended Cohn Kanade (CK+) dataset [46]. Experiments are performed in Matlab 2014a on an Intel® Core™ i5 2.27 GHz machine.

9.4.1 Experiments over the JAFFE Dataset

This experiment demonstrates robustness of Wavelets for different facial expressions. The Japanese Female Facial Expression (JAFFE) dataset [45] is a collection of 213 facial expression images. These images include 6 basic facial expressions angry, disgust fear, happy, sad and surprised along with neutral posed by 10 Japanese female models.

For training and testing cross validation is used. Dataset is divided into 10 sets of approximately equal size. Out of 10 sets, 9 sets are used for training and one set is used for testing. Whole process is repeated 10 times so that each set is used as a testing set once. Average of 10 results is considered to be percentage recognition rate. Figure 9.4 shows visual results for JAFFE dataset. Table 9.1 shows the values for confusion matrix of wavelet over JAFFE database.

Recognised Expression

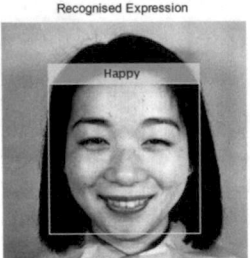

Recognised Expression

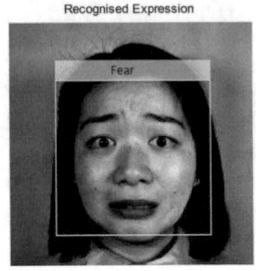

Recognised Expression

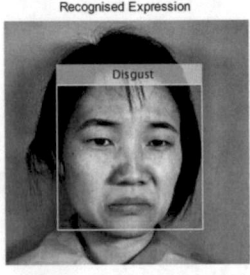

Recognised Expression

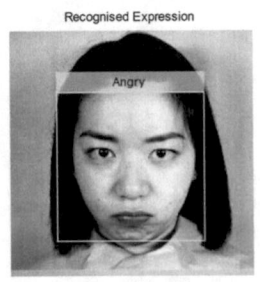

Recognised Expression

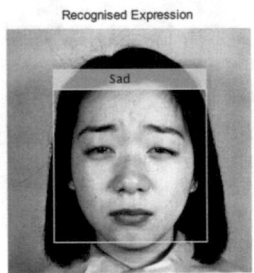

Recognised Expression

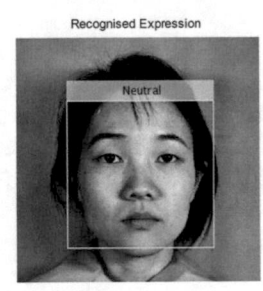

Recognised Expression

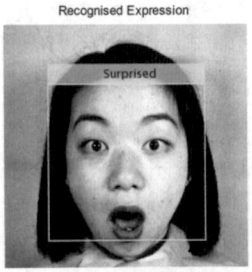

Fig. 9.4   Wavelet based emotion recognition for JAFFE dataset

Table 9.1 Confusion matrix for JAFFE dataset

	Angry	Disgust	Fear	Happy	Neutral	Sad	Surprised
Angry	96.6	0	3.4	0	0	0	0
Disgust	3.4	96.6	0	0	0	0	0
Fear	0	0	100.00	0	0	0	0
Happy	0	0	0	100.00	0	0	0
Neutral	0	0	0	3.4	96.6	0	0
Sad	0	0	0	0	0	100.00	0
Surprised	0	0	0	0	0	0	100.00

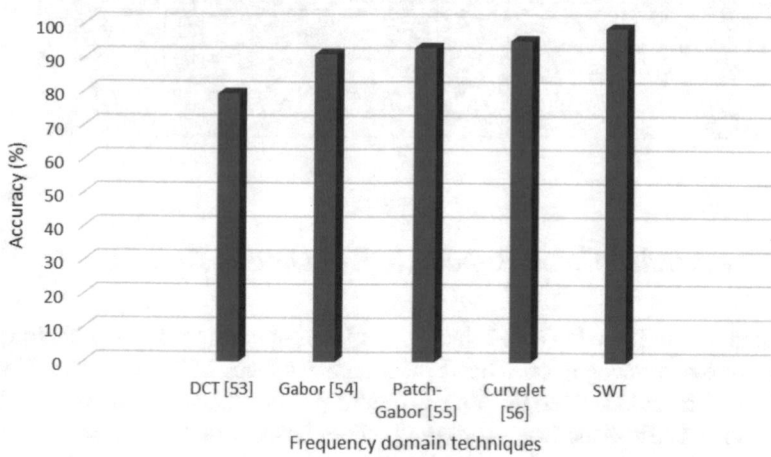

Fig. 9.5 Recognition rate of frequency domain techniques on JAFFE dataset

From Table 9.1, it is observed that wavelet shows a very high recognition rate
100% for expressions fear, happy, sad and surprised. For expressions angry, disgust
and neutral, a high recognition rate of 96.6% is achieved. Average recognition rate
achieved is 98.8%. Overall, it can be said that wavelet provides high recognition rate.
Total execution time is 54.4 s. Objective evaluation of wavelet and other frequency
domain techniques is shown in Fig. 9.5. It is clear from Fig. 9.5, discrete wavelet
transform shows high accuracy when compared to other frequency domain techniques based on discrete cosine transform [53], Gabor [54], Patch-Gabor [55] and
curvelet transform [56].

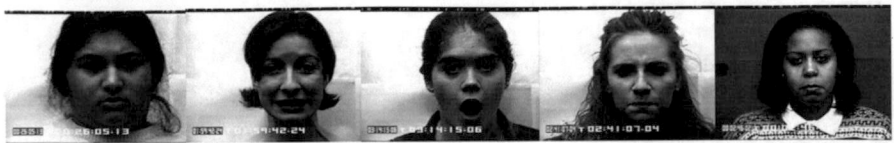

Fig. 9.6   Sample expressions of CK+ Dataset

Table 9.2   Confusion matrix for CK+ dataset

	Angry	Disgust	Fear	Happy	Neutral	Sad	Surprised
Angry	100.0	0	3.4	0	0	0	0
Disgust	0	100.0	0	0	0	0	0
Fear	0	0	90.0	3.3	0	0	6.7
Happy	0	6.7	0	93.3	0	0	0
Neutral	0	6.7	3.3	0	90.0	0	0
Sad	6.7	0	6.7	0	0	86.6	0
Surprised	0	0	0	0	0	0	100.0

9.4.2   Extended Cohn–Kanade (CK+) Dataset Results

Extended Cohn–Kanade (CK+) dataset [46] is used in numerous techniques for facial expression recognition. This dataset includes faces of 210 human subjects of age 18–50. It includes people from different group viz. men and women, Euro-American and Afro-American people and others. Images are taken from frontal view as well as from 30° angular view. A total of 1917 images are captured from 182 human subjects. Few samples of CK+ dataset are depicted in Fig. 9.6. Confusion matrix for wavelet technique is presented in Table 9.2.

From Table 9.2, it is observed that wavelet achieves 100% recognition rate for expressions angry, disgust and surprised. For the expression fear, happy and neutral, we get a high recognition rate of above than 90%. Only expression sad shows a little lower accuracy of 86.6%. From average recognition rate of 96.6%, we can say that wavelet achieves high recognition rate on CK+ dataset.

9.5 Summary

This study deploys a wavelet based technique for improved facial expression recognition. It includes four consecutive steps. First step of face preprocessing is done by face cropping. The cropped faces are down-sampled using bilinear interpolation. Discrete wavelet transform is used to extract important facial features. Extracted features are reduced by using principal component analysis to reduce execution time as well as misclassification. Reduced extracted features are supplied in a multiclass SVM classifier. This system is trained and tested over JAFFE and CK + expression datasets. This approach is compared with existing methods [53–56] and found better than those methods.

References

1. Bousmalis K, Mehu M, Pantic M (2013) Towards the automatic detection of spontaneous agreement and disagreement based on nonverbal behaviour: a survey of related cues, databases, and tools. Image Vis Comput 31(2):203–221
2. Bartlett MS, Littlewort G, Frank M, Lainscsek C, Fasel I, Movellan J (2005) Recognizing facial expression: machine learning and application to spontaneous behavior. In: 2005 IEEE computer society conference on computer vision and pattern recognition (CVPR'05), vol 2, pp 568–573
3. Tian YL, Kanade T, Cohn JF (2005) Facial expression analysis. In: Handbook of face recognition. Springer, New York, pp 247–275
4. Bettadapura V (2012) Face expression recognition and analysis: the state of the art. arXiv preprint arXiv:1203.6722, http://arxiv.org/pdf/1203.6722
5. Ekman P (1993) Facial expression and emotion. Am Psychol 48(4):384–392
6. Jain N, Kumar S, Kumar A (2019) Effective approach for facial expression recognition using hybrid square-based diagonal pattern geometric model. Multimed Tools Appl:1–17
7. Mohammadi MR, Fatemizadeh E, Mahoor MH (2014) PCA-based dictionary building for accurate facial expression recognition via sparse representation. J Vis Commun Image Represent 25(5):1082–1092
8. Liu L, Yang L, Chen Y, Zhang X, Hu L, Deng F (2019) Facial expression recognition based on SSVM algorithm and multi-source texture feature fusion using KECA. In: Recent developments in intelligent computing, communication and devices. Springer, Singapore, pp 659–666
9. Nigam S, Khare A (2015) Multiscale local binary patterns for facial expression-based human emotion recognition. In: Computational vision and robotics. Springer, New Delhi, pp 71–77
10. Nigam S, Singh R, Misra AK (2019) Local binary patterns based facial expression recognition for efficient smart applications. In: Security in smart cities: models, applications, and challenges. Springer, Cham, pp 297–322
11. Nigam S, Singh R, Misra AK (2018) Efficient facial expression recognition using histogram of oriented gradients in wavelet domain. Multimed Tools Appl 77(21):28725–28747
12. Hu M, Wang H, Wang X, Yang J, Wang R (2019) Video facial emotion recognition based on local enhanced motion history image and CNN-CTSLSTM networks. J Vis Commun Image Represent 59:176–185
13. Sidavong L, Lal S, Sztynda T (2019) Spontaneous facial expression analysis using optical flow technique. In: Modern sensing technologies. Springer, Cham, pp 83–101
14. Ekman P, Friesen WV (1978) Facial action coding system: a technique for the measurement of facial movement. Consulting Psychologists Press

15. Agrawal A, Mittal N (2019) Using CNN for facial expression recognition: a study of the effects of kernel size and number of filters on accuracy. Vis Comput:1–8
16. Tang Y, Zhang XM, Wang H (2018) Geometric-convolutional feature fusion based on learning propagation for facial expression recognition. IEEE Access 6:42532–42540
17. Zheng Z, Cao C, Chen X, Xu G (2018) Multimodal emotion recognition for one-minute-gradual emotion challenge. arXiv preprint arXiv:1805.01060
18. Li Y, Zeng J, Shan S, Chen X (2019) Occlusion aware facial expression recognition using CNN with attention mechanism. IEEE Trans Image Process 28(5):2439–2450
19. Li X, Hong X, Moilanen A, Huang X, Pfister T, Zhao G, Pietikäinen M (2018) Towards reading hidden emotions: a comparative study of spontaneous micro-expression spotting and recognition methods. IEEE Trans Affect Comput 9(4):563–577
20. Wang SJ, Yan WJ, Zhao G, Fu X, Zhou CG (2014) Micro-expression recognition using robust principal component analysis and local spatiotemporal directional features. In: Workshop at the European conference on computer vision. Springer, Cham, pp 325–338
21. Liong ST, See J, Wong K, Le Ngo AC, Oh YH, Phan R (2015) Automatic apex frame spotting in micro-expression database. In: 2015 3rd IAPR asian conference on pattern recognition (ACPR). IEEE, pp 665–669
22. Liong ST, See J, Wong K, Phan RCW (2016) Automatic micro-expression recognition from long video using a single spotted apex. In: Asian conference on computer vision. Springer, Cham, pp 345–360
23. Huang X, Zhao G, Hong X, Zheng W, Pietikäinen M (2016) Spontaneous facial micro-expression analysis using spatiotemporal completed local quantized patterns. Neurocomputing 175:564–578
24. Wang Y, See J, Phan RCW, Oh YH (2014) Lbp with six intersection points: reducing redundant information in lbp-top for micro-expression recognition. In: Asian conference on computer vision. Springer, Cham, pp 525–537
25. Wang Y, See J, Phan RCW, Oh YH (2015) Efficient spatio-temporal local binary patterns for spontaneous facial micro-expression recognition. PLoS One 10(5):e0124674
26. Happy SL, Routray A (2017) Fuzzy histogram of optical flow orientations for micro-expression recognition. IEEE Trans Affect Comput
27. Liong ST, Phan RCW, See J, Oh YH, Wong K (2014) Optical strain based recognition of subtle emotions. In: 2014 international symposium on intelligent signal processing and communication systems (ISPACS). IEEE, pp 180–184
28. Liong ST, See J, Phan RCW, Le Ngo AC, Oh YH, Wong K (2014) Subtle expression recognition using optical strain weighted features. In: Asian conference on computer vision. Springer, Cham, pp 644–657
29. Liong ST, See J, Wong K, Phan RCW (2018) Less is more: micro-expression recognition from video using apex frame. Signal Process Image Commun 62:82–92
30. Liu YJ, Zhang JK, Yan WJ, Wang SJ, Zhao G, Fu X (2016) A main directional mean optical flow feature for spontaneous micro-expression recognition. IEEE Trans Affect Comput 7 (4):299–310
31. Patel D, Hong X, Zhao G (2016) Selective deep features for micro-expression recognition. In: 2016 23rd international conference on pattern recognition (ICPR). IEEE, pp 2258–2263
32. Li Y, Huang X, Zhao G (2018) Can micro-expression be recognized based on single apex frame? In: 2018 25th IEEE international conference on image processing (ICIP). IEEE, pp 3094–3098
33. Wang SJ, Li BJ, Liu YJ, Yan WJ, Ou X, Huang X et al (2018) Micro-expression recognition with small sample size by transferring long-term convolutional neural network. Neurocomputing 312:251–262
34. Li J, Wang Y, See J, Liu W (2018) Micro-expression recognition based on 3D flow convolutional neural network. Pattern Anal Appl:1–9
35. Gan YS, Liong ST, Yau WC, Huang YC, Tan LK (2019) OFF-ApexNet on micro-expression recognition system. Signal Process Image Commun 74:129–139

36. Liong ST, Gan YS, See J, Khor HQ (2019) A shallow triple stream three-dimensional CNN (STSTNet) for micro-expression recognition system. arXiv preprint arXiv:1902.03634
37. Li H, Ding H, Huang D, Wang Y, Zhao X, Morvan JM, Chen L (2015) An efficient multimodal 2D+ 3D feature-based approach to automatic facial expression recognition. Comput Vis Image Underst 140:83–92
38. Li H, Sun J, Xu Z, Chen L (2017) Multimodal 2d+ 3d facial expression recognition with deep fusion convolutional neural network. IEEE Trans Multimed 19(12):2816–2831
39. Huynh XP, Tran TD, Kim YG (2016) Convolutional neural network models for facial expression recognition using bu-3dfe database. In: Information science and applications (ICISA) 2016. Springer, Singapore, pp 441–450
40. Hinton GE, Osindero S, Teh YW (2006) A fast learning algorithm for deep belief nets. Neural Comput 18(7):1527–1554
41. Fathallah A, Abdi L, Douik A (2017) Facial expression recognition via deep learning. In: 2017 IEEE/ACS 14th international conference on computer systems and applications (AICCSA). IEEE, pp 745–750
42. Zhong L, Liu Q, Yang P, Huang J, Metaxas DN (2015) Learning multiscale active facial patches for expression analysis. IEEE Trans Cybern 45(8):1499–1510
43. Li W, Abtahi F, Zhu Z, Yin L (2017) Eac-net: a region-based deep enhancing and cropping approach for facial action unit detection. In: 2017 12th IEEE international conference on automatic face & gesture recognition (FG 2017). IEEE, pp 103–110
44. Jan A, Ding H, Meng H, Chen L, Li H (2018) Accurate facial parts localization and deep learning for 3D facial expression recognition. In: 2018 13th IEEE international conference on automatic face & gesture recognition (FG 2018). IEEE, pp 466–472
45. Dailey MN, Joyce C, Lyons MJ, Kamachi M, Ishi H, Gyoba J, Cottrell GW (2010) Evidence and a computational explanation of cultural differences in facial expression recognition. Emotion 10(6):874–893
46. Lucey P, Cohn JF, Kanade T, Saragih J, Ambadar Z, Matthews I (2010) The extended cohn-kanade dataset (ck+): a complete dataset for action unit and emotion-specified expression. In: Computer vision and pattern recognition workshops (CVPRW), 2010 IEEE computer society conference on. IEEE, pp 94–101
47. Viola P, Jones MJ (2004) Robust real-time face detection. Int J Comput Vis 57(2):137–154
48. Peter M, Minoi JL, Hipiny IHM (2019) 3D face recognition using kernel-based PCA approach. In: Computational science and technology. Springer, Singapore, pp 77–86
49. Cortes C, Vapnik V (1995) Support-vector networks. Mach Learn 20(3):273–297
50. Iranmehr A, Masnadi-Shirazi H, Vasconcelos N (2019) Cost-sensitive support vector machines. Neurocomputing 343:50–64
51. Tavara S (2019) Parallel computing of support vector machines: a survey. ACM Comput Surv 51(6):123
52. Chen WJ, Li CN, Shao YH, Zhang J, Deng NY (2019) RTBSVM: robust twin bound support vector machine via joint feature selection. Knowl-Based Syst
53. Jiang B, Yang GS, Zhang HL (2008) Comparative study of dimension reduction and recognition algorithms of DCT and 2DPCA. In: 2008 international conference on machine learning and cybernetics, vol 1. IEEE, pp 407–410
54. Guo G, Dyer CR (2005) Learning from examples in the small sample case: face expression recognition. IEEE Trans Syst Man Cybern B Cybern 35(3):477–488
55. Zhang L, Tjondronegoro D (2011) Facial expression recognition using facial movement features. IEEE Trans Affect Comput 2(4):219–229
56. Uçar A, Demir Y, Güzeliş C (2016) A new facial expression recognition based on curvelet transform and online sequential extreme learning machine initialized with spherical clustering. Neural Comput Appl 27(1):131–142

Chapter 10
Intelligent Multimedia Applications in Wavelet Domain: New Trends and Future Research Directions

Abstract The huge amount of multimedia data available over Internet compelled to adopt new methodologies day by day. It becomes extremely complex to process and filter data as per user requirements. Hence, new tools, technologies are being used one after another. In this era of artificial intelligence, where machine and deep learning has been evolved, there is a great requirement of intelligent multimedia processing to fulfill and meet the requirements of users. With this aim, this chapter discusses a few key challenges in the visual information processing that are directly related to the societal benefits. Its major components are healthcare, education, transportation and security. A methodological enhancement of the techniques are being discussed to provide future research directions to the multimedia applications in wavelet domain.

Keywords Multimedia applications · Intelligent systems · Machine learning · Deep learning · Wavelet transforms · Image processing · Computer vision

10.1 Introduction

Intelligent multimedia systems [1] are made to assist human beings in many applications such as healthcare, transportation, education, security, etc. [2–4]. These applications require a huge amount of multimedia data processing which can be done using adaptive and intelligent algorithms [5]. With the evolution of artificial intelligence based multimedia systems and mathematical tools like wavelet transforms, it becomes necessary to integrate these to build hybrid algorithms to handle large scale data. This chapter provide an outline to the future challenges in the development of the intelligent multimedia applications. The chapter will discuss each and every key research areas in the context of modern intelligent applications and provide directions for the future research.

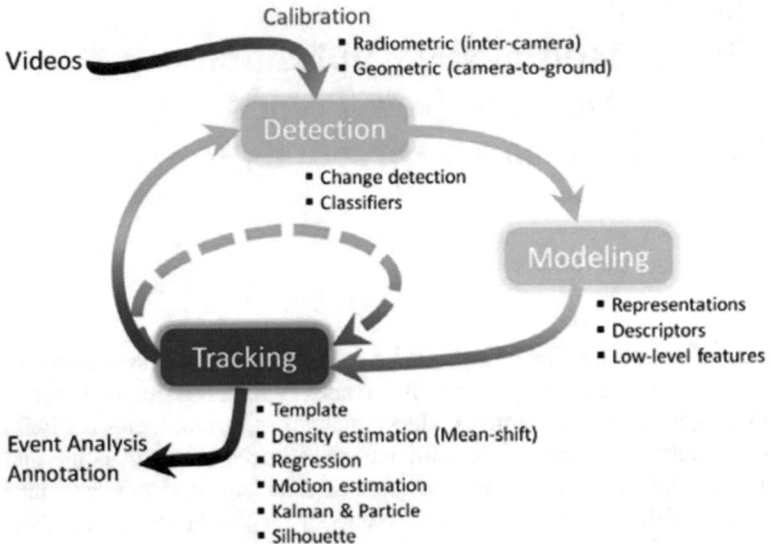

Fig. 10.1 A general video analytics framework

10.2   Video Analytics in Wavelet Domain

Data analytics has been a growing area of research and various social media platforms have been used for sharing video data. In the era of data analytics, automatic analysis of video data has become challenging. To strengthen this analysis video analytics can be used [6]. The steps involved in the video analytics have been shown in Fig. 10.1.

Video analytics includes object tracking, classification, segmentation and behavior understanding [7–9]. Wavelets have been used for understanding of video sequences and hence can be used for video analytics. Furthermore, wavelet coefficients can be used as a feature or can be easily combined with other feature descriptors like histogram of oriented gradients (HoG), local binary patterns etc. Thus, there is a great possibility to extend the multimedia applications of wavelet transforms the following areas.

10.2.1   Single and Multiple Object Tracking

Object tracking is a problem that has been handled by several researchers. However the focus has always been remain on single object tracking. Chapter 6 of this book has developed and demonstrated a new algorithm for tracking of moving human objects in video. This algorithm exploited shift invariant wavelet transform coefficients for real world single as well as multiple object tracking. From experimentation it is clear that wavelet based tracking performed well. Wavelet based tracking approach allowed to accurately track the target object in different frames. Also it is capable of handling several real world complexities such as partial or full occlusion. Experimental results show that wavelet based tracking method is better when compared to existing tracking methods such as method CBWH, method JCTH, method CT. Its better discriminating power distinguishes multiple targets from each other and hence overcomes the occlusion. The proposed method extracts effectively the features in target region, which characterize better and represent more robustly the target. However, multiple object tracking is still in developing phase. Robust algorithms are still required to track all the objects present in a scene. Crowd tracking is also important where a large amount of people wander around which makes it difficult to track each and every object in different directions.

10.2.2   Person Identification and Re-Identification

Person identification is a widespread topic in computer vision field. However, camouflaged identification is a rarely touched topic. Chapter 7 provided a camouflaged person identification method which integrates discrete wavelet coefficients with support vector machine classifier. The multi-resolution nature of wavelet transform provides invariant person identification against camouflaged scenes and do not get affected by similar background and foreground objects. Flexibility of wavelet and SVM makes this method accurate resulting in better efficiency. For objective evaluation of this method, CAMO_UOW video dataset is used. This evaluation shows that wavelet transform based methods outperform existing camouflaged person identification methods. The objective evaluation using F-measure parameter demonstrates high performance of this method. This method is capable of handling background and foregrounds ambiguity for camouflaged persons. This methodology can further be enhanced for camouflaged objects as well as other ambiguous objects. Background clutter can also be included for this purpose. This would really be an interesting topic of future research.

10.2.3   Abnormal Activity Recognition

Activity recognition methodology is required to detect abnormal human activities from video sequences. Classification based human activity recognition has been proposed in Chap. 8. It used wavelet transform and multiclass SVM classifier for this. The experiments are done on Weizmann and KTH video datasets. Nine activities are considered for objective evaluations from Weizmann dataset are walk, run, bend, gallop sideways, jumping jack, one handwave, two handwave, jump in place and skip. Six activities that have been considered from KTH dataset are handwaving, walking, running, boxing, handclapping and jogging. Performance is discussed visually and analytically both which show that wavelet outperforms other existing methods. However, abnormal activity recognition is still at nascent state. It should be addressed in detail so that all aspects of abnormal activity recognition could be handled. Real world scenarios should also be considered instead of taking few benchmark datasets.

10.2.4   Emotion Recognition

Emotion recognition using facial expression recognition is a great topic of interest. Chapter 9 incorporated a wavelet based technique for improved facial expression recognition. It includes four consecutive steps. First step of face preprocessing is done by face cropping. The cropped faces are down-sampled using bilinear interpolation. Discrete wavelet transform is used to extract important facial features. Extracted features were reduced by using principal component analysis to reduce execution time as well as misclassification. Reduced extracted features are supplied in a multiclass SVM classifier. This system is rained and tested over JAFFE and CK+ expression datasets. This approach is compared with existing methods and found better than those methods. However, other aspects of emotion recognition such as voice recognition, gaze recognition have not been touched in detail. These topics need more attention from research community.

10.2.5   Crowd Behavior Analysis

A system capable of inferring the behavior of multiple humans (often called crowd behavior analysis) would have many applications. Generally, a method for determining human behavior is comprised of detection and tracking of human objects of interest for generating motion descriptors followed by activity recognition [10–12]. The framework of crowd behavior analysis is an extension of video surveillance and requires the complete understanding of the each human behavior present in the crowd. This can be understood from the Fig. 10.2. Thus, crowd analysis is more challenging and complex than video surveillance. However, wavelet transforms can be explored for crowd behavior analysis which would be helpful in detecting social behavior in countries like India where cases of mob lynching or human stampedes have been reported at public places [13–15].

10.3   Wavelets and Deep Learning

The extensive use of wavelet transform for multimedia applications has been extended to design deep neural networks. Earlier, it has been observed that wavelets can act as a feature and well suited for many applications. This has certainly

Fig. 10.2 Steps involved in crowd behavior analysis

increased the interest to design invariant neural networks for applications such as medical image reconstruction, anomaly prediction [16, 17]. Moreover, many deep networks can be proposed as there are a number of wavelet transforms that vary from classical to new generation wavelets [18–20]. However, the computational complexity of the multiscale transforms should be taken care while developing such deep networks in wavelet domain. Generative adversarial network (GAN) is an extensive learning mechanism that has become popular due to its wide range of applications [21, 22]. A very recent application of GAN shows its importance in psychological behavior detection and used for multiscale face hallucination [23]. Thus, wavelets can be further explored to build GAN based intelligent multimedia systems.

10.4 Wavelets for Healthcare Monitoring

The analysis of human behavior differs from the analysis of other subjects in the clinical applications due to several reasons. First, human behavior, resulted by the human nervous system, is more complicated phenomena than the resulting output of other organ systems. Due to this complexity, normal behavior of a human object is very difficult to characterize. Also, this analysis is not independent of various environmental as well as individual characteristics. Hence, it is only possible with aid of special tools like the Electroencephalogram (EEG), Computed Tomography (CT), Single Photon Emission Computed Tomography (SPECT), Positron Emission Tomography (PET), Magnetic Resonance Imaging (MRI and FMRI), and Magnetic Resonance Spectroscopy (MRS) techniques. The interpersonal information is necessary for the full analysis of a human behavior. For behavior monitoring, several experiments can be designed using EEG or fMRI scans and can be tested in wavelet domain [24, 25]. Medical image fusion in wavelet domain is another area that can be explored for disease prediction. Fusion imaging has been found very useful in diseases like epilepsy etc. [26–28]. Similarly, wavelet transforms can be further used for tumor segmentation and classification [29–32].

10.5   Wavelets for Internet of Things

Internet of things (IoT) has been an emerging field of research and wavelet transforms have not been explored for this area. In order to build smart applications, one can think wavelet as a mathematical tool and can be used for data processing in IoT. Since, IoT uses different sensors to record data, wavelet transforms has great possibility to be explored for it [32–35]. An energy aware image watermarking system in wavelet domain have been developed for IoT which indicates that wavelet transforms can be explored for this domain as well.

10.6   Wavelets in Biology and Agriculture

The complex biological and agricultural data can be handled with the help of wavelet transform. The multi-scale property of wavelet is used to capture scale specific information from biological and agricultural data. Since, mathematical terminology and detailed description of wavelet transform do not make clear understanding to biological or agricultural scientists, hence wavelet has not been a popular tool among them. But applying it step by step and considering available software, it may be applied for this purpose easily. It may specifically be used for (i) Scale-specific applications in biostatistics (ii) forecasting of nonlinear time series (iii) providing DNA walks and neutral landscapes. In literatures, many works based on wavelet transforms for agriculture and biology has been reported. These are based on the health monitoring of soil, plants etc. [36, 37]. Thus, wavelets in agriculture and biology based applications can help farmers to protect plants and crops from disease and understand the soil properties for better farming.

10.7   Summary

This chapter discusses the applications of wavelet transforms for different multimedia applications. It can be easily observed that wavelet transform has a great impact on multimedia applications. The applications of wavelet transform ranges from simple image to complex vision based problems. Video analytics, healthcare, agriculture, IoT, data analytics are some of the key areas in which wavelet transforms have been applied and can be further explored. Wavelets also have great impact on GAN which is a very recently developed learning mechanism. These applications has shown that intelligent multimedia applications can be developed by using wavelet transforms by taking the advantage of their properties such as directional selectivity, shift invariance etc. It has also seen that there is a lot possibility in which elementary multimedia theory can be developed using machine and deep learning techniques. Also, integration of wavelet transform with intelligent techniques enables to utilize and enhance the performance of multimedia systems to meet the user's requirement.

References

1. De Pietro G, Gallo L, Howlett RJ, Jain LC (eds) (2018) Intelligent interactive multimedia systems and services 2017. Springer, Cham
2. Garrett BM, Callear D (2001) The value of intelligent multimedia simulation for teaching clinical decision-making skills. Nurse Educ Today 21(5):382–390
3. Aarts E (2004) Ambient intelligence: a multimedia perspective. IEEE Multimedia 11(1):12–19
4. Wactlar HD, Kanade T, Smith MA, Stevens SM (1996) Intelligent access to digital video: informedia project. Computer 29(5):46–52
5. Al-Turjman F, Alturjman S (2018) Intelligent UAVs for multimedia delivery in smart-cities applications. In: Intelligence in IoT-enabled smart cities, vol 143. CRC Press
6. Porikli F, Yilmaz A (2012) Object detection and tracking. In: Video analytics for business intelligence. Springer, Berlin/Heidelberg, pp 3–41
7. Regazzoni CS, Cavallaro A, Wu Y, Konrad J, Hampapur A (2010) Video analytics for surveillance: theory and practice [from the guest editors]. IEEE Signal Process Mag 27 (5):16–17
8. Barthélemy J, Verstaevel N, Forehead H, Perez P (2019) Edge-computing video analytics for real-time traffic monitoring in a smart city. Sensors 19(9):2048
9. Kang D, Bailis P, Zaharia M (2019) Challenges and opportunities in DNN-based video analytics: a demonstration of the BlazeIt video query engine. In: CIDR
10. Johansson A, Helbing D, Al-Abideen HZ, Al-Bosta S (2008) From crowd dynamics to crowd safety: a video-based analysis. Adv Complex Syst 11(04):497–527
11. Zaki MH, Sayed T (2018) Automated analysis of pedestrian group behavior in urban settings. IEEE Trans Intell Trans Syst 19(6):1880–1889
12. Hao Y, Xu ZJ, Liu Y, Wang J, Fan JL (2019) Effective crowd anomaly detection through spatio-temporal texture analysis. Int J Autom Comput 16(1):27–39
13. Illiyas FT, Mani SK, Pradeepkumar AP, Mohan K (2013) Human stampedes during religious festivals: a comparative review of mass gathering emergencies in India. Int J Disaster Risk Reduct 5:10–18
14. Chatterjee M (2016) Bandh politics: crowds, spectacular violence, and sovereignty in India. Distinktion J Soc Theory 17(3):294–307
15. https://www.thehindu.com/opinion/editorial/wave-of-lynchings/article24223296.ece
16. Kang E, Min J, Ye JC (2017) A deep convolutional neural network using directional wavelets for low-dose X-ray CT reconstruction. Med Phys 44(10):e360–e375
17. Kanarachos S, Christopoulos SRG, Chroneos A, Fitzpatrick ME (2017) Detecting anomalies in time series data via a deep learning algorithm combining wavelets, neural networks and Hilbert transform. Expert Syst Appl 85:292–304
18. Ye JC, Han Y, Cha E (2018) Deep convolutional framelets: a general deep learning framework for inverse problems. SIAM J Imaging Sci 11(2):991–1048
19. Duan Y, Liu F, Jiao L, Zhao P, Zhang L (2017) SAR image segmentation based on convolutional-wavelet neural network and markov random field. Pattern Recogn 64:255–267
20. Yildirim Ö (2018) A novel wavelet sequence based on deep bidirectional LSTM network model for ECG signal classification. Comput Biol Med 96:189–202
21. Goodfellow I, Pouget-Abadie J, Mirza M, Xu B, Warde-Farley D, Ozair S, Bengio Y (2014) Generative adversarial nets. In: Advances in neural information processing systems, pp 2672–2680
22. Radford A, Metz L, Chintala S (2015) Unsupervised representation learning with deep convolutional generative adversarial networks. arXiv preprint arXiv:1511.06434
23. Huang H, He R, Sun Z, Tan T (2019) Wavelet domain generative adversarial network for multi-scale face hallucination. Int J Comput Vis 127(6–7):763–784
24. Mohamed F, Ahmed SF, Ibrahim Z, Yaacob S (2018) Comparison of features based on spectral estimation for the analysis of EEG signals in driver behavior. In: 2018 international conference

on computational approach in smart systems design and applications (ICASSDA). IEEE, pp 1–7

25. Wang X, Gong G, Li N (2019) Automated recognition of epileptic EEG states using a combination of Symlet wavelet processing, gradient boosting machine, and grid search optimizer. Sensors 19(2):219

26. Chowdhury RA, Pellegrino G, Aydin Ü, Lina JM, Dubeau F, Kobayashi E, Grova C (2018) Reproducibility of EEG-MEG fusion source analysis of interictal spikes: relevance in presurgical evaluation of epilepsy. Hum Brain Mapp 39(2):880–901

27. Madabhushi A, Agner S, Basavanhally A, Doyle S, Lee G (2011) Computer-aided prognosis: predicting patient and disease outcome via quantitative fusion of multi-scale, multi-modal data. Comput Med Imaging Graph 35(7–8):506–514

28. Vollmar C, Peraud A, Noachtar S (2018) Multimodal imaging in extratemporal epilepsy surgery. Cureus 10(3)

29. Boldbaatar EA, Lin LY, Lin CM (2019) Breast tumor classification using fast convergence recurrent wavelet Elman neural networks. Neural Process Lett:1–16

30. Nazir M, Khan MA, Saba T, Rehman A (2019) Brain tumor detection from MRI images using multi-level wavelets. In: 2019 international conference on computer and information sciences (ICCIS). IEEE, pp 1–5

31. Hossain E, Hossain MF, Rahaman MA (2018) An approach for the detection and classification of tumor cells from bone MRI using wavelet transform and KNN classifier. In: 2018 international conference on innovation in engineering and technology (ICIET). IEEE, pp 1–6

32. Bahadure NB, Ray AK, Thethi HP (2018) Comparative approach of MRI-based brain tumor segmentation and classification using genetic algorithm. J Digit Imaging 31(4):477–489

33. Al-Shayea TK, Mavromoustakis CX, Batalla JM, Mastorakis G, Mukherjee M, Chatzimisios P (2019, May) Efficiency-aware watermarking using different wavelet families for the internet of things. In: ICC 2019-2019 IEEE international conference on communications (ICC). IEEE, pp 1–6

34. Guidi B, Ricci L (2019) Aggregation techniques for the internet of things: an overview. In: The internet of things for smart urban ecosystems. Springer, Cham, pp 151–176

35. Krishnaraj N, Elhoseny M, Thenmozhi M, Selim MM, Shankar K (2019) Deep learning model for real-time image compression in Internet of Underwater Things (IoUT). J Real-Time Image Process:1–15

36. Dong X, Nyren P, Patton B, Nyren A, Richardson J, Maresca T (2008) Wavelets for agriculture and biology: a tutorial with applications and outlook. Bioscience 58(5):445–453

37. Ge Y, Thomasson JA (2006) Wavelet incorporated spectral analysis for soil property determination. Trans ASABE 49(4):1193–1201

Printed in the United States
by Baker & Taylor Publisher Services